Visualizing the Semantic Web

Springer

London
Berlin
Heidelberg
New York
Barcelona
Hong Kong
Milan
Paris
Singapore
Tokyo

Vladimir Geroimenko and Chaomei Chen (Eds)

Visualizing the Semantic Web

XML-based Internet and Information Visualization

 Springer

Vladimir Geroimenko, PhD, DSc
School of Computing, University of Plymouth, Plymouth, PL4 8AA, UK

Chaomei Chen, PhD
College of Information Science and Technology, Drexel University,
Philadelphia, PA 19104-2875, USA

British Library Cataloguing in Publication Data
Visualizing the semantic web : XML-based internet and
information visualization
    1. Information display systems 2. Visualization 3. Internet
    4. XML (Document markup language)
    I. Geroimenko, Vladimir II. Chen, Chaomei, 1960–
        006
    ISBN 1852335769

Library of Congress Cataloging-in-Publication Data
Visualizing the semantic Web: XML-based Internet and information
visualization/Vladimir Geroimenko and Chaomei Chen (ed.).
        p. cm.
    Includes bibliographical references and index.
    ISBN 1-85233-576-9 (alk. paper)
    1. Web site development. 2. Visualization. 3. XML (Document markup language)
    I. Geroimenko, Vladimir, 1955- II. Chen, Chaomei, 1960-

TK5105.888 .V55 2002
005.2'76–dc21

                                                    2002021739

ISBN 1-85233-576-9 Springer-Verlag London Berlin Heidelberg
Springer Science+Business Media
springeronline.com

Typeset by Gray Publishing, Tunbridge Wells, Kent
Printed and bound at Kyodo Printing Co (S'pore) Pte Ltd
34/3830-5432 Printed on acid-free paper SPIN 11303671

Table of Contents

Preface

Vladimir Geroimenko and Chaomei Chen

The Semantic Web is a vision that has sparked a wide-ranging enthusiasm for a new generation of the Web. The Semantic Web is happening. The central idea of this vision is to make the Web more understandable to computer programs so that people can make more use of this gigantic asset. The use of metadata (data about data) can clearly indicate the meaning of data on the Web so as to provide computers with enough information to handle such data.

On the future Web, many additional layers will be required if we want computer programs to handle the semantics (the meaning of data) properly without human intervention. Such layers should deal with the hierarchical relationships between meanings, their similarities and differences, logical rules for making new inferences from the existing data and metadata, etc. Dozens of new technologies have emerged recently to implement these ideas. XML (eXtensible Markup Language) forms the foundation of the future Web, RDF (Resource Description Framework), Topic Maps and many other technologies help to erect a "multi-storey" building of the Semantic Web layer by layer by adding new features and new types of metadata. According to Tim Berners-Lee, the inventor of the current Web and the Semantic Web, it may take up to ten years to complete the building.

The new Web will be much more complex than the current one and will contain enormous amounts of metadata as well as data. How can one manage such information overflow? There are two complementary solutions. The first one is to turn machines into a new, non-human, type of Web users such that they "understand" the meaning of data on the Web and what to do with them, without any involvement of individuals. This is indeed the main purpose of developing a new version of the Web. The second solution is to make the Web more useful for human beings by presenting data and metadata in a comprehensible visual form. XML and related technologies separate data and presentation rules (HTML does not), and that allows us to present data and metadata in any desirable and visually rich form. This is where information visualization comes into the scene. Information visualization in its own right has become one of the hottest topics over the last few years. The sheer size of the Web has provided an ultimate testbed for information visualization technologies. The appeal of information visualization is so strong and far-reaching that one can find a touch of information visualization in almost every field of study concerning accessing and handling large complex information resources.

The underlying theme of this book is that the Semantic Web and information visualization share many significant issues to such an extent that they demand to be considered together. We call this unifying topic visualization of the Semantic Web. It is an emergent topic. Our book is only one of the first steps in reflecting the potential of this emerging research field. We hope that this book will stimulate and foster more studies and more books on the visualization of the Second Generation Web.

There are two major approaches to semantic web visualizations: (1) adopting and applying existing techniques and (2) developing completely new techniques specifically for the new version of the Web. Since the Semantic Web is expected to be a complex multi-layered building, its visualizations can vary greatly in their types and nature. In this book, we have tried to explore the most significant of them.

The book is arranged as follows.

Chapter 1 introduces the concept and architecture of the Semantic Web and describes the family of XML-related standards that form the technological basis of the new generation of the Web.

Chapter 2 examines how semantics has been dealt with in information visualization and in the Semantic Web. The chapter outlines the origin of information visualization and some of the latest advances in relation to the Semantic Web. An illustrative example is included to highlight the challenges that one has to face in seeking for a synergy of information visualization and the Semantic Web.

Chapter 3 presents the Cluster Map, an expressive and interactive visualization mechanism for ontological information. Its use for information-intensive tasks such as analysis, search and navigation is discussed and demonstrated by a set of case study descriptions.

Chapter 4 focuses on Topic Maps, which are a candidate technology for the Semantic Web. Topic Maps give a semantic structure to information resources and thus enhance navigation within complex data sets. The chapter presents and compares several visualization techniques for Topic Maps.

Chapter 5 introduces the concept of Web rendering, referring to a set of techniques used to show to the user the information residing on the Web and to support making sense of such information. Several criteria that may be used to classify Web visualization systems or, in general, Web rendering systems are discussed and various relevant Web systems are surveyed.

Chapter 6 investigates new technologies – SVG (Scalable Vector Graphics) and X3D (eXtensible 3D) – available for the visualization of 2D and 3D content respectively. The chapter deals with the basics of both technologies and shows that SVG and X3D, based entirely on XML, open essentially new possibilities for the visualization of the Semantic Web.

Chapter 7 reviews research in semantic information retrieval and browsing as well as visual interfaces to digital libraries and information workspaces. It describes the LVis Digital Library Visualizer system that provides a 2D and 3D visual search and browsing environment for documents (text or images) based on a semantic analysis. The chapter concludes with an outlook of semantic information retrieval and browsing in the Semantic Web of tomorrow.

Chapter 8 describes the design and construction of an application conceived to support goal-directed search of single documents. GridVis is an interactive visualization of a document's paragraph-level semantic metadata. The chapter follows the evolution of the design through user testing, empirical evaluation, and theoretical analysis. It also covers the methods used to construct high quality metadata and metadata taxonomies for corporate documents.

Chapter 9 is a brief introduction to Web Services. It presents the main technologies of Web Services and works through an extended example. Its purpose is a comparison to the Semantic Web, both in terms of intrinsic capabilities (where do they complement each other? how can they work together?) and in terms of pragmatic context (how fast are they evolving? what tools do they offer to developers?).

Chapter 10 explores recommender systems – particularly those that perform Web recommendations using collaborative filtering – and examines how they may be enhanced by the Semantic Web. The chapter discusses a number of interface issues related to filtering and recommending on the Web.

Chapter 11 investigates the possibility of developing simple but effective interfaces with interactive visually rich content that enable domain experts to access and manipulate XML metadata and underlying ontologies. Native visualizations, i.e. those that are integral parts of the process of creating and displaying XML documents, are analysed in order to utilize their potential in the interface design.

Chapter 12 explores the use of Scalable Vector Graphics (SVG) and Geographical Information Systems (GIS) in the medical world, specifically being applied to back pain data. The visualization and analytic capabilities offered by these two technologies are harnessed to provide semantically enhanced solutions for the medical community.

PART 1

Semantic, Visual and Technological Facets of the Second Generation Web

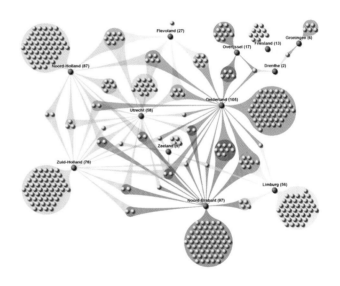

Chapter 1
The XML Revolution and the Semantic Web

Vladimir Geroimenko

1.1 From HTML to XML

The Internet and especially the World Wide Web are among the most remarkable achievements in the history of humankind. Without them, it is impossible to imagine current information services, entertainment and business. Every day more and more ordinary people are getting access to the Web and every one of them is possibly an active builder of the Web. For companies and organizations, a presence on the Web has become something equal to their existence in the modern world as such.

The great success of the Web was based on the simple idea of combining hypertext and a global Internet. This idea lead to a revolution, at the heart of which lay HTML (Hypertext Markup Language). Just by following hypertext links, everyone could get desired information from servers around the globe. In a very short period of time, the use of search engines has enhanced these possibilities dramatically. Moreover, information has also become available not only in simple "text + link" format but also in a variety of multimedia forms, such as images, animation, sound, video or virtual reality.

However, the main advantage of HTML – its simplicity – has a reverse side. HTML was created as a means of presenting information of the Web and is about the spatial layout of a presentation, styling fonts and paragraphs, integrating multimedia elements, enabling user interactivity, and the like. Only humans are able to understand the content of such presentations and to deal with them. Because of it, computers have played a passive and inadequate role in this process – just as the technical means of display, something similar to TV sets or data projectors. They had no real access to the content of a presentation because they were not able to understand the meaning of information on HTML Web pages. On the other hand, the growth of e-commerce created a need for a language that could deal not only with the design (things like "font colour" or "image size") but also with the content (things like "item price" or "sale offer") of a presentation. In other words, there was need for a markup language that would go beyond HTML limits in the following aspects. Firstly, it should describe not only the style but also the content of a Web document. Secondly, it should mark up this content in such a meaningful way that it would be understandable not only by human beings but also (to a certain extent) by computers. Thirdly, it should be sufficiently flexible to describe specific areas of interest of any of the millions of existing and future businesses, companies and organizations.

The good news was that such a language had already existed for many years. It was a metalanguage (i.e. a language for describing languages) called SGML (Standard Generalized Markup Language), which had proved useful in many large publishing applications and was actually used in defining HTML. The bad news was that this language was too complicated, and not very suitable for the Internet.

In early 1998, a new metalanguage was developed by removing the frills from SGML. XML (eXtensible Markup Language) was intended as a foundation of the next-generation Internet. Subsequently, it has spread like wildfire through all the major areas of Web-related science, industry and technology. The XML revolution began.

An XML document is easy to write and to read. Here is an example:

```
<?xml version="1.0"?>
  <VIP_customers shop="Florist">
    <customer>
      <first_name>James</first_name>
      <last_name>Wood</last_name>
      <photo filename="jwood.jpg"/>
    </customer>
  </VIP_customers>
```

Since XML is a plain text format, an XML document can be created using any available text editor and then saved as a file with an extension ".xml". In the above document, the first line called the *XML declaration* is always to be included because it defines the XML version of the document. In this example, the document conforms to the 1.0 specification of XML. The rest of the file is easily understandable by a person, even if they have never heard about XML. It is quite obvious that the file tells us about James Wood, a VIP customer of a shop called "Florist". XML uses *tags* (words or phrases in angle brackets) to mark up the meaning of the data it contains. To show precisely what piece of data they describe, tags usually appear in pairs *start tag – end tag*. The start tag and the end tag must match each other exactly (since XML is case sensitive) except for a forward slash that has to be included in every end tag after the opening angle bracket. The combination "start tag – content – end tag" called an *element* is the main building block of an XML document. Some elements include *attributes* in order to add more information about the content of an element. Attributes are "name-value" pairs enclosed within the start tag of an element. In our example, the element "VIP_customers" has an attribute with the attribute name "shop" and the attribute value "Florist". Some elements can contain no content at all and store data only in their attributes (like the element "photo" in our example: **<photo filename="**jwood.jpg**"/>**). They are called *empty elements* and combine the start and end tags in one, as shown above.

Although XML will form the basis of the new generation of the Web, it is not a replacement for HTML. They are designed for different purposes: XML for describing data, HTML for displaying data. XML cannot throw HTML aside because it needs HTML as a means of presenting the data it describes. At the same time, XML forces HTML to change itself. Everything on the future XML-based Web tends to be written or re-written using the XML syntax. And HTML is not an

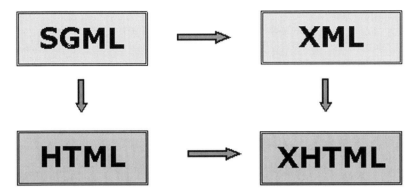

Figure 1.1 Relationships between SGML, XML, HTML and XHTML.

exception. A new generation of HTML called XHTML (eXtensible HTML) began its life as a reformulation of the latest version of HTML, namely HTML 4.0, in XML. That is, HTML will be replaced by XHTML not by XML. The latter two languages will complement one another very well on the future Web. XML will be used to structure and describe the Web data, while XHTML pages will be used to display it. Figure 1.1 shows how SGML, XML, HTML and XHTML are related to each other. It is important to note that SGML and XML are metalanguages and therefore belong to a higher level that the two languages (HTML and XHTML) are directly or indirectly defining.

Since XML is a metalanguage, it allows a company, organization or even an individual to create their own domain-specific markup language, giving them considerable flexibility and functionality. At the same time, this most useful feature of the technology can lead to a paradoxical conclusion that the use of XML technology is in principle hardly possible. Indeed, if every company uses its own XML-based language for its specific business, any meaningful communication between them will be out of the question. For example, Company 1 describes its customers and staff using XML tags **<first_name>** and **<last_name>**, Company 2 uses **<given_name>** and **<surname>**, and Company 3 goes for **<Given_Name>** and **<Surname>**. From a human point of view, these metadata tags convey the same meaning. But for computers they are different, even in the case of the languages developed by Company 2 and Company 3 (since XML is case sensitive). To avoid a "Tower of Babel" scenario, significant efforts are required in order to compensate for the unlimited freedom of creating everyone's own markup languages. Basically, there are two possible solutions to this problem. The first is to create special applications that serve as translators between corporate markup languages of interest. The second is to use existing XML vocabularies developed for horizontal or vertical industry as an intermediary language to enable communication and mutual understanding.

Since XML incorporates a revolutionary new approach to the future of the Web, it has numerous advantages and benefits. Here are only some of them:

- XML is an open industry standard defined by the World Wide Web Consortium (W3C). It is a vendor-independent language, endorsed by all the major software producers and market leaders.

- XML is a text format. Since practically all relevant software and devices are able to process text, XML is good for all platforms, devices, programming languages and software. XML is based on a new multi-lingual character-encoding system called *Unicode* and because of this enables exchange of information across national and cultural boundaries.
- XML separates the content of an XML document from its presentation rules. As a result, the content or any of its fragments can be presented in many desired forms on a variety of devices, such as computers, mobile phones, personal digital assistants or printers.
- XML contains self-describing information. Metadata tags and attributes allow not only humans but also computers to interpret the meaning of XML data.
- XML is both Web-friendly and data-oriented. It enables us to integrate data from any legacy, current and future sources such as databases, text documents and Web pages.

1.2 The XML Family

XML is simple and easy to learn. Its specification is only 26 pages long. However, XML has a huge number of other specifications that help to realize its potential – a family of XML-related languages developed by the W3C. This area is evolving so quickly, that the only way to find out the state of the art is to visit the Consortium Web site (www.w3.org) in order to comprehend the situation as it develops literally day by day. It is good to know that all results of W3C development activities are presented as *Technical Reports*, each of which can reach one of the following levels of maturity (from lower to higher): *Working Draft, Candidate Recommendation, Proposed Recommendation* and *Recommendation.* A Recommendation represents consensus within W3C and is a *de facto* Web standard.

The overview of the XML family provided below is very condensed and classifies the family members in accordance with different stages of the development of XML-based languages and documents. Salminen (2001) gives a very good summary of the XML family of W3C languages, dividing them into four groups: XML, XML Accessories, XML Transducers and XML Applications. Vint (2001) published a technical reference for the XML family of specifications that covers the latest versions of the XML-based standards in more or less complete detail. Our high-level overview of XML-related technologies, which includes their main purpose and meanings of acronyms, is intended to help understand the XML family as a technological basis of the Semantic Web. Figure 1.2 show that the Semantic Web will be built on top of the current Web using XML and its family of technologies.

The stage of **designing and creating XML-based languages and their documents** involves the following members of the XML family:

- *XML* – a metalanguage that allows the creation of markup languages for arbitrary specialized domains and purposes. This is XML as such. For a deeper understanding of the nature of XML as a metalanguage, let us point out some contradictory uses of terms. It seems to be quite common and normal to talk about specific documents being "written in XML". Strictly speaking, however, it is impossible to write even one single document in XML because XML *is not* a language. As a metalanguage, it has no tags at all for

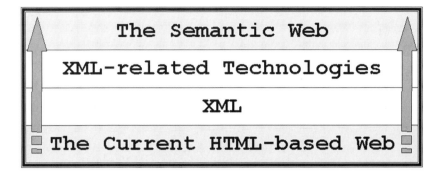

Figure 1.2   Relationships between the current Web, XML technologies and the Semantic Web.

describing any specific content and therefore can be used only as a language-definition tool. This means that one has first to develop a specialized XML-based language (something like "MyML") and only after this is it possible to create documents that are written, strictly speaking, not in XML but in MyML (using XML syntax, of course). Another very common expression is to describe any XML-based language as "an XML application". This seems hardly to be the right use of words. We agree with Misic (2001) who pointed out: "It is rather misleading to describe XHTML and other standards as XML applications. XHTML, RML, and WML are actually XML-specified languages – which is not the same as being an XML application". Almost all members of the XML family listed below are XML-specified languages, i.e. use XML syntax.

- *XML Namespaces* prevent name collision in XML documents by using qualified element and attribute names. A qualified name consists of a namespace name and a local part. The namespace name is a prefix identified by a URI (Uniform Resource Identifier) reference.
- *XML Schema* defines types of elements an XML document can contain, their relationships and the data they can include. A schema can be used for both creating and validating a specific class of XML documents. An XML document must be *well-formed*, i.e. conform to the syntactic rules of XML, and additionally it can be *valid*, i.e. conform to the rules of a schema if it has one.
- *XPath* specifies how to address parts of an XML document.
- *XPointer* extends XPath by defining fragment identifiers for URI references.
- *XLink* provides facilities for creating and describing links between XML documents, including two-way links, links to multiple documents and other types of linking that are much more sophisticated than in HTML.
- *XForms* specifies the use of Web form techniques on a variety of platforms, such as desktop computers, television sets or mobile phones.
- *XML Signature* provides syntax and processing rules for XML digital signatures.

The following members of the XML family are involved in the processes of **accessing, manipulating, transforming and rendering** XML documents:

- *DOM (Document Object Model)* is an application programming interface that describes an XML document as a tree of nodes, and defines the way the nodes are structured, accessed and manipulated.

- *XSL (eXtensible Stylesheet Language)* consists of *XSL-T (XSL Transform-ations)* and *XSL-FO (XSL Formatting Objects)* and is a language for trans-forming XML documents into other XML documents and for rendering them, for example, into HTML, Braille, audible speech and many other forms on a variety of platforms and devices (such as computers, mobile phones, printers, or TV sets).
- *XQuery* is a language for querying XML data that considers an XML file as a database.
- *CSS (Cascading Style Sheets)* is a simple language for specifying style sheets for rendering XML documents.
- *XHTML (eXtensible HTML)* is a reformulation of HTML 4.0 into XML.
- *SVG (Scalable Vector Graphics)* is a language for describing two-dimensional vector and mixed vector/raster graphics in XML.
- *SMIL (Synchronized Multimedia Integration Language)* is used to create multimedia Web presentations by integrating, synchronizing and linking independent multimedia elements such as video, sound, and still images.
- *X3D (eXtensible 3D)* is a markup language that allows VRML (Virtual Reality Markup Language) content to be expressed in terms of XML.
- *WML (Wireless Markup Language)* is a language for presenting some content of Web pages on mobile phones and personal digital assistants.
- *MathML (Mathematical Markup Language)* deals with the representation of mathematical formulae.

The following XML family members are specially intended for **adding a hierarchy of meanings (metadata) to Web data and resources:**

- *RDF* is one of the cornerstones of the Semantic Web. It defines a simple data model using triples (subject, predicate, object), where subject and predicate are URIs and the object is either a URI or a literal. It allows to describe and to retrieve Web data in a way that is similar to using catalogue cards for describing and finding books in a library.
- *RDF Schema* is a key technology for describing basic features of an RDF as well as other RDF vocabularies in order to enable computers to make inferences about the data collected from the Web.
- *DAML + OIL (DARPA Agent Markup Language + Ontology Inference Layer)* are languages for expressing ontologies that extend RDF Schema.
- *Topic Maps* are a new international standard. Written in XML, topics and topic associations build a structured semantic network above information resources. This allows the description and retrieval of Web data in a way that is similar to using the index of a book to find the pages on which a specific topic is covered.

1.3 The Concept of the Semantic Web

The concept of the Semantic Web is based on a vision of Tim Berners-Lee, the inventor of the World Wide Web and the Director of the World Wide Web Consortium. In particular, this vision was expressed in his *Semantic Web Road Map* (Berners-Lee, 1998), his book *Weaving the Web* (Berners-Lee, 1999), and his speech at the XML 2000 conference (Berners-Lee, 2000). Recently many online and magazine articles have appeared which provide a more or less clear explanation of what the Semantic Web actually is (for example, Hellman, 1999; Bosak and Bray, 1999; Dumbill, 2000, 2001; Berners-Lee, Hendler and Lassila, 2001; Palmer, 2001; Cover, 2001). Some Web sites are specially devoted the Semantic Web and its key technologies (for instance, www.semanticweb.org, www.w3c.org/2001/sw/ and www.xml.com).

The main idea of the Semantic Web is to delegate many current human-specific Web activities to computers. They can do them better and quicker than any individuals. But to enable computers to do their new jobs, humans need to express web data in a machine-readable format suitable for completely automate transactions that do not require human intervention. This can be achieved by adding more and more metadata to Web data using XML, RDF, Topic Maps and other technologies. Computers should "understand" not only what a bit of data means but also that other pieces of data, located somewhere on the Web, mean the same even if they look different (for example, `<last_name>` and `<surname>`). Shared data is one of the basic principles the Semantic Web will operate on.

The idea of the "sameness" of Web data will provide a new solution to many current problems, such as more meaningful searches on the Web. For example, if you are looking for "Wood" and specifying this word as a person's last name, you will get back only topics related to people not to timber, firewood or forests. The use of RDF, Topic Maps or other high-level metadata technologies can make Web searches even more powerful and therefore more successful. Computers will be able to automatically convert complex expression from one domain-specific XML language into another in order to process them.

Although the above considerations hopefully provide the reader with a general understanding of the concept, the question "What is the Semantic Web?" is not a simple one. Computer scientists and Web developers from different fields (e.g. e-commerce, networking, knowledge management or artificial intelligence) tend to have quite contradictory views. The new generation of the Web will be so complex and multi-faceted that it allows people with almost any background to find all that they need or want to see. The complexity of the question has led to the setting up of a specialist *Semantic Web Agreement Group (SWAG)* with the mission of defining for people what the Semantic Web is. The following definition provided by SWAG (2001) is an attempt at a clear view of the Semantic Web: "The Semantic Web is a Web that includes documents, or portions of documents, describing explicit relationships between things and containing semantic information intended for automated processing by our machines".

Despite the fact that the above definition is a clear one, it does not prevent people from having a variety of interest-specific views. For one group of researchers and developers, the Semantic Web is a brain for humankind (Fensel and Musen, 2001), for another it is a database for communicating invoices, timetables and other similar information in XML. The spectrum of such views becomes even more diverse when the matter in question is how to implement the concept of the Second-Generation Web, what technologies to use, and in what direction to move. Indeed, there are many ways of constructing the Web and many technologies that can be employed. Figure 1.3 shows some technological differences between the First and Second Generations of the Web.

It is interesting to analyse the conceptual basis of the Semantic Web from a methodological point of view because it helps in developing a deeper

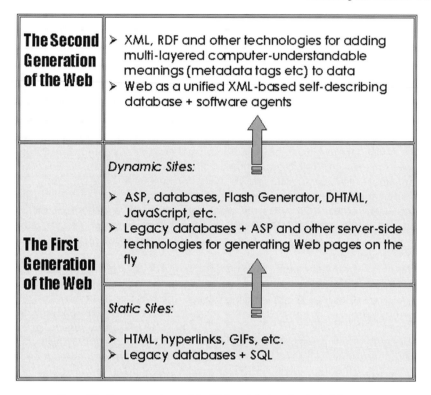

<table>
<tr><td>The Second Generation of the Web</td><td>➤ XML, RDF and other technologies for adding multi-layered computer-understandable meanings (metadata tags etc) to data
➤ Web as a unified XML-based self-describing database + software agents</td></tr>
<tr><td rowspan="2">The First Generation of the Web</td><td>Dynamic Sites:

➤ ASP, databases, Flash Generator, DHTML, JavaScript, etc.
➤ Legacy databases + ASP and other server-side technologies for generating Web pages on the fly</td></tr>
<tr><td>Static Sites:

➤ HTML, hyperlinks, GIFs, etc.
➤ Legacy databases + SQL</td></tr>
</table>

Figure 1.3   Two generations of the Web and their technological features.

understanding of the nature of this new-generation Web. As is generally known, semantics is a branch of linguistics concerned with meaning. The Semantic Web, in contrast to the current HTML-based Web, is all about the meaning of data. If, for instance, 100 means £100 it can be described in XML as **<Price currency="**GBP**">100</Price>**. But if 100 means a speed it might be marked up as **<Speed><mph>100</mph></Speed>**. Obviously, in these cases the same syntax ("100") has different semantics. It is not just a number any more, it is something meaningful and therefore much more useful. It is important to keep in mind that we are here talking about data that are meaningful not only for humans but in the first instance for computers. Human beings do not need any markup metadata tags for understanding current Web pages. For them the existing Web is already the semantic one. But for machines it is meaningless, and therefore non-semantic (perhaps, the only exception is the **<meta>** tag that can be placed in the head section of a HTML Web page in order to add non-displayable information about the author, keywords and so on). Consequently the question arises: from what point does the Web become meaningful for computers (in other words, become "Semantic") and to what extent can it be possible?

A fairly common opinion is that the point where the Semantic Web actually starts is not XML (since this language is "not semantic enough") but RDF, RDF Schema and other more specialized metadata technologies. The proposed architecture of the Second Generation Web will be discussed later in this chapter. Our view is based on a multi-levelled conceptual model of a machine-processable Web. In our opinion, since XML allows us to add meanings to Web data and these meanings can in principle be understandable by computers, we can talk about XML as the first level of the Semantic Web. This new generation of the Web begins where XML and its companion (XHTML) are replacing HTML. Of course, XML is far from being enough to construct the Semantic Web as such. The human system of meanings, and even the current Web resources, are not so simple that they can be described using XML alone. Therefore, the architects of the Semantic Web need to add more and more new levels on top of XML. It is impossible to say what kind of technology will be successfully implemented in the future in order to construct a complex hierarchical system of multi-layered semantic information that would enable computers to understand a little bit more after adding a new layer. At present, for example, RDF seems to be the most suitable technology for adding more meanings to Web data and resources. At the same time, XML Topic Maps looks like a promising candidate for this job as well.

Thus, the Semantic Web has originated in XML which provides a minimal (but not zero) semantic level. This version of the Web will be under development for a long time, adding extra levels of meaning and using new specialist technologies. As a result, computers will be able to "understand" more and to put this to good use. Although it will work, in reality we can talk about meanings, understandable by computers, only in a metaphorical sense. For machines any XML element is still meaningless. For them, the element `<Price in_GBP ="100"/>` makes no more sense than, for example, the element `<Kdg9kj Drdsf=`"100"`/>`. Paradoxically, adding new levels of semantics (using RDF or any other future technologies) does not change the situation. As long as computers do not possess a very special feature, similar to human consciousness, they will not be able to understand any meanings at all. However, by using computers the creators of the Semantic Web will be able to simulate some human understanding of meaningful Web data and, most important, to force machines to make practical use of this.

1.4 The Architecture of the Semantic Web

The first high-level plan of the architecture of the Semantic Web was by Tim Berners-Lee in his *Semantic Web Road Map* (Berners-Lee, 1998) and refined in following publications and presentations (Berners-Lee, 1999, 2000; Berners-Lee, Hendler and Lassila, 2001). According to him, the Semantic Web will be built by adding more layers on the top of existing ones and may take around ten years to complete. Figure 1.4 shows Semantic Web architectural relationships. It is based on the famous "layer cake" diagram, presented by Tim Berners-Lee at the XML 2000 conference (Berners-Lee, 2000).

Most current Semantic Web technologies belong to the XML family and it is almost certain that all future layers will be XML-based as well. XML is the foundation of the new generation of the Web. XML is powered by the URI, Namespaces and Unicode technologies. URIs are intended for identifying arbitrary resources in a unique way; they may or may not "point" to resources or serve for their retrieval. Together with XML Namespaces, they allow everyone to identify uniquely elements within an XML document, without the danger of a

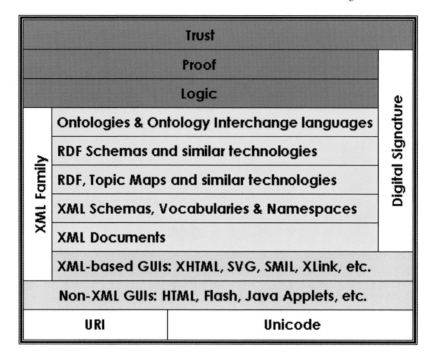

Figure 1.4   The architecture of the Semantic Web.

name collision. Unicode, as a multi-lingual character-encoding system, provides opportunities for describing Web resources in any natural language and therefore enables exchange of information across national and cultural boundaries.

XML documents form the most substantial layer of the Semantic Web, because they embrace, strictly speaking, not only documents with domain-specific content (such as product catalogues) but also almost all "technological" documents written in XML (such as XSL, RDF, or Topic Maps). XML is a universal format for storing and exchanging data and metadata on the new version of the Web.

The XML document layer interfaces with the two main types of Semantic Web users: humans and computers. Although an XML document is, as a rule, saying nothing about how to present its content to an individual, this is not a problem because plenty of formatting and rendering technologies (both legacy and XML-based) are available for displaying XML data in human-readable form (for example, Flash, Java, HTML/XHTML, XSLT, SVG, etc.). Interfacing with computers and especially autonomous software agents is a much more difficult problem. To make XML documents "understandable" and processable by computers, a hierarchy of special layers should be added in order to achieve the goal – to make the meanings of data clear to non-human users of the Web. No one knows how many extra layers will be needed in the future and what kind of new technologies should be implemented.

RDF seems to be the main building block of today's Semantic Web, giving a domain-neutral mechanism for describing metadata in a machine-processable format. RDF is built around the following three concepts: resources, properties and statements. Resources can be anything that can be referred to by a URI (from an entire web site to a single element of any of its XML or XHTML pages). A property is a specific characteristic or relation that describes a resource. RDF statements are composed of triplets: an object (a resource), an attribute (a property), and a value (a resource or free text). They are the formal implementation of a simple idea expressed in natural-language sentences of the following type: "Someone is the *creator/owner/etc.* of something else." RDF statements describe additional facts about an XML vocabulary in an explicit, machine-readable format, and therefore allow computers to understand meanings in context. In this way, they act like the human ability of implicit common-sense understanding of the underlying real-world concepts.

RDF Schemas provide appropriate data typing for RDF documents by defining domain-specific properties and classes of resources to which those properties can be applied. These classes and properties are organized in a hierarchical way by using the basic modelling primitives of the RDF Schema technology: *class* and *property* definitions, and *subclass-of* and *subproperty-of* statements.

Topic Maps are a new standard defined by the International Organization for Standardization (ISO). Like RDF, they are intended to annotate web resources in order to make them understandable by computers. Topic Maps technology can be used to build a semantic network above information resources (some sort of "GPS (Global Positioning System) of the information universe") and thus to enhance navigation in very complex data sets. A Topic Map is an XML document based on the following fundamental concepts: *topics*, *associations* and *occurrences*. Similar to an entry in an encyclopaedia, a topic can represent any subject and therefore almost everything in a Topic Map is a topic. Topics are connected by associations and point to resources through occurrences. An association expresses a relationship between topics. A topic can be linked to one or more occurrences – information resources that are somehow related to this topic. For example, "the Semantic Web" and "the Web" are topics that have an association "is a new version of" and several assurances (places where they are mentioned, including not only text but also images) in this book. The relationship between RDF and Topic Maps technologies is not simple. On the one hand, Topics Maps are in competition with RDF. They provide an effective knowledge-centric approach to metadata in contrast to the resource-centric RDF technique. On the other hand, Topic Maps may be used to model RDF and vice versa.

Ontologies are another fundamental technology for implementing the Semantic Web. They establish a common conceptual description and a joint terminology between members of communities of interest (human or autonomous software agents). An ontology is an explicit specification of a conceptualization (Gruber, 1993). An XML schema can be regarded as a primitive ontology. The construction of the new Web requires ever more expressive languages for describing and matching a variety of "horizontal" and "vertical" ontologies. The latest development in this area includes, on the one hand, generating a variety of ontologies within vertical marketplaces – such as Dublin Core, Common Business Library (CBL), Commerce XML (cXML), Open Catalog Format (OCF), and RosettaNet – and, on the other hand, creating new improved languages that extend RDF Schema by richer sets of modelling primitives for representation of Boolean expressions, property restrictions, axioms, etc. – such as OIL (Ontology Inference Layer) and DAML + OIL (DARPA Agent Markup Language + OIL).

The highest layers of the Semantic Web are yet to be fully developed. The logic layer will contain logical rules that allow computers to make inferences and deductions in order to derive new knowledge. The proof layer will implement languages and mechanisms for distinguishing between Web resources with different levels of trustworthiness. The logic and proof, together with the XML Digital Signature, will enable us to construct the "Web of Trust", where autonomous software agents will be able and allowed to undertake important tasks such as, for example, to find and buy expensive goods without any human intervention.

Thus, the Semantic Web makes maximal use of both Web resources and computers. Computers will not be just devices for posting and rendering data, but will deal with resources in a meaningful and competent way. Current technologies for adding multi-layered machine-processable semantics and heuristics make this development possible.

1.5 References

Berners-Lee T (1998) *Semantic Web Road Map.* Available:
    http://www.w3.org/DesignIssues/Semantic.html
Berners-Lee T (1999) *Weaving the Web.* Harper, San Francisco.
Berners-Lee T (2000) *Semantic Web XML2000.* Available:
    http://www.w3.org/2000/Talks/1206-xml2k-tbl/
Berners-Lee T, Hendler J, Lassila O (2001) The Semantic Web. *Scientific American*, May. Available:
    http://www.scientificamerican.com/2001/0501issue/0501berners-lee.html
Bosak J, Bray T (1999) XML and the Second-Generation Web. *Scientific American*, May. Available:
    http://www.scientificamerican.com/1999/0599issue/0599bosak.html
Cover R (2001) *XML and 'The Semantic Web'.* Available:
    http://www.coverpages.org/xmlAndSemanticWeb.html
Dumbill E (2000) *The Semantic Web: A Primer.* Available:
    http://www.xml.com/lpt/a/2000/11/01/semanticweb/index.html
Dumbill E (2001) *Building the Semantic Web.* Available:
    http://www.xml.com/pub/a/2001/03/07/buildingsw.html
Fensel D, Musen M (2001) The Semantic Web: a brain for humankind. *IEEE Intelligent Systems*,
    15(2):24–25.
Gruber TR (1993) A translation approach to portable ontologies. *Knowledge Acquisition*,
    5(2):199–200.
Hellman R (1999) A semantic approach adds meaning to the Web. *Computer*, December: 13–16.
Misic V (2001) Metalanguage clarification. *Computer*, October: 7.
Palmer S (2001) *The Semantic Web: An Introduction.* Available:
    http://infomesh.net/2001/swintro/
Salminen A (2001) *Summary of the XML family of W3C languages.* Available:
    http://www.cs.jyu.fi/~airi/xmlfamily-20010806.html
SWAG (2001) *What is the Semantic Web?* Available:
    http://swag.webns.net/whatIsSW
Vint D (2001) *XML family of specifications.* Manning Publications, Greenwich, CT.

Chapter 2
Information Visualization Versus the Semantic Web

Chaomei Chen

The appeal and potential of information visualization is increasingly recognized in a wide range of information systems. The Semantic Web sets out the blueprint of the second generation of the ever-popular World Wide Web. Information visualization aims to produce graphical representations of abstract information structure for human users, whereas the Semantic Web aims to rely on a universal descriptive framework of resources that can be utilized by software agents. On the one hand, information visualization and the Semantic Web may compliment each other on a number of fundamental issues concerning the organization of and access to large-scale information resources. On the other hand, the two distinct research fields differ in some fundamental ways in terms of how semantics is defined and represented. It is important for designers and users to be able to distinguish the key differences as well as the major similarities between the two. In this chapter, we outline the origin of information visualization and some of the latest advances in relation to the Semantic Web. An illustrative example is included to highlight the challenges that one has to face in seeking for a synergy of information visualization and the Semantic Web.

2.1 The Semantic Web

The Semantic Web is the second generation of the Web. The Semantic Web is an extension of the current web in which information is given well-defined meaning, better enabling computers and people to work in co-operation (Berners-Lee, Hendler, and Lassila, 2001). The idea is to have data on the Web defined and linked so that it can be used for more effective discovery, automation, integration, and reuse across various applications. The Web can reach its full potential if it becomes a place where data can be shared and processed by automated tools as well as by people. In 1998 Tim Berners-Lee sketched the *Semantic Web Roadmap* (Berners-Lee, 1998), which has become the most cited article about the Semantic Web.

A few topics in the Semantic Web are fundamentally related to information visualization, including topic maps and SVG. The Topic Map[1] community has been finding increasing synergy with the RDF data model.

The World Wide Web was originally built for human consumption, and although everything on it is machine-readable, this data is not machine-understandable.

---

[1]http://www.egroups.com/group/xtm-wg

15

It is very hard to automate anything on the Web. The proposed solution is to use metadata to describe the data on the Web. Metadata is "data about data", or "data describing Web resources". The distinction between "data" and "metadata" depends on a particular application – the same resource could be interpreted in both ways simultaneously.

Resource Description Framework (RDF) is to enable automated processing of Web resources. Research in RDF has identified a variety of application areas. In resource discovery, RDF may lead to better and more efficient search engines. RDF may facilitate the description of the content and content relationships available at a particular Web site or digital library, facilitate knowledge sharing and exchange, and many other appealing possibilities (Berners-Lee, 1998; Berners-Lee et al., 2001).

2.1.1 Visualization Issues

As far as the Semantic Web is concerned, visualizing the structure of a formally defined information resource domain is important not only for designers and developers of the Semantic Web, but also for the business and individual users of the first generation of the Web.

One of the most active areas of the Semantic Web is the development of a variety of tools for authoring, extraction, visualization, and inference RDF. For example, RDFSViz[2] provides a visualization service for ontologies represented in RDF Schema. The RDFSViz tool was implemented in the FRODO project (A Framework for Distributed Organizational Memories) at DFKI Kaiserslautern (German Research Centre for Artificial Intelligence). It uses the open-source graph drawing program Graphviz from AT&T and Lucent Bell Labs (see Figure 2.1 for example). W3C also provides RDF validation service,[3] which can visualize general RDF models. The OntoViz plugin[4] is a similar tool for the knowledge acquisition tool Protégé-2000. OntoViz is much more configurable than RDFSViz.

The OntoViz Tab[5] can visualize Protégé-2000 ontologies with the help of highly sophisticated graph visualization software, namely GraphViz from AT&T.

Once the metadata is available, it is relatively straightforward to use it, to visualize it. It is, however, much harder and more time- and resource-consuming to produce metadata in the first place. Even the quality of metadata generated by domain experts is subject to changes in domain knowledge. In practice, there are situations in which metadata are impossible to generate without an overall understanding of a large-scale complex body of data. Information visualization over the last decade has been devoted to searching for insightful images from such data. A more in-depth analysis of the nature of the problems may help us clarify the scope of the Semantic Web approaches, as well as how information visualization can benefit from the Semantic Web.

---

[2]http://www.dfki.uni-kl.de/frodo/RDFSViz/
[3]http://www.w3.org/RDF/Validator/
[4]http://protege.stanford.edu/plugins/ontoviz/ontoviz.html
[5]http://protege.stanford.edu/plugins/ontoviz/ontoviz.html

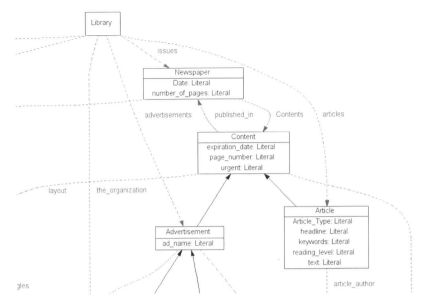

Figure 2.1   A visualization of an RDF model.

2.2 Information Visualization

Information visualization is a rapidly advancing field of study. The number of review and survey articles on information visualization is steadily increasing (Card, 1996; Hearst, 1999; Herman, Melançon, and Marshall, 2000; Hollan, Bederson, and Helfman, 1997; Mukherjea, 1999). There are currently several books on information visualization, notably (Card, Mackinlay, and Shneiderman, 1999; Chen, 1999; Spence, 2001; Ware, 2000). A related book is on algorithms for graph visualization (Battista et al., 1999). Palgrave, Macmillan's global academic publisher, has launched a new, peer-reviewed international journal *Information Visualization* in 2002.

The goal of information visualization is to reveal patterns, trends, and other new insights into a phenomenon. Information visualization focuses on abstract information. A major challenge in information visualization is to transform non-spatial and non-numerical information into effective visual form. This distinct orientation is captured by the following definition (Card et al., 1999): "Information visualization is the use of computer-supported, interactive, visual representations of abstract data to amplify cognition."

Information visualization faces some major fundamental challenges: one is to come up with a design metaphor that will accommodate such transformations from non-spatial, non-numerical data to something visible and meaningful; the other is to find ways to ensure that information visualization functions designed based on a particular metaphor indeed work.

In general, information visualization is at a crossroad, waiting for the "killer applications". Creating or even selecting an appropriate visual metaphor is not simple. A taxonomy that can help one to match a problem at hand with appropriate design metaphors remains on many people's wish list. Information retrieval has brought countless inspirations and challenges to the field of information visualization. It has played considerable roles in shaping the field. Our quest aims to go beyond information retrieval. Our focus is on the growth of scientific knowledge, the key problems to solve and the central tasks to support. Instead of focusing on locating specific items in scientific literature, we turn to higher levels of granularity – scientific paradigms and their movements in scientific frontiers.

Information visualization is particularly in need of a generic theory that can help designers and analysts to assess information visualization designs. Semiotic morphisms is a computational theory on how to preserve the meaning of signs in translating symbol systems. Recently, Joseph Goguen of the University of California at San Diego demonstrated the potential of semiotic morphisms in identifying defects of information visualization (Goguen, 2000).

According to Goguen, the fundamental issues in information visualization can be understood in terms of representation: a visualization is a representation of some aspects of the underlying information; and the main questions are what to represent, and how to represent it. Information visualization needs a theory of representation that can take account not just of the capabilities of current display technology, but also of the structure of complex information, such as scientific data, the capabilities and limitations of human perception and cognition, and the social context of work.

However, classical semiotics, which studies the meaningful use of signs, is not good enough because it has unfortunately not developed in a sufficiently rigorous way for our needs, nor has it explicitly addressed representation; also, its approach to meaning has been naive in some crucial respects, especially in neglecting (though not entirely ignoring) the social basis and context of meaning. This is why semiotics has mainly been used in the humanities, where scholars can compensate for these weaknesses, rather than in engineering design, where descriptions need to be much more explicit. Another deficiency of classical semiotics is its inability to address dynamic signs and their representations, as is necessary for displays that involve change, instead of presenting a fixed static structure, e.g., for standard interactive features like buttons and fill-in forms, as well as for more complex situations like animations and virtual worlds.

Goguen's initial applications of semiotic morphisms on information visualization have led to several principles that may be useful in assessing a range of information visualization design (Goguen, 2000). He suggested three rules of thumbs:

- Measuring quality by what is preserved and how it is preserved.
- It is more important to preserve structure than content when a trade-off is forced.
- The need to take account of social aspects in user interface design.
- The semiotics morphisms methodology is not just algebraic but also social. More in-depth studies are needed to verify the power of this approach.

2.2.1 Tracking Knowledge and Technology Trends

Tracking knowledge and technology transfer can be a challenging but potentially rewarding task if it can be accomplished on the new generation of the World

Wide Web – the Semantic Web. The aim is to transform billions of machine-readable and human-friendly documents on the first generation of the Web to machine-understandable forms in the second generation of the Web.

Knowledge visualization is not merely knowledge representation gone graphical. With knowledge visualization, the goal is to help us to track down a cognitive and intellectual movement from the available resources on the Web.

2.2.2 Citation Analysis

In information science, the term specialty refers to the perceived grouping of scientists who are specialized on the same or closely related topics of research. Theories of how specialties evolve and change started to emerge in the 1970s (Small and Griffith, 1974). Researchers began to focus on the structure of scientific literatures in order to identify and visualize specialties, although they did not use the term "visualization" at that time.

Today's most widely used citation index databases such as SCI and SSCI were conceived in the 1950s, especially in Garfield's pioneering paper (Garfield, 1955). In the 1960s, several pioneering science mapping studies began to emerge. For example, Garfield, Sher, and Torpie created the historical map of research in DNA (Garfield, H., and Torpie, 1964). Sher and Garfield demonstrated the power of citation analysis in their study of Nobel Prize winners' citation profiles (Sher and Garfield, 1966).

The 1980s saw the beginning of what turned out to be a second fruitful line of development in the use of citation to map science – author co-citation analysis (ACA). Howard White and Belver Griffith introduced ACA in 1981 as a way to map intellectual structures (White and Griffith, 1981). The unit of analysis in ACA is authors and their intellectual relationships as reflected through scientific literatures. The author-centred perspective of ACA led to a new approach to the discovery of knowledge structures in parallel to approaches used by document-centred co-citation analysis (DCA).

The author co-citation map produced by White and Griffith (1981) depicted information science over an 8-year span (1972–1979). In 1998, 17 years later, White and McCain (1998) generated a new map of information science based on a considerably expanded 23-year span (1972–1995).

An author co-citation network offers a useful alternative starting point for co-citation analysis, especially when we encounter a complex document co-citation network, and vice versa. Katherine McCain (1990) gave a comprehensive technical review of mapping authors in intellectual spaces. ACA reached a significant turning point in 1998 when White and McCain (1998) applied ACA to information science in their thorough study of the field. Since then ACA has flourished and has been adopted by researchers across a number of disciplines beyond the field of citation analysis itself. White and McCain's paper won the best JASIS paper award. With both ACA and DCA in our hands, we begin to find ourselves in a position to compare and contrast messages conveyed through different co-citation networks of the same topic. Robert Braam, Henk Moed and Anthony van Raan investigated whether co-citation analysis indeed provided a useful tool for mapping subject-matter specialties of scientific research (Braam, Moed, and Raan, 1991a, 1991b).

2.2.3 Patent Citation Analysis

Patent analysis has a long history in information science, but recently there has been a surge of interest from the commercial sector. Numerous newly formed companies are specifically aiming at the patent analysis market. Apart from historical driving forces such as monitoring knowledge and technology transfer and staying in competition, the rising commercial interest in patent analysis is partly due to publicly accessible patent databases, notably the huge amount of patent applications and grants from the United States Patent and Trademark Office (USPTO). The public can search patents and trademarks at USPTO's website http://www.uspto.gov/ and download bibliographic data from ftp://ftp.uspto.gov/pub/patdata/.

The availability of abundant patent data, the increasingly widespread awareness of information visualization, and the maturity of search engines on the Web are among the most influential factors behind the emerging trend of patent analysis. Many patent search interfaces allow users to search by specific sections in patent databases, for example by claims. Statistical analysis and intuitive visualization functions are by far the most commonly seen selling points from a salesman's patent analysis portfolio. The term visualization has become so fashionable now in the patent analysis industry that from time to time we come across visualization software tools that turn out to be little more than standard displays of statistics. Table 2.1 lists some of the prominent vendors and service providers in patent analysis.

A particularly interesting example is from Sandia National Laboratory. Kevin Boyack and his colleagues (2000) used their landscape-like visualization tool VxInsight to analyse the patent bibliographic files from USPTO in order to answer a number of questions. For example: Where are competitors placing their efforts? Who is citing our patents, and what types of things have they developed? Are there emerging competitors or collaborators working in related areas? The analysis was based on 15,782 patents retrieved from a specific primary classification class from the US Patent database. The primary classification class is class 360 on Dynamic Magnetic Information Storage or Retrieval. A similarity measure

Table 2.1   A recent surge of patent analysis

Software	Functionality	Applications	Homepage
Aurigin	Patent searching; analysis; visualization	Patent analysis; knowledge management	http://www.aurigin.com/
Delphion	Patent searching	Intellectual property management	http://www.delphion.com/
ImageSpace	Analysis and visualization	Confocal imaging	http://www.mdyn.com/
Mapit	Patent mining		http://www.mnis.net/
OmniViz Pro	Information visualization; data mining	Life sciences; chemical sciences	http://64.77.30.212/default.htm
PatentLab II	Analysis	Extracting intelligence from patent data	http://www.wisdomain.com/
SemioMap	Text analysis	Multi-layered concept maps	http://www1.semio.com/

Source: Chen (2002, Table 5.3).

was calculated using the direct and co-citation link types of Small (1997). Direct citations were given a weighting five times that of each co-citation link.

2.3 A Harmonious Relationship?

2.3.1 Beyond Information Retrieval

Science mapping reveals structures hidden in scientific literature. The definition of association determines the nature of the structure to be extracted, to be visualized, and to be eventually interpreted. Co-word analysis (Callon, Law, and Rip, 1986) and co-citation analysis (Small, 1973) are among the most fundamental techniques for science mapping. Small (1988) described the two as follows: "if co-word links are viewed as translations between problems, co-citation links have been viewed as statements relating concepts." They are the technical foundations of the contemporary quantitative studies of science. Each offers a unique perspective on the structure of scientific frontiers. Researchers have found that a combination of co-word and co-citation analysis could lead to a clearer picture of the cognitive content of publications (Braam et al., 1991a, 1991b).

Among the most seminal works in information science, the contribution of Derek de Solla Price (1922–1983) is particularly worth noting, namely his "Networks of scientific papers" (Price, 1965), *Little Science, Big Science* (Price, 1963), and *Science since Babylon*. In *Little Science, Big Science*, Price raised the profound questions: Why should we not turn the tools of science on science itself? Why not measure and generalize, make hypotheses, and derive conclusions? He used the metaphor of studying the behaviour of gas in thermodynamics as an analogy of the science of science. Thermodynamics studies the behaviour of gas under various conditions of temperature and pressure, but the focus is not on the trajectory of a specific molecule. Instead, one considers the phenomenon as a whole. Price suggested that we should study science in a similar way: the volume of science, the trajectory of "molecules" in science, the way in which these "molecules" interact with each other, and the political and social properties of this "gas".

Scientists in general and information scientists in particular have been influenced by Thomas Kuhn's structure of scientific revolutions (Kuhn, 1962), Paul Thagard conceptual revolutions (Thagard, 1992), and Diana Crane's invisible colleges (Crane, 1972). The notion of tracking scientific paradigms originates in this influence. Two fruitful strands of efforts are particularly worth noting here. One is the work of Eugene Garfield and Henry Small at the Institute for Scientific Information (ISI) in mapping science through citation analysis. The other is the work of Michel Callon and his colleagues in tracking changes in scientific literature using the famous co-word analysis. In fact, their co-word analysis is designed for a much wider scope – scientific inscriptions, which include technical reports, lecture notes, grant proposals, and many others as well as publications in scholarly journals and conference proceedings. More detailed analysis of these examples can be found in Chen (2002). The new trend today focuses more specifically on the dynamics of scientific frontiers. What are the central issues in a prolonged scientific debate? What constitutes a context in which a prevailing theory evolves? How can we visualize the process of a paradigm shift? Where are the rises and falls of competing paradigms in the context of scientific frontiers? What are the most appropriate ways to visualize scientific frontiers? What can the Semantic Web do to help us address these questions?

One of the most influential works of the 20th century is the theory of the structure of scientific revolutions by Thomas Kuhn (1922–1996) (Kuhn, 1962). Before Kuhn's structure, the philosophy of science had been dominated by what is known as the logical empirical approach. Logical empiricism uses modern formal logic to investigate how scientific knowledge could be connected to sense experience. It emphasizes the logical structure of science rather than its psychological and historical development.

Kuhn criticized that logical empiricism cannot adequately explain the history of science. He claimed that the growth of scientific knowledge is characterized by revolutionary changes in scientific theories. According to Kuhn, most of the time scientists are engaged in what is known as normal science. A period of normal science is typically marked by the dominance of an established framework. The majority of scientists would work on specific hypotheses within such frameworks or paradigms. The foundations of such paradigms largely remain unchallenged until new discoveries begin to cast doubts over fundamental issues. As anomalies build up, attention is suddenly turned to an examination of previously taken for granted basic assumptions – science falls into a period of crises. To resolve such crises, radically new theories with greater explanatory power are introduced. New theories replace the ones in trouble in a revolutionary manner. Science regains another period of normal science. Scientific revolutions, as Kuhn claimed, are an integral part of science and science progresses through such revolutionary changes.

Diana Crane is concerned with scientific ideas and how they grow into a body of knowledge in *Invisible Colleges: Diffusion of Knowledge in Scientific Communities* (Crane, 1972). She suggests that it is the "invisible college" that is responsible for the growth of scientific knowledge. An invisible college constitutes a small group of highly productive scientists. They share the same field of study, communicate with one another and thus monitor the rapidly changing structure of knowledge in their field. Howard White and Katherine McCain identified the domain structure of information science by using author co-citation analysis (White and McCain, 1998).

Steve Steinberg addressed several questions regarding the use of a quantitative approach to identify paradigm shifts in the real world (Steinberg, 1994). He examined the history of Reduced Instruction Set Computing (RISC). The idea behind RISC was that a processor with only a minimal set of simple instructions could outperform a processor that included instructions for complex high-level tasks. In part, RISC marked a clear shift in computer architecture and had reached some degree of consensus. Steinberg searched for quantitative techniques that could help his investigation. He adapted the co-word analysis technique to produce a map of the field, a visualization of the mechanisms, and a battle chart of the debate. He collected all abstracts with the keyword RISC for the years 1980–1993 from the INSPEC database, filtered out the 200 most common English words, and ranked the remaining words by frequency. The top 300 most frequently occurring words were given to three RISC experts to choose those words central to the field. Finally, words chosen by the experts were aggregated by synonyms into 45 keyword clusters. The inclusion index was used to construct a similarity matrix. This matrix was mapped by MDS with ALSCAL. The font size of a keyword was proportional to the word's frequency. Straight lines in the co-word map denoted strongly linked keywords.

The first papers to explicitly examine and define RISC appeared within the period 1980–1985. The design philosophy of RISC was opposed to the traditional computing architecture paradigm; every paper in this period was written to defend and justify RISC. The map shows two main clusters. One is on the left, surrounding keywords such as register, memory, simple, and pipeline. These are the architectural terms that uniquely define RISC. The other cluster is on the right, centred on keywords such as language and CISC. These are the words that identify the debate between the RISC and CISC camps. Language is the most frequent keyword on the map. According to Steinberg, the term language most clearly captures the key to the debate between RISC and CISC. While CISC proponents believe that a processor's instruction set should closely correspond to high-level languages such as FORTRAN and COBOL, RISC proponents argue that simple instructions are better than high-level instructions. This debate is shown in the co-word map with the connections between language, CISC, compiler, and programming. For a detailed description and a reproduction of the co-word maps, readers are referred to Chen (2002).

Chen, Kuljis, and Paul (2001) explored how to overcome some of the difficulties in visualizing under-represented latent domain knowledge through two case studies: one on knowledge representation and the other on a controversial theory on the causes of mad cow disease. Chen, Cribbin, Macredie, and Morar (Chen et al., 2002) reported two more case studies of tracking competing paradigms using information visualization. One case study was about the active galactic nuclei paradigm in astronomy and astrophysics and the other was about mad cow disease in medical science.

2.3.2 Yin and Yang

Hjorland has promoted domain analysis in information science (Hjorland, 1997; Hjorland and Albrechtsen, 1995). The unit of domain analysis is a specialty, a discipline, or a subject matter. In contrast to existing approaches to domain analysis, Hjorland emphasized the essential role of a social perspective instead of the more conventional psychological perspective.

Hjorland called his approach the activity-theoretical approach. Traditional approaches focus on individuals as single users of information in terms of their cognitive structures and strategies. The activity-theoretical approach, on the other hand, emphasizes a holistic view of information retrieval issues in a much broader context so that the needs of the user are always interpreted in the context of the discipline (see Table 2.2). The relevance of a retrieved item is linked directly to the substance of a subject matter. This view is in line with the goal of domain visualization, that is to provide a meaningful context in which scientists can explore the body of knowledge as a whole, as opposed to dealing with fragmented pieces of knowledge. Domain visualization underlines the development of a research theme in scientific literature.

The major differences between the Semantic Web and information visualization are similar. The Semantic Web emphasises formal, machine-understandable, and sometimes cognitivism-like approaches. It focuses on the form and even the meaning achieved through rigorously defined forms. In contrast, information

Table 2.2 Differences between cognitivism and the domain-specific viewpoint (Hjorland and Albrechtsen, 1995)

Cognitivism	Domain-specific view
Priority is given to the understanding of isolated user needs and intrapsychological analysis. Intermediating between producers and users emphasizes psychological understanding.	Priority is given to the understanding of user needs from a social perspective and the functions of information systems in trades or disciplines.
Focus on the single user. Typically looks at the disciplinary context as a part of the cognitive structure of an individual – if at all.	Focus on either one knowledge domain or the comparative study of different knowledge domains. Looks at the single user in the context of the discipline.
Mainly inspired by artificial intelligence and cognitive psychology.	Mainly inspired by knowledge about the information structures in domains, by the sociology of knowledge and the theory of knowledge.
The psychological theory emphasizes the role of cognitive strategies in performance.	The psychological theory emphasizes the interaction among aptitudes, strategies, and knowledge in cognitive performance.
Central concepts are individual knowledge structures, individual information processing, short- and long-term memory, categorical versus situational classification.	Central concepts are scientific and professional communication, documents (including bibliographies), disciplines, subjects, information structures, paradigms, etc.
Methodology characterized by an individualistic approach.	Methodology characterized by a collectivistic approach.
Methodological individualism has some connection to a general individualistic view, but the difference between the cognitive and the domain-specific view is not a different political perception of the role of information systems, but a different theoretical and methodological approach to the study and optimization of information systems.	Methodological collectivism has some connection to a general collectivistic view, but the difference between cognitivism and the domain-specific view is not a different political perception of the role of information systems, but a different theoretical and methodological approach to the study and optimization of information systems.
Best examples of applications: user interfaces (the outer side of information systems).	Best examples of applications: subject-representation/classification (the inner side of information systems).
Implicit theory of knowledge: mainly rationalistic/positivistic, tendencies toward hermeneutics.	Theory of knowledge: scientific realism/forms of social constructivism with tendencies towards hermeneutics.
Implicit ontological position: subjective idealism.	Ontological position: realism.

visualization emphasizes the semantics and the meaning that can be conveyed by visual-spatial models to the users. The form for information visualization is secondary. The following is an illustrative example. The question is: to what extent is the Semantic Web suitable to handle semantics associated with high-level, volatile information structures?

2.3.3 An Illustrative Example

In the following example, we illustrate the challenges one has to face in order to benefit from the best of the both worlds. This is a typical citation analysis enhanced by information visualization techniques. The goal of this study is to identify the overall structure and the central issues of patent citation analysis. A description of the procedure for a general audience can be found in Chen and Paul (2001).

In order to generate a brief snapshot of the field of patent citation analysis, we searched the Web of Science on 15 January 2002 for the period 1990 to 2001. The Web of Science allows the user to specify the appearance of keywords in a number of fields. We would like to find all the articles that not only contain the keywords patent and citation, but they must appear within the same sentence. The Web of Science allows us to specify our requirement with a search query "patent same citation" in topic, which covers the fields of title, abstract, and keyword (see Figure 2.2).

A total of 36 records were found by this query (see Figure 2.3). The hit rate is relatively small, considering some queries may result in hundreds or thousands

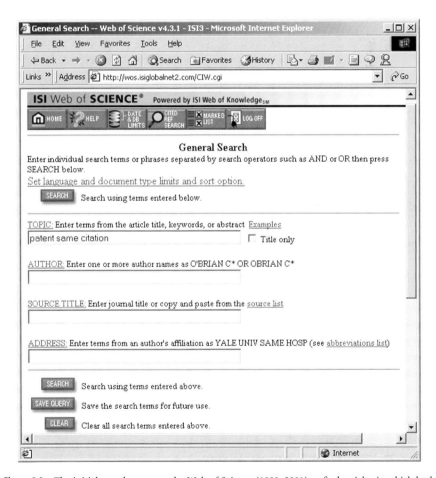

Figure 2.2   The initial search query to the Web of Science (1990–2001) to find articles in which both patent and citation appear within the same sentence in title, abstract, or keyword list. Date of search: 15 January 2002.

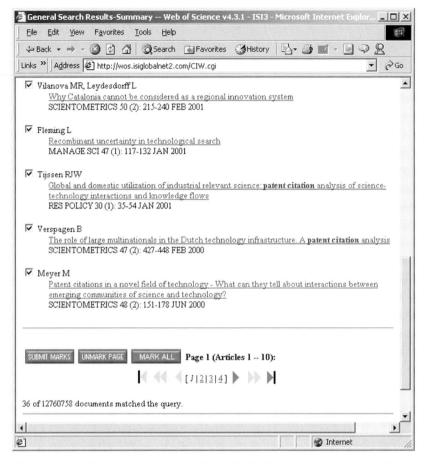

Figure 2.3   A total of 36 hits were returned by Web of Science on patent citation analysis.

of hits. A low hit rate like this reflects the size of the patent citation analysis literature. Nevertheless, these 36 records allow us to glimpse into the history and the state of the art of patent citation analysis. Each of these 32 records contains a list of references. It is this set of references that form the basis of a snapshot of patent citation analysis (see Figure 2.4).

The 36 citing documents cited 97 unique articles at least once. A snapshot of the intellectual structure was generated based on the 97-by-97 document co-citation matrix. Figure 2.5 shows the overview of the snapshot and four close-up views of individual components. Articles that have been cited more than three times are labelled in the scene. The three-dimensional landscape scene was rendered in Virtual Reality Modelling Language (VRML). The base structure is defined by Pathfinder network scaling (Chen, 1998a, 1998b; Schvaneveldt, 1990). The node-and-link structure denotes the connectivity between cited documents on patent citation analysis. The colour of a node indicates the specialty membership of the corresponding document cited. The colour is determined by

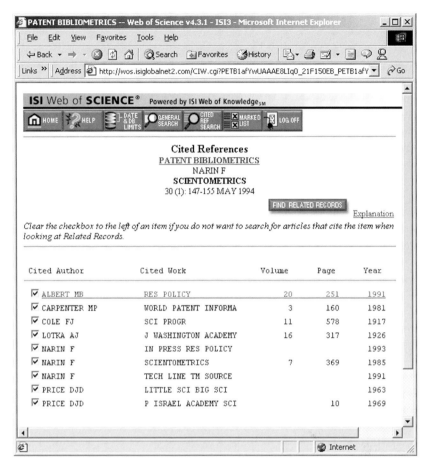

Figure 2.4 Each of the 36 records cites a list of references. The creation of a snapshot is based on inter-relationships among all the references cited collectively by the 36 publications.

the results of Principle Component Analysis (PCA); in particular, the factor loading coefficients of the three most predominant factors are mapped to the red, green, and blue strengths of the final colour. A cluster or sub-graph in red essentially corresponds to the largest predominant factor, which normally represents the strongest specialty in the field. The second strongest specialty would be in green and the third in blue. A well-balanced specialty would have a colour close to white, which is the perfect balanced colour of equal amounts of red, green, and blue. In Figure 2.5, there is a purple cluster located towards the lower left corner of the view (cluster 1); a green cluster towards the lower right corner (cluster 2); a small blue cluster in the remote distance (cluster 3); and a long-shaped cluster connecting cluster 3 to the centre of the network (cluster 5). Each cluster is also shown in insets at the corners of the figure.

The height of a vertical bar stemmed from an article is proportional to the number of times the article has been cited by the 36 citing articles as a whole.

Figure 2.5 A snapshot of the patent citation analysis field based on the co-citation visualization procedure explained in Chen and Paul (2001).

We have demonstrated the power of animated visualizations of citation landscapes in a number of case studies based on ISI's citation index databases (Chen et al., 2001, forthcoming). We are currently extending this streamlined procedure from co-citation analysis of scientific literature to patent citation analysis based on patent databases. On the one hand, we will distinguish citation networks reflected through patent applications and those from granted patents. On the other hand, we are more interested in the interrelationship and time-series relationships involving both scientific literature and patent databases.

Table 2.3 lists the six factors extracted by Principle Component Analysis. Each factor corresponds to a non-exclusive specialty, which means a document could

Table 2.3 Factors extracted by Principle Component Analysis. Each factor corresponds to a non-exclusive specialty

Component	Extracton sums of squared loadings			Rotation sums of squared loadings		
	Eigenvalue	% of variance	Cumulative %	Eigenvalue	% of variance	Cumulative %
1	47.139	48.597	48.597	46.435	47.872	47.872
2	24.338	25.091	73.688	23.171	23.887	71.759
3	8.403	8.663	82.351	7.589	7.824	79.582
4	6.584	6.787	89.138	7.550	7.784	87.366
5	3.120	3.216	92.354	3.569	3.680	91.046
6	1.451	1.496	93.850	2.720	2.804	93.850

Table 2.4 A ranked list of documents in the first specialty. Documents in this specialty should be coloured in red

Factor loading	Cited references
0.932	NARIN F, 1997, RES POLICY, V26, P317
0.906	NARIN F, 1995, RES EVALUAT, V5, P183
0.905	MARTIN B, 1996, RELATIONSHIP PUBLICL
0.905	NOYONS ECM, 1994, RES POLICY, V23, P443
0.905	VANVIANEN BG, 1990, RES POLICY, V19, P61
0.904	NARIN F, 1985, SCIENTOMETRICS, V7, P369
0.899	CARPENTER MP, 1983, WORLD PATENT INFORMA, V5, P180
0.899	SCHMOCH U, 1993, SCIENTOMETRICS, V26, P193
0.889	GIBBONS M, 1994, NEW PRODUCTION KNOWL
0.884	*IITRI, 1968, TECHN RETR CRIT EV S
0.879	PAVITT K, 1984, RES POLICY, V13, P343
0.878	NARIN F, 1994, SCIENTOMETRICS, V30, P147
0.873	BRAUN T, 1997, SCIENTOMETRICS, V38, P321

belong to more than one specialty. These six factors explained a total of 94% of variance.

To date, the nature of a specialty cannot be algorithmically identified. This is in part due to the incompleteness of the source data. For example, it contains no further information on a cited reference, no title and no abstract. This is where the Semantic Web could play a substantial role in piecing together a comprehensive description of a given reference from a number of different resources. Currently, NEC's ResearchIndex has done a great job by scanning scientific publications on the Web and building an increasingly comprehensive, online accessible bibliographic database. Table 2.4 shows a ranked list of documents in the first specialty. For example, Narin's 1997 article published in *Research Policy* has the highest factor loading coefficient 0.932, which implies that Narin's article is the most representative of this specialty. In the Semantic Web, a bibliographic agent could go out and fetch further details of this article, such as its title and abstract, behind the scenes. Furthermore, an automated summarization agent could produce a short list of keywords that can be used to characterize the nature of the specialty.

Table 2.5 lists the predominant documents in the second specialty. Price's *Little Science, Big Science* tops the list with a factor loading of 0.507. Sometimes the significance of a document like *Little Science, Big Science* cannot be fully appreciated without substantial knowledge of a domain. Documents in the second specialty should be found in green in the scene.

Table 2.6 shows a ranked list of documents from the third largest specialty. Document in this specialty should be in blue colour. Henry Small's three articles are included in the top ten of this specialty. Small is well known for his work in citation analysis using ISI's data; thus his three articles strongly indicate the nature of this specialty.

Table 2.5 A ranked list of documents in the second largest specialty. Documents in this specialty should be essentially coloured in green

Factor loading	Cited references
0.507	PRICE DJD, 1963, LITTLE SCI BIG SCI
0.408	ABERNATHY WJ, 1978, TECHNOLOGY REV JUN, P40
0.408	ALLEN T, 1977, MANAGING FLOW TECHNO
0.408	BASALLA G, 1988, EVOLUTION TECHNOLOGY
0.408	CAMERON AC, 1986, J APPLIED ECONOMETRI, V1, P29
0.408	AVETTI G, 2000, ADMIN SCI QUART, V45, P113
0.408	GILFILLAN S, 1935, INVENTING SHIP
0.408	HALL B, 2000, NBER WORKING PAPER, V7741
0.408	HARGADON A, 1997, ADMIN SCI QUART, V42, P716
0.408	HAUSMAN J, 1984, ECONOMETRICA, V52, P909
0.408	HENDERSON RM, 1990, ADMIN SCI QUART, V35, P9
0.408	KING G, 1989, INT STUD QUART, V33, P123
0.408	LEVIN RC, 1987, BROOKINGS PAPERS EC, V3, P783
0.408	MARCH J, 1958, ORGANIZATIONS
0.408	MARCH JG, 1991, ORG SCI, V2, P71
0.408	MCCLUSKEY E, 1986, LOGIC DESIGN PRINCIP
0.408	NELSON R, 1982, EVOLUTIONARY THEORY
0.408	RIVKIN JW, 2000, MANAGE SCI, V46, P824
0.408	SCHUMPETER J, 1939, BUSINESS CYCLES
0.408	SIMON H, 1996, SCI ARTIFICIAL
0.408	TUSHMAN ML, 1986, ADMIN SCI QUART, V31, P439
0.408	ULRICH K, 1995, RES POLICY, V24, P419
0.408	WEITZMAN M, 1996, P AM ECONOM ASS MAY, P207
0.399	ROSENBERG N, 1982, INSIDE BLACK BOX TEC
0.390	TRAJTENBERG M, 1990, RAND J ECON, V21, P172
0.380	ALBERT MB, 1991, RES POLICY, V20, P251
0.377	NARIN F, 1985, SCIENTOMETRICS, V7, P369
0.366	NARIN F, 1994, SCIENTOMETRICS, V30, P147
0.365	CAMPBELL B, 1989, EXPERT EVIDENCE INTE, P210
0.365	COLLINS P, 1988, RES POLICY, V17, P65
0.365	MALSCH I, 1997, NANOTECHNOLOGY EUROP
0.365	MEYERKRAHMER F, 1997, CHEM INFORMATION TEC
0.365	RIP A, 1986, MAPPING DYNAMICS SCI, P84
0.365	VANDENBELT H, 1989, EXPERT EVIDENCE INTE
0.363	MEYER M, 1998, SCIENTOMETRICS, V42, P195
0.360	*IITRI, 1968, TECHN RETR CRIT EV S

Tables 2.7–2.9 show documents in the 4th, 5th, and 6th specialty, respectively. A number of documents appear in more than one specialty. The more generic a document, the more likely that it will appear in different specialties. Table 2.10 lists documents that appear in three or more specialties, along with the three

Table 2.6 A ranked list of documents in the third largest specialty (in blue)

Factor loading	Cited references
0.824	NARIN F, 1988, HDB QUANTITATIVE STU
0.772	TRAJTENBERG M, 1990, RAND J EC, V21
0.761	FRANKLIN JJ, 1988, HDB QUANTITATIVE STU, P325
0.761	MOGEE ME, 1998, EXPERT OPIN THER PAT, V8, P213
0.761	SMALL H, 1985, SCIENTOMETRICS, V7, P391
0.761	SMALL H, 1974, SCI STUD, V4, P17
0.752	SMALL H, 1973, J AM SOC INFORM SCI, V24, P265
0.614	CARPENTER MP, 1981, WORLD PATENT INFORMA, V3, P160
0.602	*US DEP COMM, 1992, TECHN PROF REP SEM
0.602	BRAUN E, 1982, REVOLUTION MINIATURE
0.602	NARIN F, 1987, RES POLICY, V16, P143
0.602	ROGERS EM, 1984, SILICON VALLEY FEVER
0.602	SAXENIAN AL, 1991, RES POLICY, V20, P423
0.572	KRUGMAN P, 1991, GEOGRAPHY TRADE
0.333	CAMPBELL RS, 1979, TECHNOLOGY INDICATOR
0.258	PRICE DJD, 1963, LITTLE SCI BIG SCI
0.124	ALBERT MB, 1991, RES POLICY, V20, P251

articles of Henry Small. In particular, Derek Price's *Little Science, Big Science* appears in specialties 2, 3, 4, and 6.

This example shows that we can generate a snapshot of a knowledge domain based on co-citation patterns. We are currently undertaking research in order to

Table 2.7 A ranked list of documents in the 4th specialty. The colour of a document in this specialty is determined by its factor loadings in the 1st, 2nd, and 3rd specialties

Factor loading	Cited references
0.714	KRUGMAN P, 1991, GEOGRAPHY TRADE
0.672	GROSSMAN GM, 1991, INNOVATION GROWTH GL
0.631	*US DEP COMM, 1992, TECHN PROF REP SEM
0.631	BRAUN E, 1982, REVOLUTION MINIATURE
0.631	NARIN F, 1987, RES POLICY, V16, P143
0.631	ROGERS EM, 1984, SILICON VALLEY FEVER
0.631	SAXENIAN AL, 1991, RES POLICY, V20, P423
0.622	CARPENTER MP, 1981, WORLD PATENT INFORMA, V3, P160
0.436	PRICE DJD, 1963, LITTLE SCI BIG SCI
0.407	NARIN F, 1988, HDB QUANTITATIVE STU, P465
0.379	ARTHUR WB, 1989, ECON J, V99, P116
0.310	JAFFE AB, 1986, AM ECON REV, V76, P984
0.276	PAVITT K, 1982, EMERGING TECHNOLOGIE
0.251	JAFFE AB, 1993, Q J ECON, V108, P577

Table 2.8 A ranked list of documents in the 5th specialty

Factor loading	Cited references
0.391	PRICE DJD, 1965, TECHNOL CULT, V6, P553
0.293	CAMPBELL B, 1989, EXPERT EVIDENCE INTE, P210
0.293	MALSCH I, 1997, NANOTECHNOLOGY EUROP
0.293	MEYERKRAHMER F, 1997, CHEM INFORMATION TEC
0.293	RIP A, 1986, MAPPING DYNAMICS SCI, P84
0.293	VANDENBELT H, 1989, EXPERT EVIDENCE INTE
0.287	MEYER M, 1998, SCIENTOMETRICS, V42, P195
0.264	CARPENTER MP, 1981, WORLD PATENT INFORMA, V3, P160
0.258	BRAUN T, 1997, SCIENTOMETRICS, V38, P321
0.254	*US DEP COMM, 1992, TECHN PROF REP SEM
0.293	BRAUN E, 1982, REVOLUTION MINIATURE
0.293	NARIN F, 1987, RES POLICY, V16, P143
0.293	ROGERS EM, 1984, SILICON VALLEY FEVER
0.293	SAXENIAN AL, 1991, RES POLICY, V20, P423
0.253	COLLINS P, 1988, RES POLICY, V17, P65
0.235	PAVITT K, 1984, RES POLICY, V13, P343
0.197	NARIN F, 1994, SCIENTOMETRICS, V30, P147
0.162	CAMPBELL RS, 1979, TECHNOLOGY INDICATOR

extend and unify citation analysis of scientific literature and patent citation analysis. There are at least two potentially fruitful routes. First, by visualizing the interconnections between scientific literature and patent offices' databases, one can provide a more detailed understanding of the dynamics of knowledge and technology transfer. Science and technology policy decision-makers and

Table 2.9 A ranked list of documents in the 6th specialty. Small's three articles appear again in this specialty, suggesting a considerable overlap between the 3rd and the 6th specialties

Factor loading	Cited references
0.273	GROSSMAN GM, 1991, INNOVATION GROWTH GL
0.211	PRICE DJD, 1963, LITTLE SCI BIG SCI
0.199	ARTHUR WB, 1989, ECON J, V99, P116
0.177	NARIN F, 1988, HDB QUANTITATIVE STU, P465
0.140	SMALL H, 1973, J AM SOC INFORM SCI, V24, P265
0.127	FRANKLIN JJ, 1988, HDB QUANTITATIVE STU, P325
0.127	MOGEE ME, 1998, EXPERT OPIN THER PAT, V8, P213
0.127	SMALL H, 1985, SCIENTOMETRICS, V7, P391
0.127	SMALL H, 1974, SCI STUD, V4, P17
0.108	NARIN F, 1988, HDB QUANTITATIVE STU
0.106	NELSON RR, 1982, EVOLUTIONARY THEORY
0.104	*IITRI, 1968, TECHN RETR CRIT EV S
0.103	MANSFIELD E, 1991, RES POLICY, V20, P1

Table 2.10   Documents appearing in three or more specialties

Number of specialties	Occurring specialties	Documents
4	2, 3, 4, 6	PRICE DJD, 1963, LITTLE SCI BIG SCI
3	1, 2, 5	NARIN F, 1994, SCIENTOMETRICS, V30, P147
3	1, 2, 6	*IITRI, 1968, TECHN RETR CRIT EV S
3	3, 4, 5	*US DEP COMM, 1992, TECHN PROF REP SEM
3	3, 4, 5	BRAUN E, 1982, REVOLUTION MINIATURE
3	3, 4, 5	CARPENTER MP, 1981, WORLD PATENT INFORMA, V3, P160
3	3, 4, 5	NARIN F, 1987, RES POLICY, V16, P143
3	3, 4, 5	ROGERS EM, 1984, SILICON VALLEY FEVER
3	3, 4, 5	SAXENIAN AL, 1991, RES POLICY, V20, P423
3	3, 4, 6	NARIN F, 1988, HDB QUANTITATIVE STU
2	3, 6	SMALL H, 1973, J AM SOC INFORM SCI, V24, P265
2	3, 6	SMALL H, 1974, SCI STUD, V4, P17
2	3, 6	SMALL H, 1985, SCIENTOMETRICS, V7, P391

researchers would be likely to benefit from such knowledge. Researchers at CHI Research Inc. have been using citations to scientific literature in patent front page references as an indicator of the extent to which a patent is influenced by basic research. Trends in scientific literature are therefore potential predictors for the emergent trend in technological innovations. Second, a clearer understanding of trends in technological innovations marked by patents in the broader context of scientific literature and patent application information, is likely to provide strategic signposts for scientists and engineers to orient their research and development. For small businesses, who normally do not have the resources to track the trends of intellectual properties, patent analysis enhanced by information visualization technology can cut through a thick layer of obscured trends of innovations so as to steer their business in the direction of a more competitive market position.

2.4 Conclusion

The Semantic Web emphasizes that data should be machine-understandable, whereas information visualization aims to maximize our perceptional and cognitive abilities to make sense of visual-spatial representations of abstract information structures. Will they work alongside one another? Our illustrative example is intended to demonstrate that, on the one hand, the Semantic Web can largely simplify many laborious information visualization tasks today; on the other hand, the two fields differ from their philosophical groundings to tactic approaches to individual problems such as knowledge modelling and representation. A lot of theoretical and practical work remains to be done to find the right way for the two fields to work together harmoniously.

2.5 References

Battista, G. D., Eades, P., Tamassia, R., and Tollis, I. G. (1999). *Graph Drawing: Algorithms for the Visualization of Graphs.* Prentice-Hall.

Berners-Lee, T. (1998). *Semantic web roadmap.* Available: http://www.w3.org/DesignIssues/Semantic.html

Berners-Lee, T., Hendler, J., and Lassila, O. (2001). The semantic web. *Scientific American*, 5(1).

Boyack, K. W., Wylie, B. N., Davidson, G. S., and Johnson, D. K. (2000). *Analysis of patent databases using Vxinsight (SAND2000–2266C).* Albuquerque, NM: Sandia National Laboratories.

Braam, R. R., Moed, H. F., and Raan, A. F. J. v. (1991a). Mapping of science by combined co-citation and word analysis. I: Structural aspects. *Journal of the American Society for Information Science*, 42(4), 233–251.

Braam, R. R., Moed, H. F., and Raan, A. F. J. v. (1991b). Mapping of science by combined co-citation and word analysis. II: Dynamical aspects. *Journal of the American Society for Information Science*, 42(4), 252–266.

Callon, M., Law, J., and Rip, A. (Eds.). (1986). Mapping the Dynamics of Science and Technology: Sociology of Science in the Real World. London: Macmillan.

Card, S., Mackinlay, J., and Shneiderman, B. (Eds.). (1999). *Readings in Information Visualization: Using Vision to Think.* Morgan Kaufmann.

Card, S. K. (1996). Visualizing retrieved information: A survey. *IEEE Computer Graphics and Applications*, 16(2), 63–67.

Chen, C. (1998a). Bridging the gap: The use of Pathfinder networks in visual navigation. *Journal of Visual Languages and Computing*, 9(3), 267–286.

Chen, C. (1998b). Generalized Similarity Analysis and Pathfinder Network Scaling. *Interacting with Computers*, 10(2), 107–128.

Chen, C. (1999). Information Visualization and Virtual Environments. London: Springer-Verlag.

Chen, C. (2002). Mapping Scientific Frontiers: The Quest for Knowledge Visualization. London: Springer-Verlag.

Chen, C., and Paul, R. J. (2001). Visualizing a knowledge domain's intellectual structure. *Computer*, 34(3), 65–71.

Chen, C., Kuljis, J., and Paul, R. J. (2001). Visualizing latent knowledge. *IEEE Transactions on Systems, Man, and Cybernetics*. Part C, November 2001.

Chen, C., Cribbin, T., Macredie, R., and Morar, S. (2002). Visualizing and tracking the growth of competing paradigms: Two case studies. *Journal of the American Society for Information Science and Technology*, 53(8), 678–689.

Crane, D. (1972). Invisible Colleges: Diffusion of Knowledge in Scientific Communities. Chicago, IL: University of Chicago Press.

Garfield, E. (1955). Citation indexes for science: A new dimension in documentation through association of ideas. *Science*, 122, 108–111.

Garfield, E., H., Sher, I., and Torpie, R. J. (1964*). The use of citation data in writing the history of science.* Philadelphia: Institute for Scientific Information.

Goguen, J. (2000). *Information visualization and semiotic morphisms.* University of California at San Diego. Available: http://www-cse.ucsd.edu/users/goguen/papers/sm/vzln.html

Hearst, M. A. (1999). User interfaces and visualization. In B. Ribeiro-Neto (Ed.), *Modern Information Retrieval* (pp. 257–224). Addison-Wesley.

Herman, I., Melançon, G., and Marshall, M. S. (2000). Graph visualization and navigation in information visualization: A survey. *IEEE Transactions on Visualization and Computer Graphics*, (1), 24–44.

Hjorland, B. (1997). Information Seeking and Subject Representation: An Activity-Theoretical Approach to Information Science. Westport: Greenwood Press.

Hjorland, B., and Albrechtsen, H. (1995). Toward a new horizon in information science: Domain analysis. *Journal of the American Society for Information Science*, 46(6), 400–425.

Hollan, J. D., Bederson, B. B., and Helfman, J. (1997). Information visualization. In P. Prabhu (Ed.), *The Handbook of Human Computer Interaction* (pp. 33–48). The Netherlands: Elsevier Science.

Kuhn, T. S. (1962). *The Structure of Scientific Revolutions.* Chicago: University of Chicago Press.

McCain, K. W. (1990). Mapping authors in intellectual space: A technical overview. *Journal of the American Society for Information Science*, 41(6), 433–443.

Mukherjea, S. (1999). Information visualization for hypermedia systems. ACM Computing Surveys.

Price, D. D. (1963). *Little Science, Big Science.* New York: Columbia University Press.

Price, D. D. (1965). Networks of scientific papers. *Science*, 149, 510–515.

Schvaneveldt, R. W. (Ed.). (1990). Pathfinder Associative Networks: Studies in Knowledge Organization. Norwood, NJ: Ablex.

Sher, I., and Garfield, E. (1966). New tools for improving and evaluating the effectiveness of research. Paper presented at Research Program Effectiveness, Washington, DC, 27–29 July 1965.

Small, H. (1973). Co-citation in scientific literature: A new measure of the relationship between publications. *Journal of the American Society for Information Science*, 24, 265–269.

Small, H. G., and Griffith, B. C. (1974). The structure of scientific literatures I: Identifying and graphing specialties. *Science Studies*, 4, 17–40.

Small, H. S. (1988). Book review of Callon et al. *Scientometrics*, 14(1–2), 165–168.

Small, H. (1997). Update on science mapping: Creating large document spaces. *Scientometrics*, 38(2), 275–293.

Spence, B. (2001). *Information Visualization*. Addison-Wesley.

Steinberg, S. G. (1994). The ontogeny of RISC. *Intertek*, 3(5), 1–10.

Thagard, P. (1992). *Conceptual Revolutions*. Princeton, NJ: Princeton University Press.

Ware, C. (2000). *Information Visualization: Perception for Design*. San Francisco: Morgan Kaufmann.

White, H. D., and Griffith, B. C. (1981). Author co-citation: A literature measure of intellectual structure. *Journal of the American Society for Information Science*, 32, 163–172.

White, H. D., and McCain, K. W. (1998). Visualizing a discipline: An author co-citation analysis of information science, 1972–1995. *Journal of the American Society for Information Science*, 49(4), 327–356.

Chapter 3
Ontology-based Information Visualization

Christiaan Fluit, Marta Sabou and Frank van Harmelen

3.1 Introduction

The Semantic Web is an extension of the current World Wide Web, based on the idea of exchanging information with explicit, formal and machine-accessible descriptions of meaning. Providing information with such semantics will enable the construction of applications that have an increased awareness of what is contained in the information they process and that can therefore operate more accurately. This has the potential of improving the way we deal with information in the broadest sense possible, e.g. better search engines, mobile agents for various tasks, or even applications yet unheard of. Rather than being merely a vision, the Semantic Web has significant backing from various institutes such as DARPA, the European Union and the W3C, which all have formed current and future Semantic Web activities.

In order to be able to exchange the semantics of information, one first needs to agree on how to explicitly model it. Ontologies are a mechanism for representing such formal and shared domain descriptions. They can be used to annotate data with labels (metadata) indicating their meaning, thereby making their semantics explicit and machine-accessible.

Many Semantic Web initiatives emphasize the capability of *machines* to exchange the meaning of information. Although their efforts will lead to increased quality of the application's results, their user interfaces often take little or no advantage of the increased semantics. For example, an ontology-based search engine could use its ontology when evaluating the user's query (e.g. for query formulation, disambiguation or evaluation), but it could also use it to enrich the presentation of the resulting list to the end user, e.g. by replacing the endless list of hits with a navigation structure based on the semantics of the hits.

Aidministrator is a software provider in the market of information and content management. One of Aidministrator's core products is *Spectacle*. It facilitates the creation of information presentations that meet the needs of end users, e.g. a personalized navigation that reduces the need for searching and enables people to find information in a few clicks. Spectacle establishes this using the semantics of the information that can be provided by the Semantic Web. Therefore, Spectacle can be used to construct user interfaces that take advantage of the Semantic Web.

In this chapter we will present one of Spectacle's key components called the *Cluster Map*, which is used for the visualization of ontological data. First, we will give a description of Spectacle and its use of ontologies in Section 3.2. We will also explain the contents of the Cluster Map visualization and the user interface that facilitates its dynamic exploration. Section 3.3 presents three real-life case studies in which visualization plays different roles. These two sections naturally lead to a discussion in Section 3.4 on how the visualization can support several user tasks, such as analysis, search and navigation. An overview of related work, a summary and some considerations for future work conclude this chapter.

3.2 Spectacle

The Spectacle system creates an *exploration context* out of information sources, providing users with a convenient way to find and explore information. This takes into account the user's task, perspective, personal preferences, etc. This not only means that the right information should be delivered to the right user, but also that it needs to be presented (structured, formatted, etc.) in the right way. Spectacle is used both to disclose the content of databases and document repositories as well as the semantics of information from existing Semantic Web resources.

Roughly speaking, Spectacle can present information in two different ways. First, it can create hypertext interfaces, containing selected content, design and an appropriate navigation structure, based on the semantics of the information. Additionally, it can present the information in entirely novel ways, e.g. by graphical visualization, which is the topic of this chapter.

A key benefit of the first approach is that it allows for an easy and flexible presentation of the same information in different ways, for each of the envisioned tasks or user types. Furthermore, it has all the usual benefits of a generated web site and takes advantage of the expressivity and flexibility provided by Semantic Web standards such as RDF (Lassila and Swick, 1999) and RDF Schema (Brickley and Guha, 2000). A benefit of the second approach is that it has the potential of offering insights and kinds of information access, which are not possible with "conventional" publishing methods such as web sites.

Which presentation mechanism should be used depends entirely on the problem at hand; Spectacle allows to select the mechanism (or combination of mechanisms) that is the most beneficial for that problem.

3.2.1 Ontologies in Spectacle

Spectacle builds on lightweight ontologies that describe a domain through a set of classes (concepts) and their hierarchical relationships. Also known as taxonomies, such ontologies are frequently used in several domains (biology, chemistry, libraries) as classification systems. Information architects consider taxonomies as basic building blocks, representing the backbone of most web sites. Non-formal taxonomies are already widely used in web applications for product classification (e.g. Amazon) or web directories (e.g. Yahoo, Open Directory Project (ODP)). Taxonomies are also part of Semantic Web standards such as RDF and Topic Maps.

Due to the specialization relationship that is encoded in the hierarchy, the set of objects in a subclass is a subset of its superclass. The set of subclasses of a class is *incomplete* when their union does not contain all the objects of the superclass. Classes that share instances are *overlapping* if no specialization relationship holds between them. These characteristics are very common for taxonomies. However, they are difficult to show satisfactorily with normal textual representation techniques. Our visualization offers an alternative in this matter.

3.2.2 Cluster Map Basics

The Cluster Map visualizes the objects of a number of selected classes from a hierarchy, organized by their classifications.

The Cluster Map in Figure 3.1 shows a collection of job offers organized according to a very simple ontology. Each small yellow sphere represents an offer. The big green spheres represent ontology classes, with an attached label stating their name and cardinality. Directed edges connect classes, and point from specific to generic (e.g. *IT* is a subclass of *Job Vacancies*). Balloon–shaped edges connect objects to their most specific class(es). Objects with the same class membership are grouped in *clusters*. Our example contains six clusters; two of them represent overlaps between classes.

The organization of the graph is computed using a variant of the well-known spring-embedder algorithm (Eades, 1984). On the one hand the class and cluster nodes repel each other. On the other hand the edges, connecting two classes or clusters to their classes, produce an attractive force between the connected nodes; i.e. they work as "springs". The layout algorithm has been optimized for this particular kind of graph, both *qualitatively* (using the semantics of the graph to

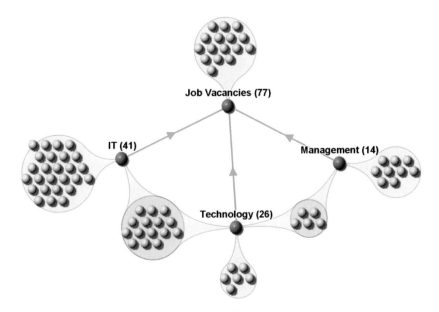

Figure 3.1   An example Cluster Map.

obtain a more insightful visualization) and *quantitatively* (obtaining a layout fast enough to permit interactive usage).

The added value of our visualization lies in its *expressivity*. The classes and their relationships (the vocabulary of the domain) are easy to detect. Also, it is immediately apparent which items belong to one or multiple classes, which classes overlap (e.g. *Technology* and *Management*) and which do not (*IT* and *Management*). The cardinality of classes and clusters is visible: the top class has the most objects, *Technology* shares more objects with *IT* than with *Management*. The subclasses of the root class are incomplete as their union does not cover the superclass: some members of *Vacancies* were not further classified.

Another interesting aspect of the visualization is that geometric closeness in the map is related to semantic closeness. This is a consequence of the graph layout algorithm. *Classes* are semantically close if they share many objects. Indeed, the more objects two classes share, the closer they are represented. *Objects* are semantically close if they belong to the same class(es). Indeed, objects with the same class membership are clustered.

The Cluster Map visualization is highly configurable. Several colour schemes support different tasks: e.g. display each class using a unique colour (Figure 3.3) or indicate cluster relevance using colour brightness (Figure 3.6). Filters can reduce the complexity of the visualization, e.g. by removing all clusters representing the overlap of less or more then *n* classes, or all clusters with cardinality above or below a certain threshold. The scalability of the visualization can be improved by displaying a cluster as a single graphical entity with its cardinality indicated (Figure 3.5).

3.2.3 User Interaction

A Cluster Map can be used as a static information visualization, as will be shown in Section 3.3. However, additional benefits are obtained when viewing it via the interactive Cluster Map viewer. The interface of this viewer has been designed to stimulate the user to *explore* the information shown.

Figure 3.2 shows a screen shot of the viewer. At the left side we see the class hierarchy from which the user can select an arbitrary combination of classes to display in the graph panel at the right. A class is added to the visualization by selecting the check box next to it, which immediately updates the graph. The contents of the map can also be changed by double-clicking on certain parts of the graph. Depending on user preference, a double-click on a class either results in the class being expanded or collapsed or in the whole visualization being replaced with a visualization of its subclasses, providing a way to semantically zoom in on the information.

There are several ways to explore the contents of a given graph. Moving the mouse pointer over objects in the graph shows information about them in the status bar (see Figure 3.2). Clicking on a class or cluster highlights related nodes and edges, giving a good overview of how its objects are distributed over the graph. Additionally, details about individual objects such as a name and a URI are shown in a table that pops up at the bottom of the screen. One can also select one or more classes in the tree at the left side. As a result, the currently visualized objects of the selected classes are highlighted. This makes it very easy to see how these selected classes relate to the currently visualized classes, without having to

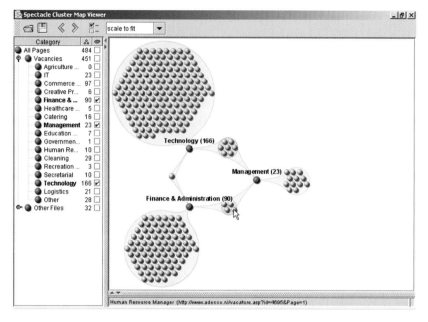

Figure 3.2   A screen shot of the Cluster Map viewer.

add them to the map. Finally, the filters described above can be applied and adapted dynamically, meaning that the visualization is updated immediately.

Often a user will want to explore several graphs, each showing a slightly different set of classes. During this interaction the user constructs a mental map of the information in the visualization (Eades et al., 1991). A number of provisions have been made to assist the user with adapting his mental map over time. When the user adds or removes classes, the system automatically calculates a layout for the new graph, reusing the layout of the old graph as much as possible. The transition of one graph to the next is animated, clearly showing the structural changes between the two graphs. During the animation, objects that appear or disappear in the graph fade in or out respectively, while objects that remain in the graph are translated to their new position. The interface provides back and forward buttons like a web browser so that the transitions can be repeated forwards and backwards. All these provisions help the user to transform his mental map. Additionally (or perhaps consequently), the animation has proved very helpful when explaining the visualization to new users.

Note that this interface adheres to Shneiderman's Visual Information-Seeking Mantra (Shneiderman, 1996) of "overview first, zoom and filter, then details-on-demand".

3.3 Cases

As we have seen, Cluster Maps contain a large amount of information. Furthermore, several strategies exist for applying them on a data set. This section

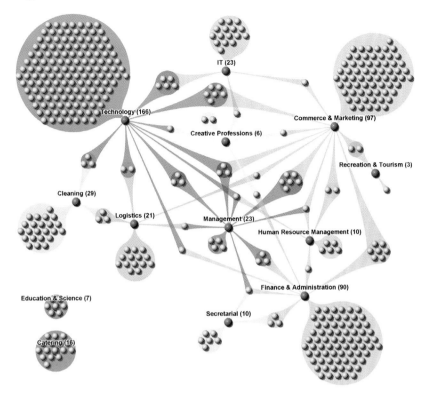

Figure 3.3   Job vacancies organized by economic sector.

demonstrates three real-life case studies where different visualization strategies were used.

The *first case study* was performed on the set of job descriptions available on the web site of a Dutch job agency. The ontology of the domain consists of several orthogonal classification dimensions such as region, relevant economic sector and required education.

Figure 3.3 visualizes the set of job offers from the perspective of the relevant economic sector: finance, IT, commerce, etc. Each yellow bullet on the map represents a job offer of the agency. It is immediately visible which classes are larger than others: most job offers are for *Technology*, while there are very few for *Creative Professions*.

Overlaps between classes represent jobs that are relevant for multiple economic sectors. For example some of the *Commerce & Marketing* jobs are also relevant for one or more other economic fields. At the other extreme, there is no job for *Education & Science* that is relevant to other sectors as well.

It is interesting to observe that jobs in the economic/administrative sector are located on the right part of the map, while the left part is occupied by more labour-oriented sectors. The semantic closeness (the overlapping nature of the sector categories) clearly results in geometric closeness in the map.

Figure 3.4 visualizes the same data set but from a totally different perspective, namely the region of the job. Since this classification criterion is largely

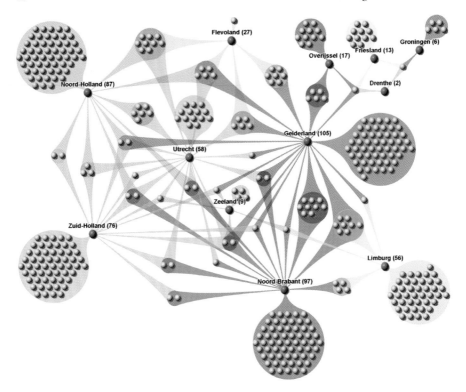

Figure 3.4 Job vacancies organized by region.

orthogonal to the previous one, the organization of the map is completely different. It is clearly visible that some regions offer more jobs than others, with most jobs being offered in Gelderland. Overlaps of classes represent jobs related to multiple regions.

An interesting observation is that the visualization more or less reflects the geography of The Netherlands. This is due to the fact that neighbouring provinces are more likely to share jobs, i.e. to be semantically related. This results in them appearing next to each other on the visualization.

The *second case study* is a comparative analysis of the web sites of two major Dutch banks, to see if they differ in their offerings. We used a simple ontology containing various bank-related topics. Both data sets were visualized according to this ontology (see Figure 3.5).

A comparison of the two visualizations reveals that one site is larger than the other. Also, the visualization suggests that the profiles of the two banks differ. The first bank seems to be oriented towards labour-related issues, while the second focuses on investment. This is shown by both the cardinality of the two major classes (*Labour* for the first bank, *Investment* for the second) and their influence on the other activities (for example the overlap between *Investment* and *Entrepreneurs* is larger for the second bank even when normalized to the cardinality of the classes).

For the *third case study* we used the web site of a travel agent, containing a separate page for each holiday offer. An ontology described this domain from

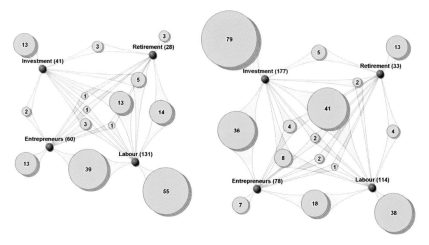

Figure 3.5 Two bank web sites visualized using the same ontology.

perspectives such as geographical location and properties of the accommodation (number of rooms, number of persons, quality). The role of the ontology in this visualization was different; while in the previous cases we viewed the data only from a single perspective, here we wish to determine the relevance of data items with respect to characteristics from different perspectives. This results in a *query* having as terms classes from the ontology.

Suppose that we are interested in all the 3-star, 2-room, 4-person accommodation in the French Loire. The classes in the ontology that correspond to these criteria are visualized in the left part of Figure 3.6. The perfect result would be represented as a cluster that connects to all four classes. However, no item in the data set satisfies all our requirements, there is no overlap between *all* the classes of interest.

Our scenario is well known in electronic commerce; when searching for a product, a customer selects a set of values that are of interest. If the query does not fully succeed then either a "no matches" message or a long list of partial

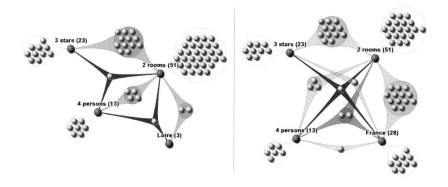

Figure 3.6 Visualizations of two consecutive query result sets.

matches is shown. The customer gets neither a clear overview of the results nor suggestions for further exploration. As a result he often abandons the site. The ideal situation would be that the customer is guided to alternatives that would come close to his needs.

With our visualization, the customer has the opportunity to analyse alternative solutions, in terms of his original query. In our example, there is a holiday destination that fulfils all the requirements except the 3-star accommodation. Also, in the case that the destination is not so important, there is one holiday offer with the required accommodation properties, but which is not in the Loire. These might be interesting options for the customer. (Note the use of colour brightness to identify the relevance of a cluster.)

Another possibility is to refine the query by using the ontological nature of the data. Although no matching destinations were found in the Loire, there is still a chance that destinations with these characteristics will exist in a broader class, i.e. the whole of France. Visualizing again the classes of interest but now in combination with France instead of Loire, there is now exactly one destination that matches completely (see the right side of Figure 3.6).

3.4 Uses of Ontology-based Visualization

So far we have demonstrated the properties and expressiveness of our visualization. In what follows we will discuss how our maps support three information seeking tasks: *data analysis*, *querying* and *navigation*.

3.4.1 Analysis

A user analyses a data set in order to get a better insight into its characteristics, to get a global understanding of the collection and to discover unexpected patterns.

The *static version* of the Cluster Map (i.e. the image itself) already contains information that can be used for analysis. The classes and their hierarchy provide an understanding of the domain of the data set. The way instances are classified results in class characteristics such as incompleteness and overlaps, showing class relations at instance level. The cardinality of classes and clusters supports quantitative analysis. Interpreting this information, one can already derive some domain-specific observations.

The *strategy* used to obtain a static Cluster Map plays an important role. Different strategies support different analysis scenarios, as shown in the previous section:

1. *Analysis within a single domain* In this case a data set is visualized from one or more perspectives, giving insight into the collection. One of our case studies investigated characteristics of a set of job offers by visualizing it according to region or relevant economic sector.
2. *Comparison of different data sets* Data sets can be compared by visualizing them using the same ontology. We have compared two banks by imposing the same ontology on their web sites and analysing the two visualizations.
3. *Monitoring* Analysing a data set at different points in time provides insight into the way it evolves. For example, one could monitor the site of a bank over time and see how its activities evolve (expand/interconnect/etc.).

The Cluster Map viewer (described in Section 3.2.3) makes analysis an interactive and explorative process. The overview, zoom and filter facilities offered by the user interface qualitatively enhance the analysis process.

3.4.2 Querying

The goal of a query task is to find a narrow set of items in a large collection that satisfy a well-understood information need (Marchionini, 1995). We will show the benefits of using the Cluster Map viewer in the four stages of the search task (Shneiderman, 1998).

Query formulation – The step of expressing an information need through a query is a difficult task. Users encounter difficulties when having to provide terms that best describe their information need (vocabulary problem). Furthermore, combining these terms in simple logical expressions using "AND" and "OR" is even more complicated. See Shneiderman (1996) for a demonstration of this problem.

In the viewer, the classes that describe the domain of a data set are explicitly shown, making the vocabulary choice much easier. There is no need to specify Boolean expressions as they are already visible on the map.

Initiation of action – Classes selected in the left panel become the terms of a query. The search is launched at a mouse-click.

Review of results – The results of the query are graphically presented to the user. For *n* selected classes the following are shown:

1. the union of the classes (disjunction of *all* query terms)
2. all intersections of the selected classes (conjunction of *some* query terms)
3. (as a particular case of (2)), the intersection of all classes (conjunction of *all* query terms), if it exists.

Note that the results of simple Boolean expressions are intuitively shown in the map. If the user wants a disjunction of the terms he will analyse all the presented objects. As an added value he will see how the corresponding classes overlap. A more interesting (and probably more frequent) case is when users want the conjunction of the terms. In that scenario, two extreme situations can happen:

1. the result set is too large (under-specification)
2. the result set is empty (over-specification).

If the result set is empty, the user can at least find objects that partially satisfy the query. The degree of relevance of certain clusters is suggested by their colour: the more relevant the darker the shade of the colour (see Figure 3.6). In the travel agent scenario, there were two destinations that were interesting if the customer dropped one requirement (quality of accommodation/ location). This is a form of *query relaxation*.

Refinement – According to the conclusions of the result interpretation, the user can narrow or broaden the scope of his search by refining the query.

If the result set is too large, the user can replace some classes with more specific subclasses. Imagine that in the travel agent scenario the customer would like to go to France and that the system returns a huge cluster that satisfies all the criteria. Instead of looking at each returned object, the customer can *refine* his query to use a more specific class, for example Loire. This would narrow the scope of the query and return a smaller set of options.

At the other extreme, in case of an empty set, some classes can be replaced by their superclass. We have demonstrated such a case for the travel agent scenario: the search for a vacation in Loire was empty for the given settings, however one destination was found in France. Note that both narrowing and broadening the scope of the query are possible due to the ontological nature of the domain description. The viewer facilitates choosing more specific or more general classes.

3.4.3 Navigation

Cluster Maps can be used for graphical navigation. We have employed them as image maps in Spectacle-generated web sites based on ontological data. Two navigation scenarios were implemented, as described below.

In the *first scenario*, the Cluster Map is used in addition to another, more traditional navigational structure (a textual tree). It plays the role of a *site map* that is invoked by the user when needed. It presents an overview of the whole data set; it shows the most important classes, their relations and instances. An interesting aspect is the way the data is accessed; one can access a whole class (click on a class) or an overlap of interest (click on a cluster). The result is a representation of the contents of the selected entity in the form of a textual list. Entries in this list present extra information about the data items as well as a link to the actual data. The role of the map is to facilitate a quick understanding of the available content and to provide quick access to individual items.

In the *second scenario*, the Cluster Map is always present as the only navigation facility. Maps gradually present deeper levels of the ontology; the user starts at the top of the ontology and can navigate towards more specific topics by clicking the classes of interest (diving into the information). At any point, the map shows the current class, its parent and its subclasses. For the current class, its elements are also presented in a textual list. This hierarchical browsing facilitates a levelled understanding of the data.

In Section 3.2.3 we demonstrated that the interactive Cluster Map viewer fulfills Shneiderman's Visual Information-Seeking Mantra. We can say the same for the interfaces created for navigation using the Cluster Map. For the first navigation scenario, the users get an overview of the content, then they can zoom in to a certain class/cluster, and access the detailed data. In the second scenario, a top-level overview of the data allows zooming in to more specific classes until the objects of interest are identified and can be accessed.

3.5 Related Work

Recently, many visualizations have been developed for web resources (see Dodge and Kitchin, 2001 for an extensive overview). Differences exist between these approaches and the Cluster Map regarding the information that is visualized and the supported tasks.

Well-known examples of visualizations of web resources are the Hyperbolic Tree (Lamping et al., 1995) for the navigation of large trees and The Brain (http://www.thebrain.com) for navigating graphs. Usually these visualizations focus on syntactic structures such as link structures. This of course has some semantics, but this is often very implicit and ad hoc. Additionally, the data structure used by these tools is often a tree or at least tree-like (it is arguable whether The Brain is really suited for navigating *arbitrary* graphs).

Of course one could use other, more semantic, input data, e.g. as is done for the WebBrain (http://www.webbrain.com), an application of The Brain on top of the Open Directory Project (ODP), or the AquaBrowser (Veling, 1997) which visualizes concept graphs. The main difference with our visualization is that these systems primarily display the abstract structure, i.e. the instances are not an inherent part of the graph but are displayed separately (usually as a textual list). A correlation between two concepts has to be explicitly made in the abstract structure in order to be shown, whereas in our visualization many class characteristics become immediately apparent because the instances are part of the visualization.

There are other visualization systems that do mix abstract structures and instances, such as the Self-Organizing Map (Kohonen, 1997) and ThemeScape (http://www.aurigin.com). These systems extract conceptual characteristics of large document sets, which is clearly outside our scope. Although scalable to very large document sets, the organization of the documents may sometimes seem arbitrary; the user has very little knowledge about why the data is organized in that particular way. Our system circumvents this because the graph structure shown *is* the main organization principle.

Finally, there are visualizations that show both abstract and instance data at the same time with an explicit organization criterion, such as Antarcti.ca's Visual Net (http://www.antarcti.ca), which has also been applied to the ODP (http://maps.map.net). This visualization can also scale to large taxonomies and document sets, but has no intrinsic way of dealing with overlapping classifications, which frequently occur in classification systems such as Yahoo or the ODP.

Concerning the tasks that are supported, a difference between our approach and most other approaches and techniques is that they primarily focus on navigation tasks, whereas our scope is much wider. That is not to say that they cannot be used for other tasks as well, only that the focus of their developers is on navigation tasks. The visualization mechanisms that offer support for analysis tasks mainly focus on showing aspects of the information *infrastructure*, not the information itself.

3.6 Future Work

Although the Cluster Map is already a very useful visualization component, many research and development issues are still open. This list gives a quick impression:

1. Improvements for showing more classes in a single image.
2. Refining the options for extending and semantically exploring the graph.
3. Adding a time dimension to the visualization, to support monitoring tasks.
4. Refining the animation in order to better aid transforming the mental map.
5. Extend the interactive viewer so that it can use more expressive ontologies such as RDF schemas, Topic Maps or other types of Semantic Web ontologies. Such a viewer could, for example, operate on top of Semantic Web repositories, such as Aidministrator's Sesame (Broekstra et al., 2001).

3.7 Summary

This chapter has demonstrated an elegant way to visually represent ontological data. We have described how the Cluster Map visualization can use ontologies to create expressive information visualizations, with the attractive property that classes and objects that are semantically related are also spatially close in the visualization. Furthermore, the available user interface provides many benefits. We have shown that a number of diverse information seeking tasks can be supported with this approach, and the real-life usability has been demonstrated by a number of case studies.

Since ontologies are expected to play a crucial role in realizing the infrastructure of the Semantic Web, we expect that these visualizations will become an important tool for various kinds of search and analysis tasks.

3.8 Acknowledgements

The authors would like to thank all their colleagues at Aidministrator for their support during the development of the Cluster Map as well as for their input on this chapter.

3.9 References

Brickley D, Guha R (2000) *Resource Description Framework (RDF) Schema Specification 1.0.* Candidate recommendation, World Wide Web Consortium.

Broekstra J, Harmelen F, Kampman A (2001) Sesame: an architecture for storing and querying RDF data and schema information. To appear in: *Semantics for the WWW*, MIT Press.

Dodge M, Kitchin R (2001) *Atlas of Cyberspace*. Addison-Wesley, London.

Eades P (1984) A heuristic for graph drawing. *Congressus Numerantium* 42:149–160.

Eades P, Lai W, Misue K, Sugiyama K (1991) Preserving the mental map of a diagram. *Proceedings of the International Conference on Computational Graphics and Visualization Techniques (COMPUGRAPHICS '91)*, pp. 34–43.

Kohonen, T (1997) *Self-organizing Maps*. Springer-Verlag, Berlin.

Lamping J, Rao R, Pirolli P (1995) A focus + context technique based on hyperbolic geometry for visualizing large hierarchies. *ACM Conference on Human Factors in Software (CHI '95)*, pp. 401–408.

Lassila O, Swick R (1999) *Resource Description Framework (RDF): Model and Syntax Specification*. Recommendation, World Wide Web Consortium.

Marchionini G (1995) *Information Seeking in Electronic Environments*. Cambridge University Press, Cambridge, UK.

Shneiderman B (1996) The eyes have it: a task by data type taxonomy for information visualizations. *Proceedings of the 1996 IEEE Symposium on Visual Languages (VL '96)*, pp. 336–343.

Shneiderman B (1998) *Designing the User Interface*. Addison-Wesley, Menlo Park, CA, pp. 509–551.

Veling A (1997) The Aqua Browser: visualization or large information spaces in context. *Journal of AGSI* 3: 136–142.

Chapter 4
Topic Maps Visualization

Bénédicte Le Grand and Michel Soto

4.1 Introduction

The standards developed in the context of the Semantic Web provide means of adding semantics to the data available on the Web. XML is a first level of semantics which allows users to structure data with regard to their content rather than their presentation. However, more semantics can be added with the Resource Description Framework (RDF) (1999) or Topic Maps (1999) standards. RDF was developed by the World Wide Web Consortium (1999) whereas Topic Maps were defined by the International Organization for Standardization (1999). The Topic Map paradigm was recently adapted to the Web by the consortium TopicMaps.Org (2001). Both RDF and Topic Maps aim at representing knowledge about information resources by annotating them.

In this chapter we focus on Topic Maps, but the techniques presented here may be applied to RDF as these two technologies are compatible; Moore (2001) stated that RDF could be used to model Topic Maps and vice versa.

Topic Maps provide a bridge between knowledge representation and information management. They build a semantic network above information resources, which allows users to navigate at a higher level of abstraction.

However, Topic Maps are high-dimensional knowledge bases and they may be very large; users may still have problems in finding relevant information within a Topic Map. Therefore, the issue of Topic Maps visualization and navigation is essential.

This chapter is organized as follows. First, we present the basic concepts of Topic Maps. Then, we discuss Topic Maps visualization requirements and study how existing visualization techniques may be applied to Topic Maps representation. We conclude by giving a few directions that could lead to the "ultimate" Topic Map visualization tool.

4.2 Topic Maps Basic Concepts

Topic Maps are a new ISO standard which allows to describe knowledge and to link it to existing information resources. Topic Maps are qualified as "GPS (Global Positioning System) of the information universe", as they are intended to enhance navigation in complex data sets.

Although Topic Maps allow to organize and represent very complex structures, the basic concepts of this model – *topics*, *occurrences* and *associations* – are simple.

A *topic* is a syntactic construct which corresponds to the expression of a real-world concept in a computer system. Figure 4.1 represents a very small Topic Map which contains four topics: *XML Europe 2000, Paris, Ile-de-France* and *France*. These topics are instances of other topics: *XML Europe 2000* is a *conference, Paris* is a *city, Ile-de-France* is a *region* and *France* is a *country*. A topic type is a topic itself, which means that *conference, city, region* and *country* are also topics.

A topic may be linked to several information resources, e.g. Web pages, which are considered to be somehow related to this topic. These resources are called *occurrences* of a topic. These occurrences are typed; in the Topic Map in Figure 4.1, occurrences of the topic *Paris* may be URLs pointing to some pictures or maps. Occurrences provide means of linking real resources to abstract concepts, which helps organize data and understand their context. It is important to notice that topics and information resources belong to two different layers. Users may navigate at an abstract level – the topic level – instead of navigating directly within data.

The concepts presented so far – topic, topic type, name, occurrence and occurrence type – allow to organize information resources with regard to a concept. However, it is interesting to describe relationships between these concepts, which is possible in Topic Maps through topic *associations*.

An association adds semantics to data by expressing a relationship between several topics, such as *XML Europe 2000 takes place in Paris, Paris is located in Ile-de-France*, etc. Every topic involved in an association plays a specific role in this association, for example, *Ile-de-France* plays the role of *container* and *Paris*

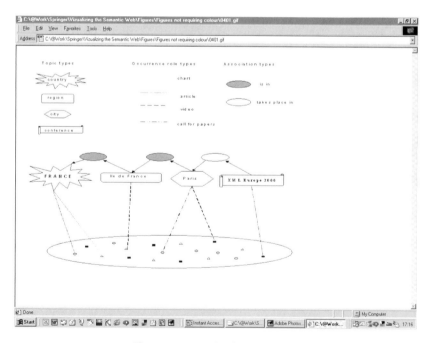

Figure 4.1 Example of a Topic Map.

plays the role of *containee*. Associations roles are also topics. Actually, almost everything in a Topic Map is a topic!

One advantage of Topic Maps is that they add semantics to existing data – by organizing and describing them – without modifying them. Moreover, one Topic Map may describe several information pools and several Topic Maps may apply to one single information pool.

In this section, we have described the basic constructs of Topic Maps: Topic Maps contain *topics* which are connected by *associations* and which point to information resources through *occurrences*. Topic Maps can enhance navigation and information retrieval in complex data sets by adding semantics to these resources. However, a topic may have a large number of dimensions, as it is characterized by its name(s), its type(s), its occurrence(s) – the resources which are related to it – and the role(s) that it plays in associations. Moreover, Topic Maps may also be complex because of their size; they may contain millions of topics and associations.

4.3 Topic Maps Visualization

As stated in the previous section, Topic Maps are very powerful but they may be complex. Intuitive visual user interfaces may significantly reduce the cognitive load of users when working with these complex structures. Visualization is a promising technique for both enhancing users' perception of structure in large information spaces and providing navigation facilities. According to Gershon and Eick (1995), it also enables people to use a natural tool of observation and processing – their eyes as well as their brain – to extract knowledge more efficiently and find insights.

In the following, we first present the goals of Topic Maps visualization. Then we review different visualization techniques that may be applied to Topic Maps.

4.3.1 Visualization Goals

The goal of Topic Maps visualization is to help users locate relevant information quickly and explore the structure easily. Thus, there are two kinds of requirements for Topic Maps visualization: representation and navigation. Good representation helps users identify interesting spots, whereas efficient navigation is essential to access information rapidly.

According to Schneiderman (1996), "the visual information-seeking mantra is: overview first, zoom and filter, then details on-demand".

4.3.1.1 Representation Requirements

First of all, we need to provide the user with an overview of the Topic Map. This overview must show the main features of the structure in order to deduce the Topic Map's main characteristics at a glance. Visual representations are particularly fitted to these needs, as they exploit human abilities to detect patterns.

The first thing we need to know about a Topic Map is what it deals with, i.e. what its main concepts are. Once they are identified, we need more structural information, such as the generality or specificity of the Topic Map. This kind of information should appear clearly on the representation so as to help users compare different Topic Maps quickly and explore only the most relevant ones in detail. The position of topics on the visual display should reflect their semantic proximity. These properties can be deduced from the computation of Topic Maps metrics, as shown by Le Grand and Soto (2001).

Moreover, Topic Maps are multidimensional knowledge bases. Topics, associations and occurrences are characterized by many parameters, which should appear somehow in the visualization.

These requirements are not compatible, as it is not possible – nor relevant – to display simultaneously general information and details. We can compare this with a geographic map; a map of the world cannot – and should not – be precise. If a user is interested in details, they must make precise their interest, for example by choosing a specific country. As in geographical maps, we need to provide different scales in Topic Maps representations.

Moreover, visualizations should be dynamic to adapt to users' needs in real time; combinations of time and space can help ground visual images in one's experience of the real world and so tap into the users' knowledge base and inherent structures.

4.3.1.2 Navigation Requirements

Good navigation allows users to explore the Topic Map and to access information quickly. Navigation should be intuitive so that it is easy to get from one place to another. Several metaphors are possible: users may travel by car, by plane, by metro or may simply be "teleported" – as on the Web – to their destination. The differences lie in what they see during their journey. From a car they see details, from a plane they have an overview, etc. Navigation is essential because it helps users build their own cognitive map – a map-like cognitive representation of an environment – and increases the rate at which they can assimilate and understand information.

Free navigation should be kept for small structures or expert users as the probability of getting lost is very high. For beginners, who do not know where to start their exploration, predefined navigation paths are preferable until topics of interest are identified.

To sum up the visualization goals, we need to represent the whole Topic Map in order to help users understand it globally. This *overview* should reflect the main properties of the structure. However, users should be able to *focus* on any part of the Topic Map and see all the dimensions they need. Providing several scales requires the use of different *levels of detail*. Finally, users should be able to navigate easily and intuitively at these different levels of detail.

In the following section, we study which visualization techniques meet our requirements and may be used to represent Topic Maps.

4.3.2 Visualization Techniques

Many visualization techniques are currently available to represent complex data. Among them, graphs, trees and maps seem to be the best suited metaphors for Topic Maps visualization.

4.3.2.1 Graphs and Trees

Representing Topic Maps as graphs seems natural as they can be seen as a network – or graph – of topics and associations. The Topic Map shown in Figure 4.1 is displayed as a graph consisting of nodes and arcs. However, this simple representation may become cluttered and difficult to interpret when the size of the structure increases. As a Topic Map may contain millions of topics and associations, it becomes necessary to use sophisticated graph visualization techniques.

Graphs and trees are suited for representing the global structure of the Topic Map. However, trees are better understood by human beings since they are hierarchical. Trees are easier to interpret than graphs. Topic Maps are not hierarchies and thus may not be – directly – represented as trees. However, it may be interesting to transform small parts of the Topic Map into trees. By doing so on a small part of the Topic Map (to avoid clutter), we may benefit from the advantages of trees.

The challenge of graph visualization is to provide graphs which display many nodes but which remain readable. A first solution, proposed by Munzner (1997), is to use hyperbolic geometry – instead of Euclidean geometry – which allows to display a very large number of nodes on the screen. Figure 4.2 is an example of a Topic Map representation as hyperbolic trees, obtained with the *K42* Topic Map engine developed by Empolis (2001).

Another solution to the lack of space on the screen is to represent the Topic Maps in three dimensions. A 3D interactive Topic Map visualization tool, *UNIVIT* (Universal Interactive Visualization Tool), was implemented by Le Grand and

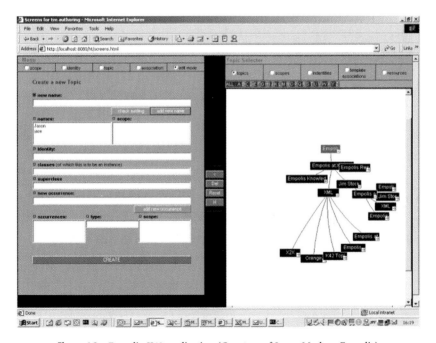

Figure 4.2 Empolis *K42* application (Courtesy of Jason Markos, Empolis).

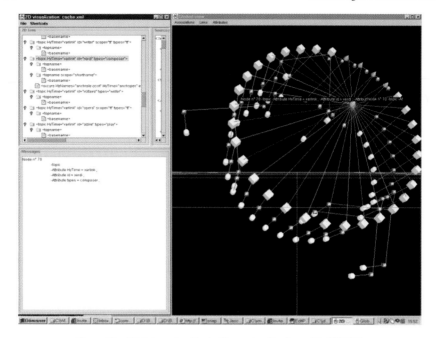

Figure 4.3   3D interactive Topic Maps visualization with *UNIVIT*.

Soto (2000). The example shown in Figure 4.3 was generated with *UNIVIT*, which uses virtual reality techniques such as 3D, interaction and different levels of detail.

Moreover, the quality of the visualization can be increased by efficient node positioning, which makes it possible to intuitively derive information from the distance between nodes. For instance:

- topics linked together by an association may be represented close to each other in the graph
- topics of the same type or pointing to the same occurrences may be clustered.

Graphs and trees meet our first requirement since they may represent the whole Topic Map. However, users also need to see detailed information about the topics they are interested in. This second requirement, which consists in representing all the different parameters of a Topic Map (name, type, etc.), may be really challenging. Figure 4.4 is a graph obtained with the *NV3D* software (Nvision Software Systems, 2000). Different shapes and colours are used to symbolize various dimensions of nodes and arcs of the graph. This kind of graph could be used to visualize a Topic Map; topics would be nodes and associations would be arcs. However, the number of different shapes, colours, icons and textures is limited. This representation is not suited for a Topic Map containing millions of topics and associations.

In order to display detailed information, it is thus necessary to focus on part of a Topic Map. The graph-like overview of the Topic Map helps users understand the structure globally and select specific topics they may be interested in. Once a topic is selected, it is easy to display very precise information about it. Figure 4.5 is a very simple representation of a topic, proposed by Le Grand (2001). The

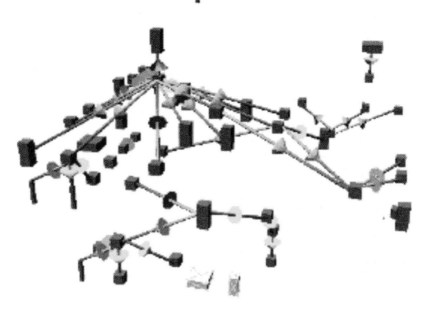

Figure 4.4   *NV3D* graph representation.

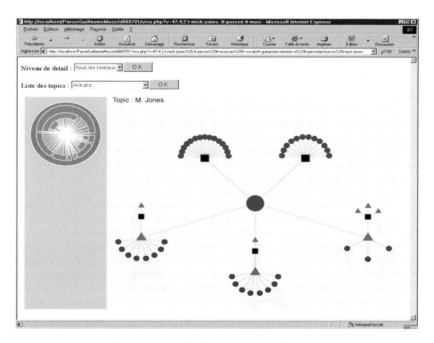

Figure 4.5   Graphical representation of a topic.

topic itself is a disc, located at the centre of the visualization. This topic may be an instance of other topics, which are above it in the graph. The associations in which this topic is involved are symbolized by triangles.

Once users' needs are clearly identified, another useful way to represent a Topic Map is to display a list – or index – from which it is possible to select a topic and see related information. The navigation is usually the same as on Web sites: users click on a link to open a new topic or association. An example of such a visualization is provided by the Ontopia (2001) *Navigator*, as shown in Figure 4.6.

We showed that the global view and precise parameters could not be displayed at the same level of detail. It is essential that users can navigate easily from one level of detail to another. Several tools already provide interactive graphical visualizations. Mondeca's (2001) *Topic Navigator* builds graph representations in real-time, according to what users are allowed or need to see (Figure 4.7). Figure 4.8 is an example of Techquila's (2001) *TM4J* Topic Map dynamic visualization using *TheBrain* software (The Brain Technologies Corporation, 2001).

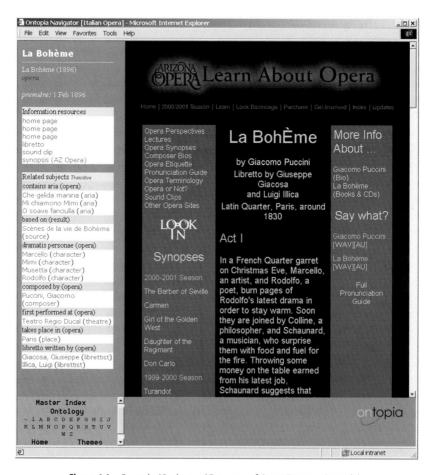

Figure 4.6   Ontopia *Navigator* (Courtesy of Steve Pepper, Ontopia).

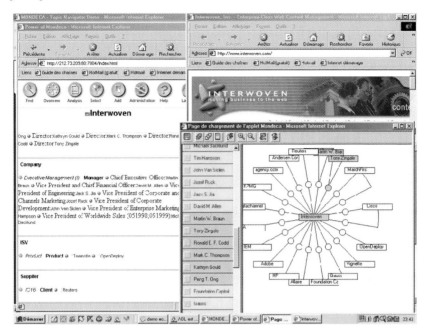

Figure 4.7   Mondeca's *Topic Navigator* (Courtesy of Jean Delahousse, Mondeca).

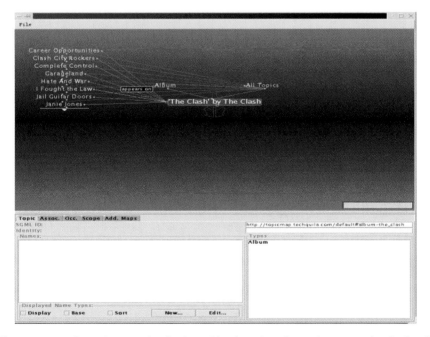

Figure 4.8   *TM4J*'s Topic Map visualization with *TheBrain* software (Courtesy of Kal Ahmed, Techquila).

4.3.2.2 Maps

Topic Maps aim at enhancing navigation within complex data sets. In the real world, maps are used to achieve this goal. It is thus natural to consider representing Topic Maps as maps.

A map should display the most significant elements of the structure. The location and the size of these elements on the map are essential. In the *Tree-Maps* proposed by Bruls et al. (2000), data is reorganized so as to reflect the relative importance of topics, as shown in Figure 4.9. These *Tree-Maps* may be used to represent Topic Maps.

One of the challenges of Topic Maps visualization as maps is to find optimal coordinates for the topics. The *Self-Organizing Maps* (SOM) algorithm, proposed by Kaski et al. (1998) can be used to achieve this by organizing the topics onto a two-dimensional grid so that related topics appear close to each other, as shown in Figure 4.10.

Factor analysis can also be used to compute topic coordinates. Davison (1992) explains how the *Multi-Dimensional Scaling* (MDS) algorithm uses similarity measures between topics to provide a 2D map of the structure. Figure 4.11 is an example of map that represents a small Topic Map about rock music.

The *ThemeScape* software by Cartia Inc. (1992) provides different types of maps. They look like topographical maps with mountains and valleys, as shown in Figure 4.12. The concept of the layout is simple: documents with similar content are placed close to each other and peaks appear where there is a concentration of closely related documents; higher numbers of documents create higher peaks. The valleys between peaks can be interesting because they contain

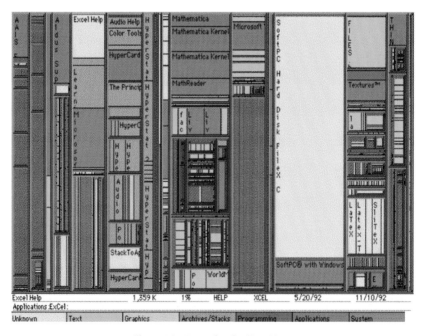

Figure 4.9   Example of a *Tree-Map*.

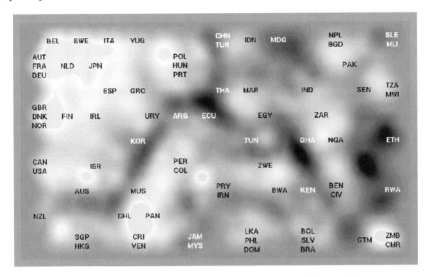

Figure 4.10   Self-organizing map (Courtesy of Sami Kaski and Teuvo Kohonen).

fewer documents and more unique content. The labels reflect two or three major topics represented in a given area of the map, providing a quick indication of what the documents are about. Additional labels often appear when we zoom into the map for greater detail. We can zoom in to different levels of magnification to declutter the map and reveal additional documents and labels.

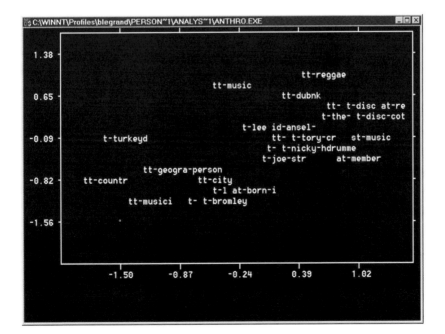

Figure 4.11   MDS map.

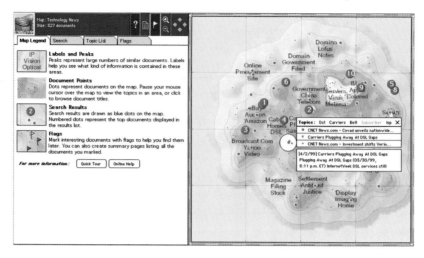

Figure 4.12   *ThemeScape* map.

This visualization is very interesting since it combines different representations in several windows. Users may choose one of them according to the selected type of information.

Visual data-mining tools depict original data or resulting models using 3D visualizations, enabling users to interactively explore data and quickly discover meaningful new patterns, trends and relationships.

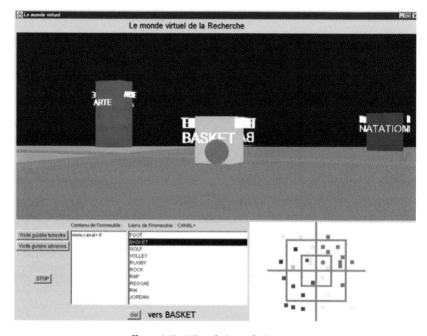

Figure 4.13   Virtual city and 2D map.

Visual tools may utilize animated 3D landscapes that take advantage of human beings' ability to navigate in three-dimensional spaces, recognize patterns, track movement and compare objects of different sizes and colours. Users may have complete control over the appearance of data. Virtual reality techniques include interactivity and the use of different *levels of detail* (LOD). Immersion in virtual worlds makes users feel more involved in the visualization.

A representation of Topic Maps as virtual cities, developed by Le Grand (2001), is shown on Figure 4.13. Topics are represented as buildings whose coordinates are computed from a matrix of similarities between topics. Users may navigate freely or follow a guided tour through the city; they may also choose to walk or fly. The properties of topics are symbolized by the characteristics of the corresponding buildings, such as name, colour, height, width, depth, etc. Occurrences and associated topics are displayed in two windows at the bottom of the screen. As human beings are used to 2D, a traditional 2D map is also provided and the two views – the map and the virtual city – are always consistent.

Users may explore the world and interact with data. However, they may get lost in the virtual world. In order to avoid these problems, predefined navigation paths are also proposed. The different levels of detail make it possible to display many scales; details appear only when the user is close to the subject of interest.

4.4 Conclusion

In this chapter, we presented Topic Maps basic concepts. These structures may be complex, thus efficient visualization techniques are essential. We reviewed different types of visualization metaphors, especially graphs, trees, maps and virtual worlds. Some of them may represent efficiently the global structure while others are better at displaying details or providing interaction with data. In fact, each technique is well-suited for a specific level of detail. The best way to benefit from the advantages of each method is thus to provide several levels of details for the representation of Topic Maps. This can be done by displaying several windows or by selecting the most appropriate representation at a given level of detail.

One visualization tool is usually adapted to display a certain amount of data. If only one tool is to be used for visualization, the Topic Map may be clustered to reach the scale at which the tool is useful, as proposed by Le Grand (2001).

4.5 References

Bruls, M., Huizing, K., van Wijk, J. J. (2000) Squarified Treemaps, *Proceedings of Joint Eurographics and IEEE TCVG Symposium on Visualization*, IEEE Press, pp. 33–42.

Cartia Inc. (1992) *ThemeScape Product Suite*. Available: http://www.cartia.com/products/index.html

Davison M. L. (1992) *Multidimensional Scaling*, Malabar, FL: Krieger.

Empolis (2001) *K42, Intelligent Retrieval with Topic Maps*. Available: http://www.empolis.com/englisch/pdf/k42_eng.pdf

Gershon, N., Eick, S. G. (1995) Visualization's New Tack: Making Sense of Information, *IEEE Spectrum*, 32, 38–56.

International Organization for Standardization (ISO), International Electrotechnical Commision (IEC), Topic Maps, International Standard ISO/IEC 13250: 1999.

Kaski, S., Honkela, T., Lagus, K., Kohonen, T. (1998) WEBSOM – self-organizing maps of document collections, *Neurocomputing*, 21, 101–117.

Le Grand, B. (2001) Extraction d'information et visualization de systèmes complexes sémantiquement structurés, PhD thesis, Laboratoire d'Informatique de Paris 6, Paris, France.

Le Grand, B., Soto, M. (2000) Information management – Topic Maps visualization, *XML Europe 2000*, Paris, France.

Le Grand, B., Soto, M. (2001) XML Topic Maps and Semantic Web mining, Semantic Web Mining Workshop, *ECML/PKDD 2001 Conference*, Friburg, Germany.

Mondeca (2001) *Topic Navigator*. Available: http://www.mondeca.com/site/products/products.html.

Moore, G. (2001) RDF and Topic Maps, an exercise in convergence, *XML Europe 2001*, Berlin, Germany.

Munzner, T. (1997) H3: Laying out large directed graphs in 3D hyperbolic space, *IEEE Symposium on Information Visualization*.

Nvision Software Systems (2000) *NV3D Technical Capabilities Overview*. Available: http://www.nv3d.com/html/tco.pdf

Ontopia (2001) *Ontopia Topic Map Navigator*. Available: http://www.ontopia.net/solutions/navigator.html

Shneiderman, B. (1996) The eyes have it: A task by data type taxonomy for information visualizations, *Proceedings of 1996 IEEE Visual Languages*, Boulder, CO, pp. 336–343.

Techquila (2001) *TM4J, A Topic Map Engine for Java*. Available: http://www.techquila.com

The Brain Technologies Corporation (2001) Available: http://www.thebrain.com

TopicMaps.Org XTM Authoring Group (2001) *XTM: XML Topic Maps (XTM) 1.0: TopicMaps.Org Specification*. Available: http://www.topicmaps.org/xtm/index.html

World Wide Web Consortium (1999) *Resource Description Framework (RDF) Model and Syntax Specification*, W3C.

Chapter 5
Web Rendering Systems: Techniques, Classification Criteria and Challenges

Stephen Kimani, Tiziana Catarci and Isabel Cruz

5.1 Introduction

Access to information scattered all over the world is becoming increasingly common since the Web is the widest information repository. However, finding, organizing, and classifying the information of interest among the massive amount of information are very hard tasks. Other challenges include the broad user base, which mainly consists of users with little or no background in computer science. The new goal is direct interaction with the final user (the person who is searching for information, and is not necessarily familiar with computer technology), for expressing information requests and conveying results. Direct manipulation is typically achieved in visual environments. The well-known high bandwidth of the human-vision channel allows both recognition and understanding of large quantities of information in no more than a few seconds.

One of the basic ideas underlying the sophisticated visualization mechanisms proposed for the Web is representing the data in a form that matches human perceptual capabilities, so that users may easily grasp the information of interest. Proposed visualizations range from advanced techniques to visualize large networks in a screen shot, to animated spaces where related information may be organized, analysed and linked by means of different visual mechanisms to sense-making tools, which help users understanding information by associating and combining it. Such tools represent retrieved information to make patterns visible, or they allow the construction of new information patterns from old ones by exploiting the power of visual attributes of the representation, which may be quickly detected by the eye.

One of the most used techniques to support Web navigation and avoid the "being lost in hyperspace" problem, is the so-called "focus + context" (Shneiderman, 1998). If, while surfing the Web, the user comes to a particular node and feels lost, some idea of the position of the node in the overall information space will help orient the user. However, despite the many different approaches already available, there are open problems still to be solved. In particular, each system seems to be an ad-hoc development. There is a lack of precise theory relating visualizations, users and tasks, with the final goal of automatically or semi-automatically producing effective visualizations depending on the classes of users and the types of tasks. Also, significant measures of effectiveness, adequacy, completeness, and correctness of visual representations have not been defined yet. Similarly, self-adaptive systems (i.e. systems which change their look and feel depending on the user's characteristics) are still in their infancy.

In this chapter, the concept of *Web rendering* is introduced, referring to a set of techniques used to show to the user the information residing on the Web and to support making sense of such information. In particular, we focus on visual rendering, therefore various techniques for visualizing the Web are discussed. The chapter also introduces several criteria that may be used to classify Web visualization systems, or in general, Web rendering systems. Then, various relevant Web systems are surveyed. Finally, existing challenges are highlighted.

5.2 Web Rendering Techniques

We use the term *rendering* to denote the mapping from the information space to one representation of that space that can be perceived by the user. The final goal is to show the information residing on the Web to users so that they can effectively make use of the information. In particular, we are interested in *visual rendering*; visual rendering refers to rendering in which the most important transmission channel is the visual one.

In our case, we consider such a mapping to have three main components: visual encoding, metaphor, and conceptual techniques. However, it should be mentioned that all the three components do not necessarily have to be defined.

Visual encoding refers to the way in which data are displayed on the screen. It entails the use of graphical properties such as points, lines, areas, volumes, colour, shape, position, size, greyscale, orientation, and texture to represent data attributes and/or relationships. Virtually, every rendering technique supports some basic visual encoding that operates from the information space to the visual space. Such an encoding yields the basic visual structure of the underlying information. In this basic case, no metaphors or conceptual techniques are used. An example is when the visual structure is essentially a graph, which is a common occurrence given the interconnection of data on the Web. In particular, the graph is usually a tree, a network or a variant such as "pre-trees" (Mukherjea et al., 1995) and multi-trees (Furnas and Zacks, 1994). Trees are used to represent information whose structure is hierarchical. Trees can be visualized in two main ways: connection/node-link diagrams and containment/enclosure (Card et al., 1999).

Networks are more complicated than trees due to the possibility of having cycles within the data. In fact one of the consequences of the presence of cycles is that enclosure cannot be used to represent networks. Networks rely on connection representation (node-link diagrams). Nodes and links may be labelled, unlabelled, ordinal, or quantitative. Links may be directed or undirected (Card et al., 1999).

Examples of Web systems with renderings whose perception primarily relies on visual encoding are SeeNet3D (Cox et al., 1996; Eick, 1996) and Star Tree (Inxight, 2001; Lamping et al., 1995). Figure 5.1 shows a visualization of communication networks taken from Eick (1996). Related work on the layout of geographic and communication networks is presented in (Brandes et al., 2000; Munzner and Burchard, 1995).

Unlike visual encoding, metaphors and conceptual techniques operate beyond just primarily mapping the basic Web information structure.

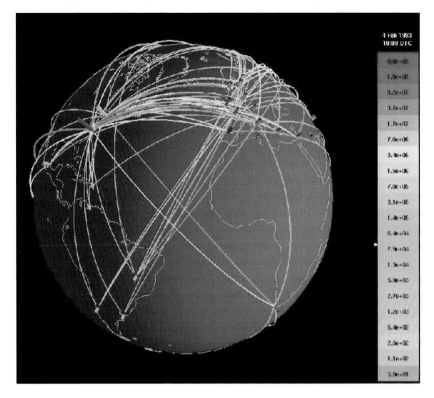

Figure 5.1 Visualization of communication networks (Eick, 1996).

Metaphors are used to establish a correspondence between the information space and a realm well known to the user. Examples of metaphor-based systems are WebBook and Web Forager (Card et al., 1996), DeckScape (Brown and Shillner, 1995), and Galaxies and ThemeView^{TM} (Pacific Northwest National Laboratory, 2002; Wise et al., 1995).

WebBook is an application that uses a book metaphor in order to enable the user to access and view Web pages. Each page in the WebBook represents a Web page. Figure 5.2 shows the WebBook. The Web Forager is an intuitive workspace in which the user can interact with the WebBook and other relevant objects in the same environment, as seen in Figure 5.3.

DeckScape, which is an experimental World Wide Web browser for navigating and organizing Web pages, adopts a deck metaphor. In this context, a deck is a window that is used to hold a collection of Web pages. The deck displays only one page at a time, as seen in Figure 5.4. The deck also displays a list of contents/ links to the pages it contains.

Galaxies and ThemeView^{TM} are deployed as part of the SPIRE project by Pacific Northwest National Laboratory. Visualization in Galaxies is based on a galaxy metaphor. Each document is bound to a single "docustar". Related documents are placed close to one another (clustered), while unrelated documents are placed far apart. Figure 5.5 shows Galaxies being used to visualize cancer information. Formerly known as ThemeScape, ThemeView^{TM} is

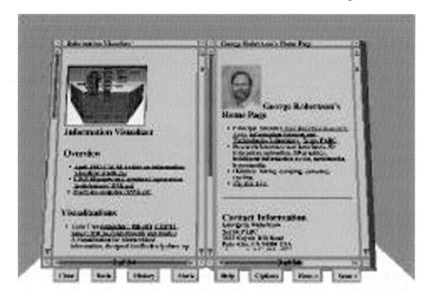

Figure 5.2   WebBook (Card et al., 1996).

a 3D visualization based on a terrain metaphor, as seen in Figure 5.6. ThemeView™ provides a visual overview of the major topics contained in a set of documents.

Conceptual techniques refer to various mechanisms used to elicit data semantics. The techniques include clustering, layering, ISA hierarchies, etc. Following is a discussion of some specific conceptual techniques that are used in the development of Web systems.

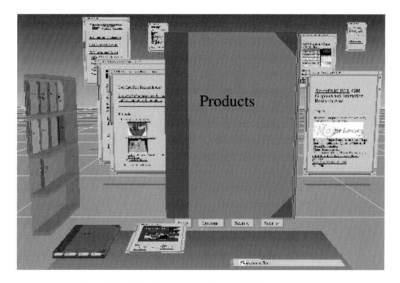

Figure 5.3   Web Forager workspace (Card et al., 1996).

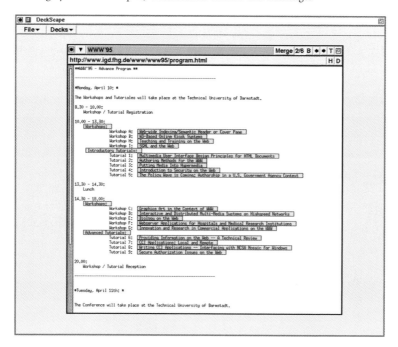

Figure 5.4 DeckScape with a single deck named "WWW'95", which has six pages. The current page, whose URL is http://www.igd.fhg.de/www/www95/program.html, is the second Web page in the deck (Brown and Shillner, 1995).

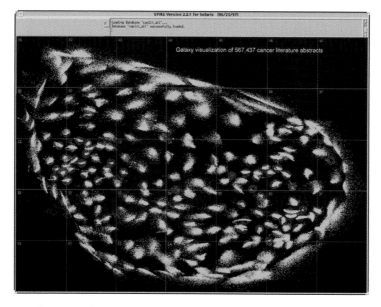

Figure 5.5 Galaxies visualization of cancer information (Pacific Northwest National Laboratory, 2002).

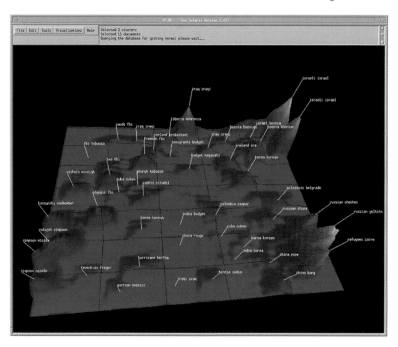

Figure 5.6 ThemeView™ visualization of news (Pacific Northwest National Laboratory, 2002).

5.2.1 Concept Maps

Concept maps (Gaines and Shaw, 1995a) are used to structure information in order to identify the interrelationships among concepts within a domain. They have an associated straightforward visual representation. A concept map is a sorted hyper-graph data structure with typed nodes. Some of the nodes may be linked. Each node has a type, a unique identifier, and content. A node may enclose other nodes. Links may be non-directional, directional or bi-directional. Arrowed or non-arrowed lines are used to visually represent links. In some cases/ applications, links take a type. In a visualization, concept maps can be used to provide a mapping between the visual structures and their semiotic infrastructure. The mapping can be made effective by ensuring that the visual attributes of the nodes (and typed links) are in one-to-one correspondence with their types. Some of the visual attributes that may be used include colour, shape and thickness. The attributes that are not used for representing the type may be used to represent other aspects of the concept map. However, such usage should be done carefully so as not to obscure the primary type mapping (visual attribute to type).

Concept maps have been applied in areas such as education, policy studies and the philosophy of science. Concept maps have also been used to visualize the Web. WebMap (Gaines and Shaw, 1995b) is a Web system that is based on concept maps.

5.2.2 Topic Maps

Topic maps refer to an ISO standard (ISO/IEC 13250 Topic Maps, 1999) that provides a paradigm for describing knowledge structures and associating the structures with information resources. Topic maps define a semantic layer above the information space. In this space, locations are topics in which the distances between the topics are measurable in terms of interposing topics that must be traversed in order to move from one topic to another. There are also relationships that define paths from topic to topic.

It is worth taking a brief look at some of the terminologies used in topic maps (Pepper and Rath, 1999; Rath, 2001). A subject is anything whatsoever about which anything whatsoever may be said or conceived by any means whatsoever. A topic is a resource for mapping the system's representation of some subject. The topic acts as a proxy for that subject. An occurrence is any information that is specified as relevant to a given subject. An association is a description of a relationship between two or more topics. Each such topic plays a role as a member of the association. A topic characteristic is anything that may be asserted by a human being about a topic. It can be a topic name, a topic occurrence or a role played by a topic in a certain association. A scope is a specification of the extent of validity of a topic characteristic assignment. Le Grand and Soto (2000) describe a system that uses topic maps to represent the Web information space.

5.2.3 Clustering/Abstraction

It should be mentioned that abstraction usually goes under the name of clustering in the context of Web visualization (Mendelzon, 1996). Clustering entails grouping related or similar objects/items. On the whole, clustering may be hierarchical or non-hierarchical. In exploiting clustering to visualize the Web, some important requirements include determining the relevance/weight of the attributes of the items in the information space, adopting an appropriate clustering method and similarity measure, and the development of effective visualizations mapping the underlying clustering. An example of systems based on this approach is Navigational View Builder (Mukherjea and Foley, 1995).

While it is true that clustering may be used to minimize screen clutter by keeping the number of objects on the screen small, care should be taken not to ignore design issues. In line with the foregoing, Tufte (1990) observes that "clutter and confusion are failures of design not attributes of information".

5.2.4 Concept Analysis

Concept analysis is a relatively new discipline that enables the automatic classification of knowledge and documents (Kent and Neuss, 1995). It has its origins in the mathematical theory of lattices and category theory. The basic components of concept analysis are objects, attributes and conceptual classes. A formal context is a triple (G, M, I) describing the relationship I between two sets G, M. Intuitively, G is an object and M an attribute. A conceptual class consists of a group of objects that have one or more common attributes. The definition of a conceptual class should include the common attributes, which are encoded in the superordinate (a higher conceptual class), and the distinguishing attributes, which differentiate the defined conceptual class from the superordinate. The process of subordination of conceptual classes and collocation of objects from the more general classes to the more specialized classes is called generalization-specialization.

The conceptual classes generated form a lattice. At the top is the set of all objects where there are no attributes specified, and then each concept is specialized by supplementing its set of attributes with some more, forming a more specialized conceptual class containing fewer objects. This lattice structure may be used to represent the structure of the World Wide Web. WAVE, an acronym for Web Analysis and Visualization Environment (Kent and Neuss, 1995), is a Web system based on concept analysis.

There also exist methods that may be used to develop sophisticated renderings. For instance, the site outlining method (Takeda and Nomiyama, 1998) whose discussion follows.

5.2.5 Site Outlining

Related to site outlining is the concept of information outlining (Morohashi et al., 1995). Information outlining is an integrated paradigm for querying, viewing, and navigating data. Each information request is formulated as a view. A view comprises a data model and a visual representation, whereby the visual representation is an appropriate/effective visualization for the data model. A data model is often a relation or an ordered set of tuples, whereas a visual representation is a graphical representation (such as a bar graph, pie chart, or map). In practice, a view is implemented by a window-based GUI (Graphical User Interface) called a viewer. Moreover, a view is associated with an information extraction method that maps the underlying data to a data model.

Site outlining takes information outlining a step further in that it incorporates dynamically and asynchronously changing information sources by introducing versions (or snapshots) and their respective information outlining views. A site could be a World Wide Web page, metadata representations, a search engine, a channel, or any program so long as it generates a specific form of information as its output for a user's query or interaction. Koichi Takeda and Hiroshi Nomiyama (1998) have developed a system based on the site outlining approach. In their system, viewers are typically simple graphical representations such as bar charts and maps. For a wide range of information, the system offers multiple viewers. In the context of Web-based information, whose range is also non-trivial, it might be worth considering the introduction of standard and effective Web renderings either as an option or as an alternative to the multiple viewers.

Each of the three rendering components, visual encoding, metaphors, and conceptual techniques has its place in a visual display. It is interesting to realize that a Web system can exploit or define all three rendering components on the same display. WebBook and Web Forager (Card et al., 1996) is an example of such a system.

5.3 Classification Criteria for Web Systems

In this section we propose criteria that may be used to classify Web systems.

Web systems may be classified according to generation dynamics. Under this criterion, Web renderings may be categorized as hand-crafted (static) or automatically generated (dynamic).

A hand-crafted rendering each time presents a discrete representation of an evolving information space. In such a system, careful advance acquisition and analysis of the overall information structure are carried out. Based on the foregoing analysis, a corresponding rendering is constructed by a designer using appropriate tools. Once constructed and installed, it does not change until the designer reconstructs it. Such renderings are often fairly complex and usually target specific applications. Static renderings may be appropriate for enabling the user to understand the overall structure of the information space. An example of a system with static renderings is the Navigational View Builder (Mukherjea and Foley, 1995).

An automatically generated rendering is constructed on-the-fly by the underlying system. The system relies on a set of pre-supplied layout parameters, rules and components to be able to construct the rendering. Dynamic renderings may be appropriate for traversing documents in the navigational history/profile. Examples of systems with dynamic renderings are WEBNET (Cockburn and Jones, 1996) and MosaicG (Ayers and Stasko, 1995).

It is worth mentioning that dynamic renderings offer the user more significant control over the system than static renderings. The user also is able to get more updated information from the rendering. However, with dynamic renderings, the system may take a significant amount of time to produce the rendering. This basically depends on the underlying rendering algorithms and the processing complexity. As for static renderings, a careful selection of a reasonably efficient generation mechanism is done in advance. Moreover, if transitions in a dynamic rendering are not smooth, then the user may lose the mental map of the space. Hand-generated renderings remain static until the designer constructs them again.

Another criterion that may be used to classify Web rendering systems is the type of adaptivity the systems support. Adaptivity involves the incorporation of a user model into the framework of the system, at least to some extent. In such a setting, the user can make changes to one or more of the following elements: portion(s) of data, mapping, and visual views. Adaptivity may take the form of personalization or transformation.

In personalization, the system updates itself in order to suit the needs of an individual user or a class of users. The system comprises or generates multiple versions of the rendering, based on the subset of users. Personalization may be manual, semi-automatic or automatic.

Manual personalizations simply carry out alterations to the rendering as specified by a human web administrator. Approaches such as STRUDEL (Fernandez et al., 1997) and XML annotations (Khare and Rifkin, 1997) might be good avenues for developing manually adaptive renderings.

Semi-automatic personalizations refer to systems that are restricted regarding changes that they can make to the rendering. The systems need the approval of a human web administrator before carrying out alterations to the rendering.

Commercial sites, such as amazon.com (http://www.amazon.com), presumably support this form of adaptivity.

On the other hand, automatic personalizations carry out changes to the rendering on their own. Letizia (Lieberman, 1995) supports automatic personalization.

A transformation refers to an evolution of the rendering based on the analysis of, ideally, all users. Transformations may be of benefit to even first time or new visitors since the evolution takes into account "all" users. Perkowitz and Etzioni (1999) describe a system whose adaptivity is a transformation. Another system that supports the same type of adaptivity is Footprints (Wexelblat and Maes, 1997).

At this point, it is worth taking a look at the concept of customization. Customization allows users to specify or modify some aspects of the system. Customization may be basic or "intelligent". In systems that support basic customization, the user specifies in an explicit way how the output will look. In "intelligent" customization, the user partially contributes to the specification of the appearance of the output. The system makes some deductions on the most appropriate visualization. Examples of systems that support "intelligent" customization are DARE (Catarci et al., 1999; Catarci and Santucci, 2001) and Delaunay (Cruz and Leveille, 2001).

DARE is a visualization system that is built on a knowledge base of rules. DARE enables the user to specify various rules on a database in order to develop a visual representation of the database. DARE analyses whether such a visual representation is correct, complete and effective. In case the user's representation falls short of certain adequacy requirements, the system builds and proposes an adequate visual representation. Delaunay uses an automatic component to determine certain visual attributes that are under-specified, taking into account sound principles of visualization.

In the discussion on adaptivity and customization, many of the systems given are not for visualizing the Web. Nonetheless, the underlying adaptivity and customization methods may be applied or carried over to Web visualizations and renderings.

Web systems may also be classified based on their primary interaction style. Web systems enable the user to interact with them in a variety of ways. The main interaction styles supported by Web systems are direct manipulation, menus and form fill-ins. A particular Web system may support one or more of such interaction styles.

Systems that support direct manipulation are characterized by: visual representation of the objects and actions of interest; rapid, incremental, reversible operations whose effect on an object is immediately apparent; and replacement of complex syntax by physical actions or button presses (Shneiderman, 1998).

In Web systems that support interaction through menus, the actions that the user can undertake are displayed on the screen in the form of a menu. When the user selects and invokes one of the appropriate actions, the rendering responds accordingly. The use of menus tends to be especially prevalent in representing high-level operations or system-level operations (such as starting and exiting the application).

Some Web systems enable interaction through form fill-ins. These interaction widgets are more or less embedded in the interface. Through form fill-ins, the user may specify rendering parameters such as queries, thresholds and mappings.

The classification can be based on whether interaction with the rendering primarily relies on direct manipulation or otherwise (mainly menus and form fill-ins). Examples of Web systems whose main interaction style is by direct manipulation are Star Tree (Inxight, 2001), WebBook and Web Forager (Card et al., 1996) and Natto View (Shiozawa and Matsushita, 1997; The Natto View, 2002). The latter form of interaction hosts systems such as TileBars (Hearst, 1995) and WebTOC (Nation et al., 1997).

5.4 Web Rendering Systems

In this section, a discussion of some noteworthy Web systems that have been proposed in the literature is given.

5.4.1 Star Tree Viewer

Star Tree Viewer (Inxight, 2001) is a Java-based tool for visualizing large collections of information in 2D using the hyperbolic lens interaction mechanism.

The system visually encodes various aspects. The nodes represent Web documents. Lines/links are used to express the existence of some relationship amongst documents. Nodes are linked in a hierarchical, tree structure. The node at the centre/root represents the home page of the Web site. The colours of the nodes may be varied to reflect various aspects of the represented Web documents. In some cases, an icon may be appended at the left end of a node to represent the type of Web document the node represents (such as HTML, sound or image files). The colour of a link may be varied to express the type of relationship that exists between the documents. However, it should be pointed out that such customization is done by the engineer/designer who sets up the system. Star Tree does not support adaptivity.

The primary mode of interaction is by direct manipulation. Double-clicking a node opens the Web document represented. The user may drag the nodes around to change the focus of the tree. However, the focus change does not affect the overall structure of the tree.

5.4.2 Navigational View Builder

Navigational View Builder (Mukherjea and Foley, 1995) uses various conceptual techniques, such as clustering and hierarchization, to make overview diagrams more understandable/effective. The foregoing techniques exploit a combination of structural and content analysis of the underlying space.

Navigational View Builder also supports the application of visual encoding on the rendering. The designer of the navigational views can specify the bindings between the information attributes and the visual attributes. For instance nodes, as icons, could be used to represent Web files (documents or media). The node type could be used to represent a file type. The node size could represent file size. The node shape could be bound the type of file author. Colour hue could be used to encode the theme/topic of the file. Colour saturation could represent the last

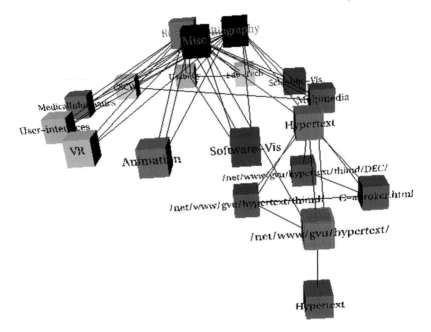

Figure 5.7 A view from the Navigational View Builder showing the details of the Hypertext research field. Colours represent research areas. Nodes whose details are currently shown are greyed out (Mukherjea and Foley, 1995).

modified time. Lines could be used to represent links. Solid lines could represent links between two HTML files. Other types of links could be bound to dashed lines. Figure 5.7 shows a visualization of research areas in which the details of the Hypertext research area are displayed.

Navigational View Builder does not support adaptivity and uses static renderings. Interaction with the renderings is mainly by direct manipulation. The system also provides minimum interaction support through menus.

5.4.3 WebOFDAV

WebOFDAV (Huang et al., 1998) uses the Online Force-Directed Animated Visualization (OFDAV) navigational approach, which does not require the structure of the entire information space to be predefined/known. On the contrary, it provides for the visualization of the available subspace based on the user's orientation/focus or the user's requirements. There is continuous, incremental computation and generation of viewing frames that maintain the current region of focus. A corresponding subgraph of this subspace is called a logical viewing frame and is defined by its focus nodes. WebOFDAV incrementally computes and generates a sequence of such frames/maps that maintain the current region of the information space that the user is browsing in. The continual, incremental calculation and generation of frames/maps offer smooth transitions between views in the navigation process and are therefore expected to preserve the user's mental map. The system uses a force-directed algorithm, which is based on physical laws behind spring and gravitational forces, to generate the frames (subgraphs) and a logical neighbourhood. The logical neighbourhood of the focus nodes gives the users a sense of their orientation and helps them in deciding their direction.

WebOFDAV also exploits visual encoding to represent various aspects. Previous traversals can be traced by following a graphical history trail that contains previous focus nodes. The colour of the nodes is used to reflect various aspects, as seen in Figure 5.8. In the figure, current focus nodes are drawn with a white

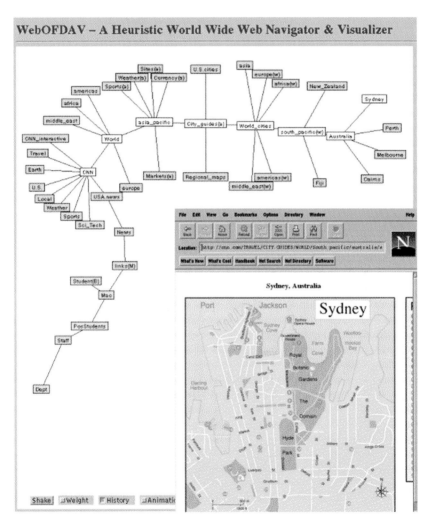

Figure 5.8 The WebOFDAV system in which current focus nodes have a white background, previous focus nodes have a light blue background, and nodes that have not been traversed are drawn with a yellowish background (Huang et al., 1998).

background, previous focus nodes are drawn with a light blue background, and nodes that have not been traversed are drawn with a yellowish background.

The system is non-adaptive. Primary interaction is by direct manipulation. However, the system also provides a simple menu for some of the operations.

5.4.4 WebMap

WebMap (Gaines and Shaw, 1995b) uses the technique of concept maps. In line with the foregoing, WebMap relies on KMap, which is one of the major tools used to support the definition of concept maps. KMap also supports the integration of the concept maps with other applications. WebMap may be viewed as a concept map-centred experience born out of taking KMap and making it available on the Web in a variety of ways including: as a client helper, as an active browser controller, as a concept map creator, and as an auxiliary HTTP server.

The system uses visual encoding to add meaning to the visualization. Web documents are bound to nodes whilst edges represent relationships or links amongst Web documents. Figure 5.9 shows WebMap in use together with the Netscape browser. Some customization is possible at the designer level. Primary interaction with the system is by direct manipulation.

5.4.5 LIP6 Visualization Tool

Le Grand and Soto (2000) from Laboratoire d'Informatique de Paris 6 (LIP6), Université Pierre et Marie Curie, have developed a tool that uses topic maps to visualize large information structures. Besides providing fairly reasonable support for hierarchical data, the tool also accommodates cases where there are non-hierarchical links, referred to as "cross-connections". The tool has been designed using XML and the Document Object Model (DOM). Two views are provided: a traditional 2D view and a 3D view. The 2D view is intended for simplicity. Figure 5.10 shows a 2D view with a tree and an XML source file. The 3D view is aimed at providing a global view of the structure of the information space. The 3D view makes use of Cone Trees as a representation of the basic structure, as seen in Figure 5.11.

The tool also exploits visual encoding. Topics are represented by nodes. The tool uses colours, shapes and textures to represent topic types. Associations are represented either as arcs or as nodes. In the arc representation, association types may be symbolized by line styles (such as full line and dotted line). As for the representation of associations by nodes, association types may be symbolized using the same approach as topics. It is worth mentioning that representing associations by nodes is more appropriate for associations that involve more than two topics.

One of the future directions of the tool is to enable users to specify themes of interest. The tool does not support adaptivity. Direct manipulation is the main style of interaction. Zooming, translations, rotations and filtering are some of the specific ways in which the user can interact with the system. The tool also provides minimum menu-based interaction support.

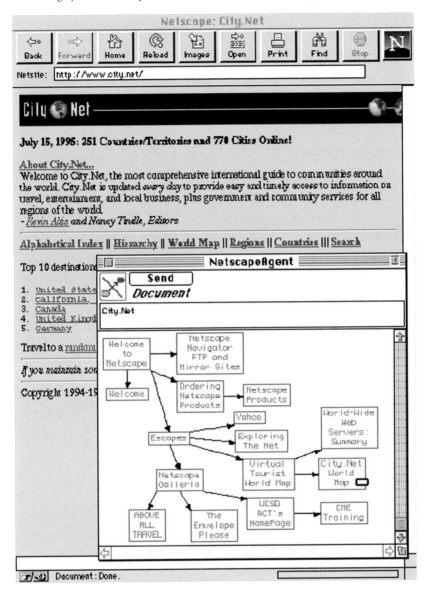

Figure 5.9   WebMap with concept maps being generated by the browser (Gaines and Shaw, 1995b).

5.4.6 HyperSpace

HyperSpace (Wood et al., 1995) is a Web visualization system based on Narcissus (Hendley et al., 1995). Essentially, HyperSpace uses self-organizing schemes and neural networks to arrange World Wide Web objects. The system provides a visualization showing the organization of areas in the Web space. The space is

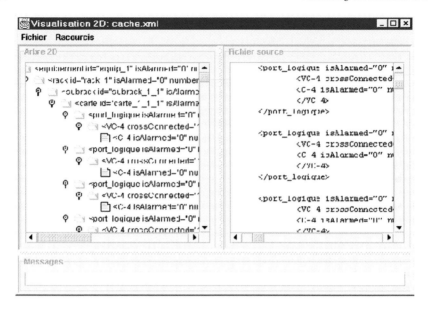

Figure 5.10   LIP6 visualization tool's 2D view showing a tree and XML file (Le Grand and Soto, 2000).

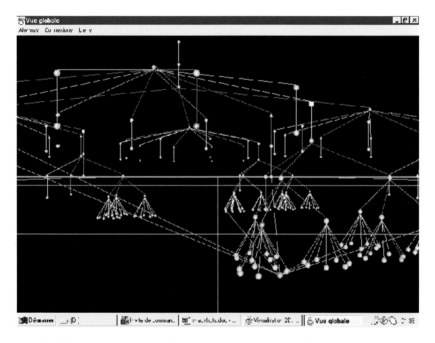

Figure 5.11   LIP6 visualization tool's 3D view with "cross-connections" (Le Grand and Soto, 2000).

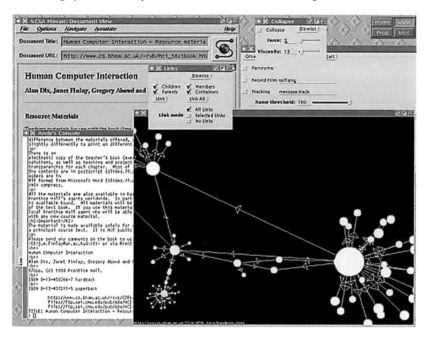

Figure 5.12 The HyperSpace system with the viewer window, browser, and control panels (Wood et al., 1995).

formatted according to a user-defined structure but not according to geographical location.

HyperSpace visually encodes various Web entities. A Web page is represented by a sphere. The size of the sphere depends on the number of links and a random spatial position. Hyperlinks are represented as lines between the spheres. Figure 5.12 shows the system's environment. Initially, these spheres and lines are placed randomly in a 3D substrate. The visualization is then allowed to self-organize based on physics in the real world. Nodes are expected to repel each other, whereas links provide attraction. Consequently, unrelated areas are pushed apart, whereas highly interrelated areas are clustered in the same region of the Web space. It should be mentioned that the visualization is generated based on static data.

HyperSpace allows the user to specify various visualization parameters. Moreover, the system also allows the user to manipulate the forces acting on the Web objects. The developers of HyperSpace have stated their intention to add more customization features to the system, for instance allowing the user to specify name, shape, size and colour of a particular node.

HyperSpace offers embedded form fill-ins for parameter manipulation. It also supports interaction by direct manipulation.

5.4.7 Natto View

Natto View (Shiozawa and Matsushita, 1997; The Natto View, 2002) is a collection of various techniques for visualizing and dynamically interacting with graph-structured information spaces such as the World Wide Web. Objects from the target information space are placed and visualized in a 3D environment.

In the system, visual encoding does play a major part. A node is used to represent a Web document. Lines/links represent relationships among Web documents. The principal style of interaction with the visualization is by direct manipulation. The nodes are arranged on a plane that can be organized according to the needs of the user. Initially, all nodes lie on the plane. As the user lifts a focused node up, the nodes to which it links are lifted up together, and thus complicated networks are disentangled dynamically, as seen in Figure 5.13. Due to the 3D perspective, the user can view both the details of information connections near the selected node and the global context of the large information space like a fisheye lens model. Natto View also provides some interaction through menus. The system does not support adaptivity.

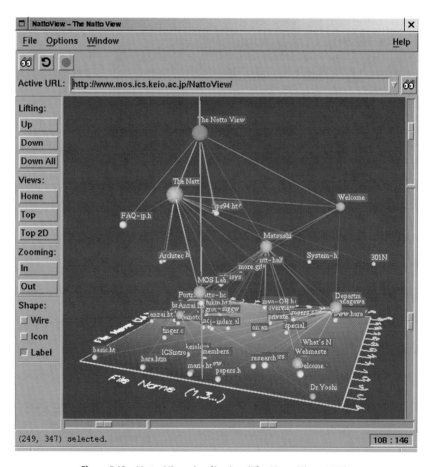

Figure 5.13   Natto View visualization (The Natto View, 2002).

Figure 5.14 Time Tube with disk trees showing the evolution of a Web site within a four-week period (Chi et al., 1998).

5.4.8 Time Tube

Time Tube (Chi et al., 1998) uses disk trees to visualize Web site evolution over a period of time. The disk tree visualization holds information related to various Web site attributes such as access frequency, paths taken, and the age of information.

The visualization also exploits visual encoding. A Web site is mapped to a disk. The centre of the disk represents the root page. Hyperlinks are bound to the tree that branches out around the root. Various instances of the same Web site are visualized by drawing several disks in parallel along a time axis on the X-axis, as seen in Figure 5.14. It is worth mentioning that the X-axis is coded twice since tree links use the X-axis and the Y-axis. Web page access frequency is bound to line size and brightness. Moreover, the lifecycle stage of a Web page is indicated by colour whereby red indicates a new page, green indicates a continued page and yellow indicates a deleted page.

The user can primarily interact with the tube by direct manipulation. For instance, the user can rotate the tube, extract slices from the tube, and zoom into slices. The system also provides menus for some operations.

The system can support authors and Web masters in the production and organization of Web content. It can also enable Web navigators to make sense of Web information. Moreover, the system may enable researchers to get a better understanding of the interconnection of information on the Web.

5.4.9 WebBook and Web Forager

The system (Card et al., 1996) utilizes information foraging theory, an approach aimed at learning how strategies and technologies for information seeking, gathering and utilization are adapted to the flux of information (Pirolli and Card, 1995).

The WebBook may be viewed as a 3D interactive book of Web pages. It enables the user to interact with Web pages at a higher level of aggregation than Web pages. On the one hand, WebBook uses the book metaphor with a view to exploiting human perceptual and cognitive systems. On the other hand, Web-Book provides more than a book in the real world offers. The system exploits visual encoding to make the visual environment easier to understand. A page in WebBook is bound to a Web page. Web page links are colour-coded: red links indicate Web pages on another page in the book, whereas blue links indicate Web pages that are outside the book.

The Web Forager is an application that enables interaction with the WebBook and other objects in a 3D workspace. The workspace has an intuitive hierarchical arrangement in terms of interaction rates. The hierarchical levels are the focus place (the large book/WebBook or page), an intermediate memory space (the air and the desk), and a tertiary place (the bookcase).

Direct manipulation is the primary means of interacting with the system. However, there is also some menu-based interaction support.

5.4.10 Cat-a-Cone

Cat-a-Cone (Hearst and Karadi, 1997) uses an interface that integrates browsing and querying. There is a graphical representation of the category hierarchy and also a graphical representation of the associated document collections. The former graphical representation is aimed at supporting browsing whilst the latter is intended for querying. Category labels are placed in a ConeTree whereas retrieval results are placed in a virtual book. Figure 5.15 shows the Cat-a-Cone environment.

The ConeTree can also provide the context in which the category labels occur. The meaning of unfamiliar or ambiguous categories can be made clearer by displaying their ancestors, siblings and descendants.

The virtual book is a modification of the WebBook and Web Forager project. In most hierarchical visualization systems, documents are associated with each node of the category hierarchy. Clicking on a node would reveal the documents assigned to the node. For Cat-a-Cone, documents are associated with searches. On opening a "page" of retrieval results, the parts of the hierarchy that correspond to the set of categories that have been assigned to the document are shown in the ConeTree. Using the virtual book, the user can "flip" through a set of pages.

In the book, the left-hand page would show the title of the document and the list of category labels associated with that document. The right-hand page would display the contents of the document. The cover of the book would show the query that produced the retrieval results.

As the user flips through the pages of the book, the categories are updated accordingly. This animation helps the user to retain context.

The user can principally interact with the system by direct manipulation. However, the system also provides menus for some of the operations.

5.4.11 WAVE

WAVE (Kent and Neuss, 1995) is aimed at providing mechanisms for refined categorization and management of Web-based information. It employs autonomous agents that acquire raw data, automatically analyse, and classify the same. In the same vein, the system supports interactive presentation and

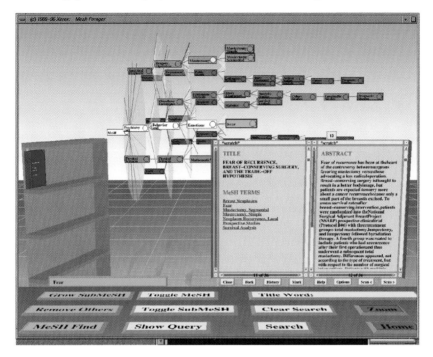

Figure 5.15   The Cat-a-Cone system in which the ConeTree contains category labels and the WebBook displays retrieval results (Hearst and Karadi, 1997).

exploration of results. The system uses a Web spider, document indexing tools, and software agents to gather Web-based information. A Web spider is a program that recursively retrieves Web documents. For analysis and classification purposes, WAVE borrows from the fields of Concept Analysis and Library Science.

WAVE aims at organizing Web objects into conceptual classes that unveil all the similarities and differences fundamental to their comprehension or interpretation by the user. In line with the foregoing, the system uses the conceptual scaling aspect of concept analysis. A conceptual scale is a single, isolated and distinct property, trait or use. Among the Web objects that can be scaled are location of HTML documents, URLs of Web objects, subject, content, topic, size and time. Kent and Neuss (1995) regard the process of organizing Web objects with conceptual scales as "an act of interpretation".

WAVE allows the user to choose the conceptual scales to use. The choice is a specification of a certain view of the entire Web space. The system builds nested line diagrams to abstractly represent the conceptual scales. In such diagrams, the hierarchical arrangement of the user-specified conceptual scales can be visualized, with the nodes representing the conceptual scales. The abstract representation is ultimately mapped to a graph in 3D space. The system relies on a conventional graph layout algorithm to calculate where to position the nodes.

It is worth observing that the nodes represent conceptual scales and thus Web objects. WAVE renders nodes as 3D objects. Visual encoding can further be used to elicit the semantics of the underlying information. For instance, attributes such as size, shape and colour of the 3D objects can be varied to reflect various aspects of the corresponding Web objects. The user can directly interact with the objects in the 3D space.

5.4.12 TileBars

The TileBars (Hearst, 1995) display paradigm offers a compact way of visualizing faceted query term hits for Web documents. The paradigm goes beyond visualizing only the strengths of query matches. TileBars enables the user to visualize the relative length of the results/documents, the relative frequency of query terms, and the distributional properties of query terms with respect to the document and each other.

Query results are visually encoded in an interesting manner, as seen in Figure 5.16. Each result/document is represented by a rectangular bar. The bar is subdivided into rows that correspond to the query terms. The bar is also subdivided into columns, where each column refers to a passage within the

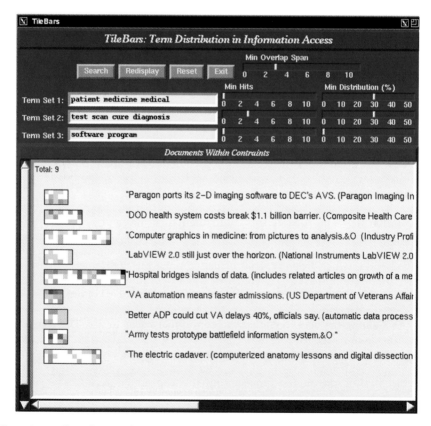

Figure 5.16   TileBars' retrieval results based on the query "patient medicine medical AND test scan cure diagnosis AND software program" with relatively strict distribution constraints (Hearst, 1995).

document. The representation can help the user to visualize the distribution of each topic in each of the documents. Moreover, the greyscale level of the squares depicts the frequency of each topic i.e. number of times the query occurs in that segment of text. Darker squares indicate more frequent matches while lighter squares indicate less frequency. The visualization is generated dynamically.

The system is non-adaptive. The user can interact with the system through embedded form fill-ins and menus.

5.4.13 WebTOC

WebTOC (Nation et al., 1997) offers a visualization of the contents of a Web site. It has two main parts: the WebTOC Parser and the WebTOC Viewer. The WebTOC Parser starts with a Web page, analyses the local links and generates a hierarchical representation of the Web documents local to the site. The WebTOC Viewer displays the generated representation as a Table of Contents (WebTOC) for the Web site using a standard Web browser, as seen in Figure 5.17.

The system applies visual encoding on the Web documents. Site documents are represented as lines of text. The textual lines behave like normal hypertext links. Moreover, each of the local documents is represented by a coloured line. The colour of the line corresponds to the file type of the document. The length of the line represents the size of the document. Lines can be collapsed into a thicker line (or "size bar") to show the overall size of the linked documents. Each size bar has a shadow under it whose size depicts the number of items/links subordinate to the document it represents. This helps the user to see items that have many or few subordinate links. It should be pointed out that the user might choose to view just the coloured lines for an overall view and for easier size comparison.

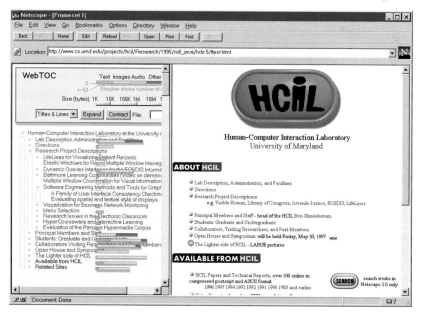

Figure 5.17 WebTOC Web site visualization (Nation et al., 1997).

WebTOC does not support adaptivity. The system provides embedded form fill-ins to enable the user to specify various parameters.

5.5 Challenges

Towards visualizing the World Wide Web, there are various challenges that need to be taken into consideration. Some of the challenges can affect almost any type of system whereas others are specific to the field of visualization. In this section, we present existing challenges, first focusing on specific challenges and then on more general challenges.

The display space available for outputting the rendering or the visualization is limited. Even after applying various information "reduction" techniques, the amount of information to be displayed usually still out-weighs the available screen space. This is especially the case with Web-based information.

In visualization, various visual cues are normally used to represent some of the aspects of the underlying information. While it is true that the use of visual cues might assist the user in interpreting the rendering, too many cues would cause the user to experience mental overload. There are limits to the amount of visual cues the user may be able to interpret or handle at a particular point in time.

Web renderings should exhibit the meaning of the information they intend to represent. Many Web systems do not effectively map or make apparent the semantics of the underlying information. It would be interesting to have Web systems extract and map the semantics either semi-automatically or automatically. However, it should be mentioned that the implementation of such systems is a real challenge.

Another specific challenge is that of interactivity. Web renderings normally turn out to be non-trivial graphical elements. It is expected that the user will interact with these graphics in real time. Actions initiated on the Web system by the user, demand some form of immediate feedback from the rendering. Changes performed on the visual environment should be a reflection of the changes taking place in the information realm in real time and vice versa.

In this chapter, various Web rendering techniques have been discussed. It would be interesting and challenging to design a Web system based on multiple rendering techniques. Consequently, the constituent Web rendering would be multi-layered. Moreover, the respective Web system could be made flexible so that some of the layers could be removed or reintegrated. The flexibility could be invoked based on rationale such as optimization and user preferences.

There is no unified or general theory or framework upon which systems for visualizing the Web can be developed. In fact, most Web systems are based on ad-hoc and somewhat disparate proposals.

On the other hand, there are challenges that are general. One of the general challenges is that of disorientation. The World Wide Web hosts massive quantities of information. Web systems that have limited user support lead to a situation whereby users gain little knowledge, if any, of the spatial and temporal contexts in which they are. As a result, Web users tend to lose their sense of orientation, previous traversals, and direction.

Moreover, most Web systems do not effectively address the issue of cognitive overhead. This refers to the extra effort and concentration that is essential to maintain multiple tasks and trails simultaneously. Often, Web users have to put in some additional effort to create a mental map of the traversed locations and relations amongst the locations. Cognitive overhead is related to how the user seeks a balance between the gains of accumulated knowledge, on the one hand, and the losses from increased distraction as the result of pursuing a link, on the other hand.

Very few Web systems support adaptivity. If Web systems are to be user-centred, then the user will need first to be modelled in some way, and that model taken as input to the rendering process to produce the Web visualization.

Many existing Web renderings and visualizations have not been subjected to extensive usability experiments. The lack of a general framework for developing Web systems and the complexity of Web visualizations make the usability evaluation problem a challenging one. An overall framework for defining and establishing usability metrics for Web visualization systems would be complex, but worthwhile undertaking.

5.6 Acknowledgements

Isabel Cruz's research was supported in part by the Advanced Research and Development Activity (ARDA) and the National Imagery and Mapping Agency (NIMA) under Award Number NMA201-01-1-2001 and by the National Science Foundation under Award EIA-0091489.

The views and conclusions contained in this document are those of the authors and should not be interpreted as necessarily representing the official policies or endorsements, either expressed or implied, of the National Imagery and Mapping Agency or the U.S. Government.

5.7 References

Ayers E., Stasko J. (1995) Using graphic history in browsing the World Wide Web. Georgia Institute of Technology, College of Computing, Technical Report GIT-CC-95-12.

Brandes U., Shubina G., Tamassia R. (2000) Improving angular resolution in visualizations of geographic networks. *Proceedings of the Joint Eurographics IEEE TCVG Symposium on Visualization*, Amsterdam, Springer-Verlag, pp. 23–32.

Brown M.H., Shillner R.A. (1995) DeckScape: An experimental Web browser. *Computer Networks and ISDN Systems* 27(6), 1097–1104.

Card S.K., Mackinlay J.D., Shneiderman B. (Eds) (1999) *Readings in Information Visualization: Using Vision to Think*, Morgan Kaufmann.

Card S.K., Robertson G., York W. (1996) The WebBook and the Web Forager: An information workspace for the World Wide Web. *Proceedings of ACM CHI Conference on Human Factors in Computing Systems*, Vancouver, ACM Press, pp. 111–117.

Catarci T., Santucci G. (2001) The prototype of the DARE System. In T.K. Sellis, S. Mehrotra (Eds) *Proceedings of the 2001 ACM SIGMOD International Conference on Management of Data*, Santa Barbara, CA, ACM Press.

Catarci T., Santucci G., Costabile M.F., Cruz I.F. (1999) Foundations of the DARE system for drawing adequate representations. *Proceedings of the International Symposium on Database Applications in Non-Traditional Environments*, Kyoto, Japan, IEEE Press.

Chi E.H., Pitkow J., Mackinlay J., Pirolli P., Gossweiler R., Card S.K. (1998) Visualizing the evolution of web ecologies. *Proceedings of ACM CHI Conference on Human Factors in Computing Systems*, New York, ACM Press, pp. 400–407.

Cockburn A., Jones S. (1996) Which way now? Analysing and easing inadequacies in World Wide Web navigation. *International Journal of Human–Computer Studies* 45(1), 105–129.

Cox K.C., Eick S.G., He T. (1996) 3D geographic network displays. *ACM SIGMOD Record* 25(4), 50–54.

Cruz I.F., Leveille P.S. (2001) As you like it: Personalized database visualization using a visual language. *Journal of Visual Languages and Computing* 12(5), 525–549.

Eick S.G. (1996) Aspects of network visualization. *Computer Graphics and Applications* 16(2), 69–72.

Fernandez M.F., Florescu D., Kang J., Levy A.Y., Suciu D. (1997) System demonstration – Strudel: A web-site management system. In J. Peckham (Ed) *Proceedings of the 1997 ACM SIGMOD International Conference on Management of Data*, Tucson, AZ, ACM Press, pp. 549–552.

Furnas G.W., Zacks J. (1994) Multitrees: Enriching and reusing hierarchical structure. *Proceedings of ACM SIGCHI Conference on Human Factors in Computing Systems*, Boston, ACM Press, pp. 330–336.

Gaines B., Shaw M. (1995a) Concept maps as hypermedia components. *International Journal on Human–Computer Studies* 43(3), 323–361.

Gaines B., Shaw M. (1995b) WebMap: Concept mapping on the web. *World Wide Web Journal* 1(1), 171–183.

Hearst M.A. (1995) TileBars: Visualization of term distribution information in full text information access. *Proceedings of the ACM SIGCHI Conference on Human Factors in Computing Systems*, Denver, CO, ACM Press, pp. 59–66.

Hearst M.A., Karadi C. (1997) Cat-a-cone: An interactive interface for specifying searches and viewing retrieval results using a large category hierarchy. *Proceedings of the 20th Annual International ACM SIGIR Conference*, Philadelphia, PA, ACM Press, pp. 246–255.

Hendley R.J., Drew N.S., Wood A.M., Beale R. (1995) Narcissus: Visualizing information. *Proceedings of IEEE Symposium on Information Visualization*, Atlanta, GA, IEEE Press, pp. 90–96.

Huang M.L., Eades P., Cohen R.F. (1998) WebOFDAV – Navigating and visualizing the Web on-line with animated context swapping. *Computer Networks and ISDN Systems* 30(1–7), 638–642.

Inxight (2001) http://www.inxight.com

ISO/IEC 13250 Topic Maps (1999) http://www.y12.doe.gov/sgml/sc34/document/0129.pdf

Kent R., Neuss C. (1995) Creating a Web analysis and visualization environment. *Computer Networks and ISDN Systems* 28(1–2), 109–117.

Khare R., Rifkin A. (1997) XML: A door to automated Web applications. *IEEE Internet Computing* 1(4), 78–87.

Lamping J., Rao R., Pirolli P. (1995) A focus + context technique based on hyperbolic geometry for visualizing large hierarchies. *Proceedings of ACM CHI Conference on Human Factors in Computing Systems*, ACM Press, pp. 401–408.

Le Grand B., Soto M. (2000) Information management – Topic Maps visualization. *Proceedings of XML Europe 2000*, Palais des Congres, Paris, France, Graphic Communications Association.

Lieberman H. (1995) Letizia: An agent that assists web browsing. *Proceedings of the 14th International Joint Conference on Artificial Intelligence*, Montreal, Canada, Morgan Kaufmann, pp. 924–929.

Mendelzon A. (1996) Visualizing the World Wide Web. *Proceedings of the Workshop on Advanced Visual Interfaces*, Gubbio, Italy, ACM Press, pp. 13–19.

Morohashi M., Takeda K., Nomiyama H., Maruyama H. (1995) Information Outlining – Filling the gap between visualization and navigation. *Proceedings of the International Symposium on Digital Libraries*, Tsukuba, Japan, University of Library and Information Science, pp. 151–158.

Mukherjea S., Foley J. (1995) Visualizing the World Wide Web with the Navigational View Builder. *Computer Networks and ISDN Systems* 27(6), 1075–1087.

Mukherjea S., Foley J., Hudson S. (1995) Visualizing complex hypermedia networks through multiple hierarchical views. *Proceedings of ACM CHI Conference on Human Factors in Computing Systems*, Denver, CO, ACM Press, pp. 331–337.

Munzner T., Burchard P. (1995) Visualizing the structure of the World Wide Web in 3D hyperbolic space. *Proceedings of VRML'95 Symposium*, San Diego, CA, ACM Press, pp. 33–38.

Nation D., Plaisant C., Marchionini G., Komlodi A. (1997) Visualizing Websites using a hierarchical table of contents browser: WebTOC. *Proceedings of the 3rd Conference on Human Factors and the Web*, Denver, CO, Quest Communications International Inc.

Pacific Northwest National Laboratory (2002) http://www.pnl.gov

Pepper S., Rath H.H. (1999) Topic Maps: Introduction and allegro. *Markup Technologies 99*, Philadelphia, Graphic Communications Association.

Perkowitz M., Etzioni O. (1999) Towards adaptive web sites: Conceptual framework and case study. *Computer Networks and ISDN Systems* 31(11–16), 1245–1258.

Pirolli P., Card S.K. (1995) Information foraging in information access environments. *Proceedings of ACM CHI Conference on Human Factors in Computing Systems*, Denver, CO, ACM Press, pp. 51–58.

Rath H.H. (2001) Semantic resource exploitation with Topic Maps. In H. Lobin (Ed.) *Proceedings of the GLDV-Spring Meeting 2001*, Giessen University, p. 315.

Shiozawa H., Matsushita Y. (1997) WWW visualization giving meanings to interactive manipulations. *HCI International 1997*, San Francisco, CA, Elsevier Science, pp. 791–794.

Shneiderman B. (1998) *Designing the User Interface: Strategies for Effective Human–Computer Interaction*, Addison-Wesley.

Takeda K., Nomiyama H. (1998) Site outlining. IBM Tokyo Research Laboratory, Technical Report RT0229.

The Natto View (2002) http://www.mos.ics.keio.ac.jp/groups/IPS/NattoView

Tufte E.R. (1990) *Envisioning Information*, Graphics Press.

Wexelblat A., Maes P. (1997) Footprints: History-rich Web browsing. *Proceedings of the Conference on Human Factors in Computing Systems (CHI'99)*, Pittsburgh, PA, ACM Press, pp. 270–277.

Wise J.A., Thomas J.J., Pennock K., Lantrip D., Pottier M., Schur A., et al. (1995) Visualizing the non-visual: Spatial analysis and interaction with information from text documents. *Proceedings of IEEE Symposium on Information Visualization*, Atlanta, GA, IEEE Press, pp. 51–58.

Wood A.M., Drew N.S., Beale R., Hendley R.J. (1995) Hyperspace: Web browsing with visualization. *Online Poster Proceedings of the Third International World Wide Web Conference*, Darmstadt, Germany, http://www.igd.fhg.de/archive/1995_www95/proceedings/posters/35/index.html.

Chapter 6
SVG and X3D: New XML Technologies for 2D and 3D Visualization

Vladimir Geroimenko and Larissa Geroimenko

6.1 Introduction

Since XML separates content from presentation rules, any appropriate language and technology can be used for displaying the content of an XML document in a visually rich form. Leading Web technologies such as Sun Java (java.sun.com) or Macromedia Shockwave (www.macromedia.com) provide developers with good opportunities to create interactive visualizations on the Web. However, some essentially new visualization technologies are emerging, which are entirely based on XML and therefore can be considered as native to the Semantic Web.

6.2 SVG

Scalable Vector Graphics (SVG) is the newest language for describing two-dimensional graphics in XML. Its first draft was issued by W3C (The World Wide Web Consortium) in February 1999; SVG 1.0 was released as a W3C Recommendation (i.e. a Web standard) in September 2001. The latest, up-to-the-minute information about this technology can be found on the W3C Web site (www. w3.org/TR/SVG). Some books and online articles specially devoted to SVG are also available (Eisenberg, 2001, 2002; Quint, 2001; Thomas, 2000; Watt, 2001).

SVG is completely based on XML and this is its main advantage. It lets authors handle Web graphics in the same way as text and data – using XML as the universal format. SVG benefits from its tight integration with other members of the XML family of technologies such as DOM (Document Object Model), CSS (Cascading Style Sheets), XSL (Extensible Stylesheet Language), RDF (Resource Description Framework), SMIL (Synchronized Multimedia Integration Language), XLink and XPointer.

Since SVG conforms to the DOM, the JavaScript language can be used to access and manipulate any SVG file components at runtime. Web users are able to interact with an SVG image on the basis of the same event model as for HTML pages, i.e. to use functions such as "onmouseover" or "onclick". It is important to note that every element (a shape or text) and every attribute of an element is accessible and can be manipulated, for example, animated. XSL allows the creation of SVG documents on the fly and their transformation into any desired format. RDF adds metadata to SVG files and describes them in the same way as any other text or data resources on the Semantic Web, which therefore can be searched, "comprehended" and processed by computers. SMIL is an XML-based language that allows integrating SVG with other Web resources into an interactive multimedia presentation. XLink and XPointer provide a mechanism for linking from within SVG files to other SVG files, SMIL presentations, HTML pages and other documents on the Web.

Some further advantages of an XML-based graphics format are as follows:

- Any XML-enabled software and tools can be used for authoring, reading and manipulating SVG images.
- Because SVG is entirely text-based, it allows for searching text elements within graphics and therefore makes the graphical content of the next generation Web searchable.
- SVG is resolution and media independent. SVG drawings fit any screen of any device (from small mobile phone displays to large TV monitors), they are fully scalable for zooming and panning, and can also be printed with the highest possible resolution.
- Through scripting, SVG supports dynamic content, animation and interactivity. It allows to create SVG drawings on the fly using a database or an XSL stylesheet.
- Last but not least, SVG is not a proprietary format but an open standard.

SVG supports three types of graphics objects (vector graphic shapes, images and text) that can be grouped, styled, transformed and composed with other rendered objects. It contains six predefined objects – basic shapes: rectangle `<rect>`, circle `<circle>`, ellipse `<ellipse>`, polyline `<polyline>`, polygon `<polygon>` and path `<path>`.

If you are familiar with XML, an SVG file is easy to read. Its editing and hand-coding using any ordinary text editor is much more intuitive than writing HTML and can be fun.

Consider an example. The file "Hello.svg" contains the following code that defines the SVG drawing shown in Figure 6.1:

```
<?xml version="1.0" standalone="yes"?>
<!DOCTYPE svg PUBLIC "-//W3C//DTD SVG 20000802//EN"
"http://www.w3.org/TR/2000/CR-SVG-20000802/DTD/
svg-20000802.dtd">
<svg width="17cm" height="14cm">
<rect style="fill:red;" x="4cm" y="1.5cm" width="3cm"
height="3cm"/>
<rect style="fill:yellow; stroke:navy; stroke-width:
0.5cm;" x="9cm" y="1cm" width="5.5cm" height="2.5cm"/>
<ellipse style="fill:green;" cx="8cm" cy="9cm" rx="5.5cm"
ry="2.5cm"/>
<text style="fill:black; font-family:Verdana; font-size:
24pt;" x="3cm" y="6cm">Hello, the SVG World!</text>
</svg>
```

Since SVG is an XML-based language, the first line of the SVG file is the declaration that identifies it as an XML file. The next line provides version information and the URL of the Document Type Definition (DTD) – a standard set of rules for writing SVG. The `<svg>` tag tells a browser or standalone viewer

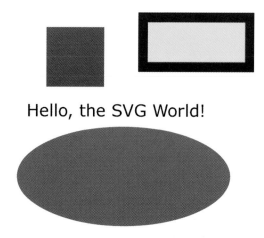

Figure 6.1   A sample SVG drawing.

that this file is an SVG document and also includes the attributes width and height that define the canvas of the SVG document. All the SVG content is placed between the <svg> and </svg> tags. The <rect/> tag is the code that defines a rectangle and declares its properties: the width and height, the fill (the fill colour of the rectangle), the stroke (an outline of the rectangle, its width and colour). It is interesting to note that SVG uses ordinary Cascading Style Sheet syntax within the style attribute. The <ellipse/> tag defines an ellipse by the coordinates of its centre and by its radius in a horizontal (rx) and vertical (ry) direction. The <text> tag contains text as character data and defines its fill colour, font family, font size and position on the screen (using the x and y attributes).

SVG is the language of choice for 2D visualizations on the Semantic Web. Both SVG tags and RDF metadata are readable and understandable not only by humans but also by computers, making SVG drawings suitable for automated search and processing. Any element and attribute of an SVG document can be accessed and changed programmatically using any XML-enabled software and technologies. Tight integration with DOM, XSL, SMIL, RDF, other current or future XML technologies and also any XML document makes SVG visualizations into an integral part of the Semantic Web.

6.3 X3D

Many Web developers believe that the second-generation Web will implement not only semantics but also 3D. "Web3D" is a term that refers to all technologies that enable interactive 3D graphics on the Web, including open and proprietary formats. The most comprehensive explanation of a wide range of Web3D technologies is provided by Walsh and Bourges-Sévenier (2001). The latest information about all aspects of Web3D technologies can be found on the Web site of the Web3D Consortium (www.web3d.org). The Consortium was formed to provide a forum for the creation of open standards for Web3D specifications.

The first successful specification developed by the Web3D Consortium was VRML (Virtual Reality Modelling Language) and this is why the Consortium was formerly called the VRML Consortium. VRML is the leading technology for the presentation of three-dimensional images on the Web. As a simple language for publishing 3D Web pages, VRML is a 3D analogue to HTML. The first version (VRML 1.0) was released in May 1995; the second version (VRML 2.0) was issued in August 1996 and became an international standard (known informally as VRML97) in December 1997. VRML97 is still the current version, but the third version of VRML is being developed by the Web3D Consortium.

The adoption of a name for the new version of VRML is a little confusing. Sometimes, especially in the past, it was (and still is) called VRML200x where the "x" will show the year this version will be approved (as of today, the planned completion date of the specification is August 2002, and so it might be named "VRML2002"). At present, VRML200x is also very often called X3D (eXtensible 3D). According to the X3D Task Group of the Web3D Consortium, X3D is the next-generation open standard for 3D on the Web that will replace VRML but keep compatibility with existing VRML content and browsers (X3D FAQ, 2001).

The Web3D Consortium considers X3D as a next generation version of VRML97, in particular, an XML representation of the VRML scene graph. To be precise, the X3D specification is just a part of the next version of VRML. This version includes the following three encoding formats of the abstract functionality (the 3D scene graph): the UFT-8 encoding (VRML97 style encoding), the XML encoding (X3D as such) and binary encoding. Special tools enable an automated translation between different encoding formats. In principle, it does not matter what name is finally adopted for the third generation of the open source VRML standard: VRML2002, X3D or, for instance, X3D/VRML200x. In any case, its next version will include X3D in order to express the geometry and behaviour capabilities of VRML97 using XML. Moreover, the new version will go beyond the limits of VRML97 by adding new graphical, behavioural and interactive objects (Hayes, 2001; Ressler, 1999, 2000a).

Let's consider an example to see the differences between the VRML97 encoding and the X3D encoding of a scene graph that defines a simple VR world, shown in Figure 6.2. This navigable 3D world consists of a red sphere and two lines of text and also includes nodes that define the user's initial viewpoint and allowed

Figure 6.2   A sample X3D world.

types of navigation. The Group and children nodes are used to group other nodes. The Transform node places the text in the desired position within the virtual world. Although the VRML code is pretty easy to understand, generally speaking it is foreign to Web developers with the exception of the VRML community.

```
#VRML V2.0 utf8
Group {
  children [
    Viewpoint {
      orientation 0 1 0 1.57
      position 6 -1 0
    }
    NavigationInfo {
      type [ "EXAMINE" "ANY" ]
    }
    Shape {
      geometry Sphere {
      }
      appearance Appearance {
      material Material {
        diffuseColor 1 0 0
    }
      }
    }
    Transform {
      rotation 0 1 0 1.57
      translation 0 -1.5 3
      children [
    Shape {
      geometry Text {
        string [ "Hello," "the X3D world!" ]
      }
      appearance Appearance {
        material Material {
        diffuseColor 0.2 0.6 1
        }
      }
    }
      ]
    }
  ]
}
```

The same virtual world can be encoded using X3D, as shown below. In this case, the audience that is able to read and understand the code is much wider because it includes everyone who is familiar with XML (and also XML-enabled software, tools and autonomous agents). The following code illustrates the use of X3D tags and attributes. Similar to an SVG or any other XML file, it starts with the XML declaration and the Document Type Definition. The VRML nodes from the above VRML97 example are presented as X3D tags written in XML and node fields as tag attributes.

```
<?xml version="1.0" encoding="UTF-8"?>
<!DOCTYPE X3D PUBLIC
"http://www.web3D.org/TaskGroups/x3d/translation/
x3d-compact.dtd"
"file:///C:/www.web3D.org/TaskGroups/x3d/translation/
x3d-compact.dtd">
<X3D>
    <head>
    </head>
    <Scene>
      <Group>
        <Viewpoint orientation="0 1 0 1.57" position="6 -1
        0"/>
        <NavigationInfo type="quot;EXAMINE quot; quot;
        ANYquot;"/>
        <Shape>
          <Sphere/>
          <Appearance>
            <Material diffuseColor="1 0 0"/>
          </Appearance>
        </Shape>
      <Transform rotation="0 1 0 1.57" translation="
      0 - 1.5 3">
        <Shape>
          <Text string="quot;Hello,quot; quot;the X3D
          world!quot;"/>
          <Appearance>
            <Material diffuseColor="0.2 0.6 1"/>
          </Appearance>
        </Shape>
      </Transform>
    </Group>
  </Scene>
</X3D>
```

Several thousands of similar translations between X3D and VRML97 are presented on Don Brutzman's X3D translation pages (Brutzman, 2001), including the entire set of VRML examples in the *VRML 2.0 SourceBook* (Ames, Nadeau and Moreland, 1997) translated into X3D.

Thus, X3D provides tight integration between 3D technology and the XML family of standards such as XML Schema, XML DOM, XSL or SVG. Since X3D is written in XML, an X3D document can be validated against an appropriate XML Schema. It can be transformed into other XML documents (for example, SVG) using XSL and its X3D data can be assessed and manipulated using the DOM. Similar to SVG, XML has many other advantages of being an XML-based language, for example, an X3D world can be viewed on any device with any screen size. In other words, "the future of the Web is XML and the future for 3D on the Web is X3D" (Ressler, 2000b). To continue this thought, it is right to add that the future for 2D on the Web is SVG. X3D and SVG technologies, based entirely on XML, open essentially new possibilities for the visualization of the Semantic Web.

6.4 References

Ames A, Nadeau J and Moreland J (1997) *VRML 2.0 SourceBook*. Wiley.
Brutzman D (2001) *Examples*. Available:
    http://www.web3d.org/TaskGroups/x3d/translation/examples/toc.html
Eisenberg D (2001) *An Introduction to Scalable Vector Graphics*. Available:
    http://www.xml.com/pub/a/2001/03/21/svg.html
Eisenberg D (2002) *SVG Essentials*. O'Reilly and Associates.
Hayes H (2001) 3D comes into focus on the Web. *Federal Computer Week*, 26 March. Available:
    http://fcw.com/fcw/articles/2001/0326/tec-3d-03-26-01.asp
Quint A (2001) *SVG: Where are we now?* Available:
    http://www.xml.com/pub/a/2001/11/21/svgtools.html
Ressler S (1999) *X3D, Next Generation VRML*. Available:
    http://web3d.about.com/library/weekly/aa070799.htm
Ressler S (2000a) *A Simple Introduction to X3D*. Available:
    http://web3d.about.com/library/weekly/aa080900a.htm
Ressler S (2000b) *Looking at 3D and VRML*. Available:
    http://web3d.about.com/library/weekly/aa112900a.htm
Thomas K (2000) *Extreme SVG: A programmer's guide to Scalable Vector Graphics*. TBO Books.
Walsh A and Bourges-Sévenier (2001) *Core Web3D*. Prentice-Hall.
Watt A (2001) *Designing SVG Web Graphics: Visual Components for Graphics in the Internet Age*. New
    Riders Publishing.
X3D FAQ (2001) Available: http://www.web3d.org/TaskGroups/x3d/faq/

PART 2
Visual Techniques and Applications for the Semantic Web

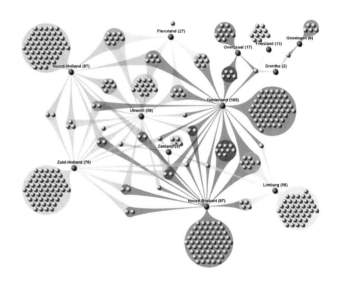

Chapter 7
Visual Interfaces for Semantic Information Retrieval and Browsing

Katy Börner

7.1 Introduction

Today, an unimaginable amount of human knowledge is available in digital libraries, repositories, on the Internet, etc. Computers have become the entry point to a worldwide network of information, services, and other people. However, the Web is extremely unstructured and heterogeneous, making the efficient and effective discovery of relevant data, services, or expertise rather difficult. In sum, we are facing unparalleled challenges and opportunities for universal knowledge collection, access, and management.

Currently, various indexing systems, cataloguing systems, and search engines exist, but their ability to retrieve relevant data from diverse, distributed databases with different formats and multimedia data (text, images, audio, video) is very limited. Among the well-known problems for traditional information systems are the vocabulary inconsistency between user queries and data presentation (Bates, 1998), and the approaches simple keyword-matching usage of exploiting the frequency of co-occurrence of terms.

The vision shared by major information retrieval (IR) experts, as well as the developers of the new "Semantic Web", is a network of distributed repositories where multilingual, multimedia documents can be searched within and across differently indexed and structured collections (Schatz and Chen, 1996). To make this vision come true, technologies are needed that search repositories despite not only variations in protocols and formats, but also variations in content and meaning. Several approaches to semantic information retrieval and browsing have been proposed and are reviewed in Section 7.2.

Visual interfaces exploit powerful human visual processing to ease information filtering and browsing. By connecting information to space, they also support browsing, i.e. the exploration of information space in order to become familiar with it and to locate information of interest. Browsing requires a working knowledge of both applied knowledge organization (typically alphabetical or hierarchical) and the means to navigate in it (Chen et al., 1998). Section 7.3 reviews related research on visual interfaces for digital libraries and information workspaces.

Section 7.4 explains the inner workings of the LVis Digital Library Visualizer. It details data analysis and data visualization and presents two prototypical interfaces, the first to citation data from the Science Citation Index and the second to images from the Dido image library. The section concludes with a discussion on how to further adapt visual interfaces to the human cognitive and perceptual system.

The potential of the Semantic Web to improve semantic information retrieval and browsing is discussed in Section 7.5.

7.2 Semantic Information Retrieval and Browsing

Diverse techniques have been proposed to automatically summarize the semantics of a document set. Among them are symbolic machine learning techniques for automatic text classification; graph-based clustering and classification; linguistic approaches; ontologies; and statistics-based multivariate techniques such as multidimensional scaling, latent semantic analysis (LSA), self-organizing maps, and genetic programming. LSA as used in the LVis Digital Library Visualizer, linguistic approaches, and ontologies are reviewed subsequently.

The reader is invited to consult Börner, Chen and Boyack (2003) for an extensive review of diverse data analysis, clustering, and visualization techniques such as factor analysis, multidimensional scaling, latent semantic analysis, pathfinder network scaling, self-organizing maps, etc.

Genetic algorithms are based on principles of evolution and heredity and can be seen as general-purpose search methods that feature stochastic, global search processes. They have been applied for document clustering (Raghavan and Agarwal, 1987), to weight Boolean queries, and to improve recall and precision in information retrieval (Petry et al., 1993). Genetic algorithms have also been combined with neural networks to improve information retrieval (Chen and Kim, 1994).

7.2.1 Linguistic Approaches

Lexical ambiguity is a fundamental problem in IR. Many words are used ambiguously. Statistical approaches to linguistic annotation can help to disambiguate based on existing terminological resources in order to develop more satisfactory indexing techniques for IR:

> ... Linguistic annotation covers any descriptive or analytic notations applied to raw language data. The basic data may be in the form of time functions – audio, video and/or physiological recordings – or it may be textual. The added notations may include transcriptions of all sorts (from phonetic features to discourse structures), part-of-speech and sense tagging, syntactic analysis, "named entity" identification, co-reference annotation, and so on.[1] (Steven Bird, 2001)

Linguistic annotation can be done via segmentation, morphological analysis, syntactic tagging, and semantic tagging. First, the text is segmented into sentences, words, and other units (e.g. by punctuation). Each word is then analysed and annotated with its lexical description(s), typically the base form and

---

[1]http://morph.ldc.upenn.edu/annotation/

a morphosyntactic description of the word. Lexical information is then converted to syntactic tags which often depend on the application.

The Interspace project enables concept navigation across repositories using "scalable semantics" (Schatz, 1995). The system prototype semantically indexes real collections of millions of documents. It applies artificial intelligence techniques for phrase extraction and statistically correlates relationships between these concepts within the collection using context co-occurrence.

7.2.2 Ontologies

Ontologies establish a shared conceptualization between members of a community of interest. Examples of ontologies are catalogues, IR indexes, entity-relationship models in database design, dictionaries, thesauri from the computational linguistics community, object-oriented class definitions from the software engineering community, and so on. Ontologies can be represented as logic-based (first-order logic), frame-based (frame logic), or web-based (RDF, KIF).[2]

An example is the Unified Medical Language System (UMLS) Semantic Network[3] under development by the National Library of Medicine as part of the Unified Medical Language System project. UMLS defines 134 semantic types that are linked by 54 important relationships in the biomedical domain and provides a consistent categorization of all concepts represented in the UMLS Metathesaurus.

The growth and dynamic range of digitally available data and the Web make it difficult to maintain manually created thesauri or ontologies that aim to cover a broad spectrum of dramatically changing topics. Automatic techniques promise to alleviate the need for time-consuming human analysis and avoid human limitations and biases. Consequently, the semi-automatic generation, mapping, and evolution of ontologies are hot research topics in Artificial Intelligence research. For example, Ding and Engels (2001) adopted co-occurrence theory to develop a lightweight domain ontology (see also Ding, 2001).

Heflin and Hendler (2000) developed SHOE[4], a web-based knowledge representation language that supports multiple versions of ontologies. SHOE uses XML-like tags and agent technology to understand specific types of web pages (e.g. university course descriptions), to mark them up with semantic information, and to draw inferences over the collection for interesting search problems, such as student academic planning.

ScholOnto is an ontology-based DL server designed to support scholarly interpretation and discourse. It enables researchers to describe and debate, via a semantic network, the contributions of a document and its relationship to the literature (Shum, Motta and Domingue, 2000).

7.2.3 Latent Semantic Analysis

Latent semantic analysis (LSA), also called latent semantic indexing (LSI), is a vector space retrieval method that overcomes the so-called vocabulary mismatch

---

[2]http://www.ladseb.pd.cnr.it/infor/Ontology/Papers/OntologyPapers.html
[3]http://www.nlm.nih.gov/pubs/factsheets/umlssemn.html
[4]http://www.cs.umd.edu/projects/plus/SHOE/

problem (Deerwester et al., 1990; Landauer, Foltz and Laham, 1998). By considering the context of words, LSA overcomes two fundamental problems faced by traditional lexical matching schemes: synonymy (variability of word choice, e.g. "dad" vs. "papa") and polysemy (a word with multiple meanings, e.g. "bank", "crane").

LSA uses an advanced statistical technique, singular value decomposition (SVD), to extract latent terms. SVD, a form of factor analysis, constructs an n-dimensional, abstract term-document space in which each original term and each original (and any new) document are presented as vectors.[5] In SVD, a rectangular term-by-document matrix X is decomposed into the product of three other matrices: W, S, and P' with $\{X\} = \{W\}\,\{S\}\,\{P\}'$. W is an orthonormal matrix and its rows correspond to the rows of X, but it has m columns corresponding to new, specially derived variables such that there is no correlation between any two columns, i.e. each is linearly independent of the others. P is an orthonormal matrix and has columns corresponding to the original columns but m rows composed of derived singular vectors. The third matrix S is an m-by-m diagonal matrix with non-zero entries (called singular values) along only one central diagonal. A large singular value indicates a large effect of this dimension on the sum-squared error of the approximation. The role of these singular values is to relate the scale of the factors in the other two matrices to each other such that when the three components are matrix multiplied, the original matrix is reconstructed.

A latent term may correspond to a salient concept described by several keywords (e.g. the concept of information retrieval). Each document is represented by a number of those latent terms. The key innovation of LSA is to retain only the n most salient latent terms. All small singular values are set to zero and semantic relationships from the term-document matrix are preserved while term usage variations are suppressed.

The amount of dimensionality reduction (i.e. the choice of n) is an open and critical issue in the factor analytic literature. Ideally, n should be large enough to fit the real structure in the data, but small enough such that noise, sampling errors, or unimportant details are not modelled (Deerwester et al., 1990). Often, good retrieval and browsing performance is used as an operational criterion. The reduced dimensionality solution then generates a vector of n real values to represent each document. The reduced matrix ideally represents the important and reliable patterns underlying the data in X.

Similarity between existing documents and a new document/query can be computed on the basis of the three matrices as follows:

1. Multiply matrix W (its rows correspond to the terms [rows] of X) by the reduced matrix S.
2. Normalize resulting vectors (i.e. divide each vector by its length). This way all vectors are mapped onto a hypersphere.
3. Determine the document–document matrix of inner products that defines the similarities between all documents.

The dot product between two row vectors of the reduced matrix reflects the degree to which two documents have a similar pattern of terms. The matrix XX' is the square symmetric matrix containing all these document–document dot

---

[5]Readers interested in the existence and uniqueness of the SVD may consult (Deerwester et al., 1990).

products. Since S is diagonal and W is orthonormal, the following holds: $XX' = WS2W'$. Thus the i, j cell of XX' can be obtained by taking the dot product between the i and j rows of the matrix WS. That is, if one considers the rows of WS as coordinates for documents, dot products between these points facilitate comparison between documents.

The construction of the SVD matrix is computationally intensive and is typically done in a pre-processing step. SVD on an m-by-n matrix is worse than quadratic in complexity on the smallest dimension. Yet, an effective dimensionality reduction helps to reduce noise and automatically organizes documents into a semantic structure more appropriate for information retrieval. This is a prime strength of LSA – once the matrix has been calculated, retrieval based on a user's query is very efficient. Relevant documents are retrieved, even if they did not literally contain the query words. The LSA matrix can also be used to calculate term-by-term or document-by-document similarities for use in other layout routines.

LSA has been successfully applied to information filtering and retrieval in Generalized Similarity Analysis (Chen, 1997, 1999), StarWalker (Chen and Paul, 2001), and the LVis – Digital Library Visualizer (Börner, 2000a; Börner, Dillon and Dolinsky, 2000) among others.

7.3 Visual Interfaces

A considerable body of research aims at processing, analysing, and visualizing large amounts of diverse online data.[6] Given the typical user's inability to specify information needs, it is widely recognized that information retrieval is an iterative process. Most direct manipulation interfaces provide users with overview, zoom, and filter functionalities, as well as details on demand as proposed by Shneiderman (1996).

Sensemaking theory (Russell et al., 1993) as well as information foraging theory (Pirolli and Card, 1995) identify four main human activities for iterative information gathering: (1) searching for specific answers using keyword or relevance feedback searches; (2) browsing or exploring an information space without a specific question or representation in mind; (3) using overviews to discover areas of high information density or relevance and to ease navigation tasks in browsing and search; and (4) utilization of information workspaces to aggregate and assimilate relevant information. Users seem to shift frequently between these activities in response to the information gathered and the information task. Ideally, information visualization facilitates and supports all four activities.

7.3.1 Visual Interfaces to Digital Libraries

Visual interfaces to digital libraries aim to support search and browsing activities. Diverse data mining and visualization algorithms can be applied to extract salient semantic structures and/or co-citation relationships among

---

[6]Note that the analysis and visualization of the entire set of documents stored in a digital library is a special case of visualizing the retrieval result – namely, one in which all documents are retrieved.

documents and to layout documents spatially, helping users to visualize, locate, and remember documents more quickly. Several systems provide spatial cues by presenting documents in three-dimensional (3D) space and enabling the user to "walk" through this space.

Some of the first visual interfaces to DLs are: a two-dimensional (2D) map proposed by Orendorf and Kacmar (1996) as a method to structure DLs and their content and to ease document location and access; SemNet (Fairchild, Poltrock and Furnas, 1988); Cone Trees (Robertson, Mackinlay and Card, 1991); a spatial data management system (Herot, 1980), Populated Information Terrains (Benford, Snowdon and Mariani, 1995); VR-VIBE (Benford et al., 1995); and Bead (Chalmers, 1992, 1993), which uses statistical techniques to analyse and group documents based on their semantic similarity and to create visualizations of bibliographies. The section "Three-Dimensional Information Spaces"[7] in Martin Dodge's *Atlas of Cyberspaces* (2002). See also Crossley et al.'s (1999) Knowledge Garden provides an environment where people can meet colleagues and share relevant information.

Research by Chen (1999) aims to allow people to explore and navigate intuitively in a semantically organized information space. Latent Semantic Analysis and Pathfinder Network Scaling (Schvaneveldt, 1990) were applied to create a semantically organized information space providing access to 169 long papers from the ACM SIGCHI conference proceedings (1995–1997) and all papers from the ACM Hypertext conference proceedings (1987–1998). The approach was implemented in StarWalker, a system that uses Blaxxun's community platform to display citation networks as a set union of all possible minimum spanning trees (Chen and Carr, 1999). StarWalker is the very first system that uses a tightly coupled spatial-semantic model as focal point in a multi-user environment. Chen et al. (1999) showed that the proliferation of information visualization (IV) models can play a significant role in extending and enriching the design of inhabited, multi-user virtual environments. In StarWalker, multiple users can simultaneously examine a complex visualization of a static data set. Social navigation is supported by the visibility of other participants and the ability to chat.

All systems mentioned thus far extract the semantic structure or co-citation networks of specific document sets. Because of the computational expense of the applied data analysis algorithms, the resulting visualizations are mostly static.

7.3.2 Information Workspaces

Research on information workspaces, as introduced by Card and his colleagues (1991), is related to visual interfaces to DLs as it refers to an environment, such as the Information Visualizer (Card et al., 1991), in which documents of interest can be compared, manipulated, and stored for future use. Diverse workspaces have been proposed. Among them are Balley's (1994) Workscape, which enables the 3D spatial layout of documents; WebBook and Web Forager (Card, Robertson and York, 1996), which provides an information workspace for the WWW; the Cat-a-cone interface (Hearst and Karadi, 1997), which uses a 3D+ animated WebBook to visualize a moderate number of documents; PadPrints

---

[7]http://www.cybergeography.org/atlas/info_spaces.html

(Hightower et al., 1998), which uses the Pad++ zoomable interface[8] to implement a thumbnail image-based web history mechanism; Data Mountain (Robertson et al., 1998), which is an alternative Web browser system that offers a generic 3D space where users can freely place thumbnail images of web pages for which they wish to keep references; the Task Gallery (Robertson et al., 2000), which extends the desktop metaphor into a 3D workspace represented as a long gallery with paintings symbolizing different tasks; and David Gelernter's Scopeware,[9] which organizes documents chronologically. These systems differ in the way documents are organized (by users in piles, automatically in a list, partition, or hierarchy, etc.) and how documents are presented (as text, icons, image thumbnail representations, etc.). All the systems mentioned make use of spatial cognition.

However, visual interfaces thus far had only limited success. One reason for this is the fact that they do not provide the user-centred cues that help in remembering locations (Tan et al., 2001); see also the discussion in Section 7.4.4.

7.4 LVis Digital Library Visualizer

The LVis Digital Library Visualizer system was developed in interdisciplinary collaboration by Börner, Dillon and Dolinsky in 1999/2000. It uses LSA (see Section 7.2.3) to extract the semantic similarity of documents; applies clustering techniques and a so-called utility measure to select the partition that best reveals the semantic structure of a document set; and visualizes the result in a two-dimensional desktop screen or in a three-dimensional virtual reality environment. Two prototype interfaces have been implemented that are intended to ease browsing through retrieval results of citation data and image data. Subsequently, data analysis and visualization are explained in detail and examples of the two prototype systems are given. This section concludes with a discussion of how to increase the fit between human information seeking and available technologies.

7.4.1 Data Analysis

Data analysis comprises parsing the textual representations of documents (e.g. document author(s), title and source, addresses, abstract, keywords), analysing the semantic relationships between documents using LSA, and determining the best partition of the data set.

Latent Semantic Analysis: The SVDPACK by M. Berry (1993) was used to determine the semantic similarity between documents. The SVDPACK comprises four numerical (iterative) methods for computing the singular value decomposition of large sparse matrices using double precision. From this package, a sparse SVD via single-vector Lanczos algorithm was selected because of its comparatively low memory and processing requirements by low to moderate accuracies. In the case of digital libraries, terms may stand for words in abstracts

---

[8]http://www.cs.umd.edu/hcil/pad++/
[9]http://www.scopeware.com/ by Mirror World Technologies.

or titles, author names, or cited references.[10] Only author names, titles, abstracts, and cited references occurring in more than one document are included in the analysis.[11]

Hierarchical Clustering: Nearest-neighbour-based, agglomerative, hierarchical, unsupervised conceptual clustering is applied to create a hierarchy of clusters grouping documents of similar semantic structure. Clustering starts with a set of singleton clusters, each containing a single document $d_i \in D$, $i = 1, \ldots N$; where D equals the entire set of documents and N equals the number of all documents. The two most similar clusters over the entire set D are merged to form a new cluster that covers both. This process is repeated for each of the remaining $N - 1$ documents. A complete linkage algorithm is applied to determine the overall similarity of document clusters based on the document similarity matrix. Merging of document clusters continues until a single, all-inclusive cluster remains. At termination, a uniform, binary hierarchy of document clusters is produced.

Selection of the Best Partition: The partition showing the highest within-cluster similarity and lowest between-cluster similarity is determined by means of a *utility* measure

$$utility = \frac{wSim}{wSim + bSim}$$

that contrasts the sum of within-cluster similarities *wSim* with the sum of between-cluster similarities *bSim*.

7.4.2 Data Visualization

Documents are presented visually in a way that reveals their semantic similarities. Rather than being a static visualization of data, the interface is self-organizing and highly interactive. Data are displayed in an initially random configuration, which sorts itself out into a more-or-less acceptable display via a force-directed placement (FDP) algorithm (Battista et al., 1994; Fruchterman and Reingold, 1991). The algorithm works by computing attraction and repulsion forces among nodes. In our applications (see Section 7.4.3), the nodes represent articles or images, which are attracted to other nodes (articles/images) to which they have a (similarity) link and repelled by nodes (articles/images) to which there is no link. Initially, the nodes are placed randomly and are then moved according to the attraction and repulsion forces upon them until a local energy minimum is achieved. If the algorithm does not produce a visually acceptable layout, or if the user wishes to view the results differently, nodes can be grabbed and moved.

FDP algorithms cannot handle larger data sets. Therefore, we recently proposed *Semantic Treemaps* (Feng and Börner, 2002) to visualize the cluster structure of documents as well as the semantic relationships of documents in each cluster.

---

[10]In order to prevent articles with too large a number of citations or too great a length from having differential effects on the model, rows or columns of the term-by-document matrix can be reweighted. Weights can also be used to impose specific preconceptions about the importance of particular terms.
[11]We do not exclude common words (like "a", "and", etc.), stem words, or map variants of words to the same root form.

7.4.3 Prototype Systems

Two prototype systems have been implemented using the data organization and visualization methods described above.

The first system visualizes query results of citation data from the *Science Citation Index Expanded* (SCI-EXPANDED) as published by the Institute for Scientific Information (ISI). This index provides access to current bibliographic information and cited references in more than 5,600 journals. The second system enables users to browse search results from the Dido Image Bank at the Department of History of Art at Indiana University. Dido stores about 9,500 digitized images from the Fine Arts slide library collection of over 320,000 images.[12]

Note that document retrieval can be done with existing search engines or based on LSA. Computationally expensive data analysis is done in a pre-processing step. Both systems are implemented in Java and run locally at Indiana University's School of Library and Information Science (SLIS).

7.4.3.1 LVis Interface to the Science Citation Database

Querying SCI-EXPANDED via the ISI Web of Science interface[13] results in an often huge number of matching documents (maximally 500 are accessible) organized into lists of ten that can be marked, saved, and downloaded for detailed study.

To demonstrate a visual browser for this type of database, a query result data set named DAIV188 containing 188 articles matching the topic "data AND analysis AND information AND visualization" will be used. It was retrieved from SCI-EXPANDED in June 1999. The documents are represented in the usual Web of Science data output format (including author(s), article title and source, cited references, addresses, abstract, language, publisher information, ISSN, document type, keywords, times cited, etc.), as shown in Figure 7.1.

ISI data provides access to co-citation linkages. However, there are very few co-citation links in each retrieval result set. For example, exactly four articles in the set of 188 articles cite another article in this set. Therefore, LSA was applied over keywords and abstracts of articles to extract their semantic similarity. After clustering, the 167th partition was selected for visualization. It shows the highest utility value partition containing 19 clusters grouping from one to 53 articles.

Figure 7.2 shows all 188 articles. Book articles are represented by a rectangle. Journal articles are denoted by an oval. Each article is labelled by its first author. Lines between articles denote co-citation links.

The 2D layout of articles corresponds to the document–document similarity matrix as well as to the forces applied by the FDP algorithm to generate an acceptable layout. Cluster boundaries are represented by rectangles. Their colour denotes the level of similarity among articles (lighter colours denoting higher similarity). Each cluster is labelled by the keyword used most often in the documents it groups.

Users can click on articles to retrieve detailed information displayed in an additional Web browser window. Note that there are three clusters labelled

---

[12]http://www.dlib.indiana.edu/collections/dido/
[13]http://webofscience.com/

```
FN ISI Export Format
PT J
AU Small, H
TI Visualizing science by citation mapping
SO JOURNAL OF THE AMERICAN SOCIETY FOR
   INFORMATION SCIENCE
LA English
DT Article
NR 46
SN 0002-8231
PU JOHN WILEY & SONS INC
C1 Inst Sci Informat, ...
ID SCIENTIFIC LITERATURES; COMBINED COCITATION;
   WORD ANALYSIS; INFORMATION; RETRIEVAL; MAP
AB Science mapping is discussed in the general
   context of information visualization. ...
CR *I SCI INF, 1997, NAT SCI IND DISK 198
   AMSLER RA, 1972, UNPUB APPL CITATION
   BALDI S, 1995, P 5 BIENN C INT SOC, P43 ...
TC 3
...
PY 1999
...
```

Figure 7.1 Partial ISI article representation.

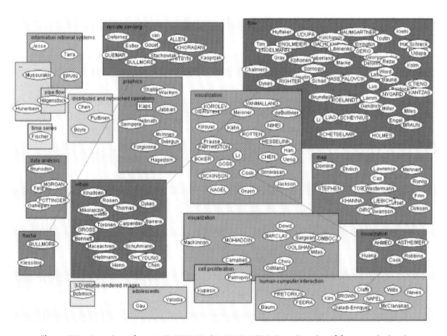

Figure 7.2 Java interface to DAIV188. (© 2000 ACM, Inc. Reprinted by permission.)

MONET, CLAUDE

Haystacks in the Snow.1891

o/c. 65.4 x 92.1 cm., N.Y.,

Met.Mus.,Metropolitan.12.4/3/79.RB.96

19.PTG.FRANCE

Figure 7.3   "Monet.Haystacks in the Snow" image and textual description.

"visualization". Closer examination reveals that two of these clusters contain articles on visualizations in chemistry and physics. The third cluster groups articles that deal more generally with the analysis and visualization of information.

7.4.3.2 LVis Interface to the Dido Database

The Dido database permits convenient access and use of images for teaching and research purposes via a Web interface.

Each image in Dido is stored together with its thumbnail representation as well as a textual description (see Figure 7.3).

Upon querying Dido, a list of textual image representations is returned, based on string matching between search string and textual image description. Thumbnail representations can be clicked on to retrieve an image.

LVis was used to provide a visual interface to the retrieved image data sets. In a first step, SVD as well as the clustering techniques are applied to organize Dido images into clusters of semantically similar images. For demonstration purposes, the set of 21 images matching the keyword "MONET" was retrieved and is displayed in Figure 7.4.

The cluster contains 21 images including two portraits of Claude Monet drawn by Edouard Manet. Thumbnail representations of images fetched from the Dido database show some of Monet's favourite themes such as haystacks, cathedrals, and water lilies. Each cluster is labelled with the word that occurs most often in the titles of its images – in this example the name of the artist.

In addition, a 3D CAVE interface has been implemented and evaluated (see Figure 7.5). Results are reported in Börner et al. (2000). An alternative 3D desktop interface to image data retrieved from Dido enables multiple participants to examine and discuss search results collaboratively (Börner, 2001a).

7.4.4 Finding the Perfect Match

Ideally, visual interfaces to digital data should match human perception and cognition capabilities as closely as possible. However, research is frequently "technology-driven" instead of "human-centred".

For example, it is not clear how closely spatial layouts of documents produced by current data analysis and layout algorithms resemble human sorting

Figure 7.4 The MONET cluster. (© 2000 ACM, Inc. Reprinted by permission.)

behaviour. There are very few studies that compare the results of algorithms (in terms of document–document similarity or spatial data layout) with how human subjects organize documents. An inter-algorithm comparison based on the application of diverse algorithms to one data set was presented in Börner et al. (2003).

Figure 7.5 Chinese paintings displayed in a 3D virtual CAVE environment.

A comparison of results generated by LSA and by human sorting is reported by Börner (2000b). However, more detailed studies are required to determine and improve those algorithms to support human information-seeking behaviour.

So far concept-based (textual) image retrieval and content-based image retrieval (image recognition) have developed in parallel, with little interaction between the two groups of researchers and their literature (Enser, 1993). For example, LVis is limited to textual analysis – the textual representation of images is used exclusively to determine semantic similarity. LVis supports human browsing of retrieved images based on visual features. Browsing enables users to recognize rather than formulate a precise query in advance. This seems to be of particular relevance for information image retrieval. This combination of textual search and visual browsing was shown to be the most effective method for finding images of interest in a study by Chang, Eleftheriadis and McClintock (1998). Still, it seems to be desirable to combine text analysis and image processing techniques – potentially augmenting both processes by intermediate results to improve retrieval and browsing.

Spatial organizations of digital documents are supposed to ease document access, management, and relocation. However, the problems of spatial navigation in 3D (Darken, Allard and Achille, 1998; Darken and Sibert, 1996), particularly using 2D input devices, often outweigh the advantage of having an additional dimension. Abstract, large-scale information landscapes are especially difficult to navigate. The large scale requires the user to integrate the information provided by successive viewpoints into a coherent mental representation, often called a "cognitive map" (Chase, 1986), which is then used for navigation. Landmarks and their layouts have been identified as critical for navigation (Golledge, 1995; Lynch, 1960; Vinson, 1999); see also Thorndyke and Hayes-Roth's (1982) work on differences in spatial knowledge acquired from maps and navigation. Darken and Sibert (1996) explored cognitive and design principles as they apply to large virtual spaces. Furnas (1997) explored view traversability and navigability for effective navigation through large data structures.

Experiments on navigation through 3D document visualizations of document databases have also been conducted by Vincow and Wickens (1998). Subjects navigated through a semantically-organized 1000-document information space; and the influence of frame of reference (egocentric, immersed perspective or more exocentric, bird's-eye perspective) and use of map on document search and spatial judgement tasks were investigated. Performance was best with the exocentric display. Interestingly, in this experiment the map hindered rather than helped. Related research on frames of reference indicates that local information is best made available via an egocentric perspective, whereas global information should be provided by an exocentric perspective (Wickens et al., 1994).

7.5 Information Retrieval and Browsing in the Semantic Web: An Outlook

Currently, information in repositories, digital libraries, and on the Web is consumed and more or less successfully digested by humans. Computers have a hard time making "sense" of digital data; their ability to support humans via agent programs or direct manipulation interfaces, or a combination of the two, is rather limited.

The Semantic Web as envisioned by Berners-Lee and his colleagues (2001) "... is an extension of the current web in which information is given well-defined meaning, better enabling computers and people to work in cooperation." It will provide access to human readable and machine understandable information. By using ontologies, different data formats can be implemented, translated, and utilized, making semantic search and browsing over different formats for diverse DLs possible.

However, the question of how to provide the necessary (shared or translatable) semantics to make it all work is still open. The most promising approach seems to be the creation of decentralized databases and their interconnection via "semantic translators". The databases would be built by small communities (e.g. companies, scholarly communities, etc.) using vocabulary and semantics specific to their domain. The different databases could then be interlinked via "semantic translators" provided by specialized companies using semi-automatic approaches. Efforts such as the Stanford Scalable Knowledge Composition (SKC) project[14] and the Bremer Semantic Translation project[15] are already tackling the interoperability between different ontologies.

Exactly one semantic translator would be needed to connect a new database to a universal web of knowledge and services. A query would be translated among diverse databases and processed differently. This way, the Semantic Web would facilitate cross-disciplinary search, communication, and understanding and could "profoundly change the very nature of how scientific knowledge is produced and shared, in ways that we can now barely imagine" (Berners-Lee and Hendler, 2001).

In parallel to the development of the Semantic Web, computers are evolving from mere number crunchers to facilitators of human–human interaction and human–information access. Digital libraries can be viewed as managed and organized information spaces. Meaningful spaces evolve into places in which people can meet and access and manage information collaboratively. Visual interfaces to digital libraries introduce the concept of (semantic) proximity, which DLs and the Web have not provided, but which is successfully used in real-world libraries. Arranging documents in space according to their semantic proximity ensures easy access to related work and to people interested in the same topic (Börner, 2001b; Börner et al., 2002). In the near future, instead of examining long scrolling lists of matching documents, we may visit virtual, semantically organized data landscapes in which matching documents are highlighted for easy access and other users can be queried for suggestions.

7.6 Acknowledgements

We wish to thank the students involved in the LVis project: Andrew J. Clune, Ryan Schnizlein, Ho Sang Cheon, Kevin Kowalew, Sumayya A. Ansari, and Tyler Waite as well as Elin Jacob who gave very detailed and insightful comments on an earlier version of this paper.

We are grateful to Helen Atkins, ISI, and Eileen Fry from Indiana University for their insightful comments on this research as well as their support in using

---

[14]http://WWW-DB.Stanford.EDU/SKC/
[15]http://www.semantic-translation.com/

the Science Citation Index Expanded and the Dido Image Bank. Dave Pape is the software architect for XP, the underlying framework used to implement LVis in the CAVE. The SVDPACK by Michael Berry was used for computing the singular value decomposition. This research was supported by a High Performance Network Applications grant of Indiana University, Bloomington.

7.7 References

Ballay, J. M. (1994). Designing Workscape: An interdisciplinary experience. *Proceedings of CHI'94 Conference*, Boston, MA, ACM Press, pp. 10–15.

Bates, M. J. (1998). Indexing and access for digital libraries and the Internet: Human, database, and domain factors. *Journal of the American Society for Information Science*, 49(13), 1185–1205.

Battista, G., Eades, P., Tamassia, R., and Tollis, I. G. (1994). Algorithms for drawing graphs: An annotated bibliography. *Computational Geometry: Theory and Applications*, 4(5), 235–282.

Benford, S., Snowdon, D., Greenhalgh, C., Ingram, R., Knox, I., and Brown, C. (1995). VR-VIBE: A virtual environment for co-operative information retrieval. *Computer Graphics Forum*, 14(3), 349–360; http://www.crg.cs.nott.ac.uk/~dns/vrvibe.html

Benford, S., Snowdon, D., and Mariani, J. (1995). Populated information terrains: First steps. In R. A. Earnshaw, J. A. Vince and H. Jones (Eds.), *Virtual Reality Application*, Academic Press, pp. 27–39.

Berners-Lee, T., and Hendler, J. (2001). Publishing on the Semantic Web. *Nature*, 410, 1023–1024; http://www.nature.com/nature/debates/e-access/Articles/bernerslee.htm

Berners-Lee, T., Hendler, J., and Lassila, O. (2001). The Semantic Web. *Scientific American*, 284(5), 43–43; http://www.scientificamerican.com/2001/0501issue/0501berners-lee.html

Berry, M. (1993). *SVDPACKC (Version 1.0) User's Guide*, University of Tennessee Tech. (CS-93-194).

Börner, K. (2000a). Extracting and visualizing semantic structures in retrieval results for browsing. *Proceedings of ACM Digital Libraries*, San Antonio, TX, 2–7 June, pp. 234–235, ACM Press.

Börner, K. (2000b). Searching for the perfect match: A comparison of free sorting results for images by human subjects and by Latent Semantic Analysis. *Proceedings of Information Visualization 2000, Symposium on Digital Libraries*, London, England, 19–21 July, pp. 192–197, IEEE Press.

Börner, K. (2001a). Adaptation and evaluation of 3-dimensional collaborative information visualizations. *Proceedings of Workshop on Empirical Evaluations of Adaptive Systems, 8th International Conference on User Modelling*, Bavaria, Germany, 13–17 July, pp. 33–40, Lawrence Erlbaum Associates.

Börner, K. (2001b). iScape: A collaborative memory palace for digital library search results. *Proceedings of International Conference on Human–Computer Interaction*, Smith, M. J., Salvendy, G., Harris, D., and Koubek, R. J. (Eds) *Vol. 1: Usability Evaluation and Interface Design*, New Orleans, LA, 5–10 August, Lawrence Erlbaum Associates, pp. 1160–1164.

Börner, K., Chen, C., and Boyack, K. (2002). Visualizing knowledge domains. *Annual Review of Information Science and Technology*, 37 (to appear).

Börner, K., Dillon, A., and Dolinsky, M. (2000). LVis – Digital Library Visualizer. *Proceedings of Information Visualization 2000, Symposium on Digital Libraries*, London, England, pp. 77–81, IEEE Press.

Borner, K., Feng, Y., and McMahon, T. (2002). Collaborative visual interfaces to digital libraries. Proceedings of the Second ACH+IEEE Joint Conference on Digitial Libraries, Portland, Oregon, USA, 14–18 July (to appear).

Card, S .K., Robertson, G. G., and Mackinlay, J. D. (1991). The Information Visualizer: An information workspace. *Proceedings of ACM Conference on Human Factors in Computing Systems (CHI '91)*, ACM Press, pp. 181–188.

Card, S. K., Robertson, G. G., and York, W. (1996). The WebBook and the Web Forager: An information workspace for the World-Wide Web. *Proceedings of the ACM Conference on Human Factors in Computing Systems (CHI '96)*, Vancouver, Canada, 13–18 April 1996, ACM Press, pp. 111–117; http://www.acm.org/sigchi/chi96/proceedings/papers/Card/skc1txt.html

Chalmers, M. (1992). BEAD: Explorations in information visualization. *Proceedings of SIGIR '92*, Copenhagen, Denmark, June 1992, ACM Press, pp. 330–337.

Chalmers, M. (1993). Visualization of complex information. In L. J. Bass, J. Gornastaev and C. Unger (Eds.), *Third East–West International Conference on Human–Computer Interaction (EWHCI '93)*, Lecture Notes in Computer Science 753. New York: Springer Verlag, pp. 152–162.

Chang, S.-F., Eleftheriadis, A., and McClintock, R. (1998). Next-generation content representation, creation and searching for new media applications in education. *IEEE Proceedings, Special Issue on Multimedia Processing and Technology*, 86(5), 884–904.

Chase, W. G. (1986). Visual information processing. In K. R. Boff, L. Kaufman and J. P. Thomas (Eds.), *Handbook of Human Performance, Vol. 2: Cognitive Processes and Performance*. Chichester: Wiley.

Chen, C. (1997). Tracking latent domain structures: An integration of Pathfinder and Latent Semantic Analysis. *AI and Society*, 11(1–2), 48–62.

Chen, C. (1999). Visualizing semantic spaces and author co-citation networks in digital libraries. *Information Processing and Management*, 35(2), 401–420.

Chen, C., and Carr, L. (1999). *Trailblazing the literature of hypertext: Author co-citation analysis (1989–1998)*. Paper presented at the 10th ACM Conference on Hypertext (Hypertext '99), Darmstadt, Germany, ACM Press, pp. 51–60.

Chen, H., and Kim, J. (1994). GANNET: a machine learning approach to document retrieval. *Journal of Management Information Systems*, 11(3), 7–41.

Chen, C., and Paul, R. J. (2001). Visualizing a knowledge domain's intellectual structure. *Computer*, 34(3), 65–71.

Chen, H., Houston, A., Sewell, R., and Schatz, B. (1998). Internet browsing and searching: User evaluations of category map and concept space techniques. *Journal of the American Society for Information Science, Special Issue on "AI Techniques for Emerging Information Systems Applications"*, 49(7), 582–603.

Chen, C., Thomas, L., Cole, J., and Chennawasin, C. (1999). Representing the semantics of virtual spaces. *IEEE Multimedia*, 6(2).

Crossley, M., Davies, J., McGrath, A., and Rejman-Greene, M. (1999). The knowledge garden. *BT Technology Journal*, 17(1).

Darken, R. P., and Sibert, J. L. (1996). Navigating large virtual spaces. *International Journal of Human–Computer Interaction*, 8(1), 49–71.

Darken, R. P., Allard, T., and Achille, L. B. (1998). Spatial orientation and wayfinding in large-scale virtual spaces: An introduction. *Presence*, 7(2), 101–107.

Deerwester, S., Dumais, S. T., Landauer, T. K., Furnas, G. W., and Harshman, R. A. (1990). Indexing by latent semantic analysis. *Journal of the American Society for Information Science*, 41(6), 391–407.

Ding, Y. (2001). IR and AI: The role of ontology. *Proceedings of 4th International Conference of Asian Digital Libraries*, Bangalore, India, 10–12 December.

Ding, Y., and Engels, R. (2001). IR and AI: Using co-occurrence theory to generate lightweight ontologies. *Proceedings of Workshop on Digital Libraries (Dlib2001), 12th International Conference on Database and Expert Systems Applications (DEXA2001)*, Munich, Germany, 3–7 September.

Dodge, M. (2002). *An Atlas of Cyberspaces*. Available: http://www.geog.ucl.ac.uk/casa/martin/atlas/

Enser, P. G. B. (1993). Query analysis in a visual information retrieval context. *Journal of Document and Text Management*, 1, 25–52.

Fairchild, K., Poltrock, S., and Furnas, G. (1988). SemNet: Three-dimensional graphic representations of large knowledge bases. In R. Guidon (Ed.), *Cognitive Science and its Applications for Human–Computer Interaction*, Lawrence Erlbaum Associates, pp. 201–233.

Feng, Y., and Börner, K. (2002). Using semantic treemaps to categorize and visualize bookmark files. In Erbacher, R. F., Chen, P. C., Grohn, M., Roberts, J. C., Wittenbrink, C. M. (Eds) *Proceedings of SPIE Conference on Visualization and Data Analysis*, San Jose, CA, 20–25 January, SPIE – The International Society for Optical Engineering. Vol. 4665. pp. 218–227.

Fruchterman, T. M. J., and Reingold, E. M. (1991). Graph drawing by force-directed placement. *Software-Practice and Experience*, 21(11), 1129–1164.

Furnas, G. W. (1997). Effective view navigation. *Proceedings of CHI '97*, Atlanta, GA, ACM Press; http://www.acm.org/sigchi/chi97/proceedings/paper/gwf.htm

Golledge, R. G. (1995). Primitives of spatial knowledge. In T. L. Nyerges, D. M. Mark, R. Laurini and M. J. Egenhofer (Eds.), *Cognitive Aspects of Human–Computer Interaction for Geographic Information Systems*. Dordrecht: Kluwer, pp. 29–44.

Hearst, M., and Karadi, C. (1997). Cat-a-Cone: An interactive interface for specifying searches and viewing retrieval results using a large category hierarchy. *Proceedings of 20th Annual International ACM/SIGIR Conference*, Philadelphia, PA, 27–31 July 1997, ACM Press, pp. 246–255; http://www.sims.berkeley.edu/~hearst/papers/cac-sigir97/sigir97.html

Heflin, J., and Hendler, J. (2000). Dynamic ontologies on the Web. *Proceedings of 17th National Conference on Artificial Intelligence (AAAI-2000)*, Menlo Park, CA, AAAI/MIT Press, pp. 443–449.

Herot, C. F. (1980). Spatial management of data. *ACM Transactions of Database Systems*, 5(4), 493–513.

Hightower, R. R., Ring, L. T., Helfman, J. I., Bederson, B. B., and Hollan, J. D. (1998). Graphical multiscale Web histories: A study of PadPrints. *Proceedings of 9th ACM Conference on Hypertext and Hypermedia (Hypertext '98)*, New York, NY, ACM Press, pp. 58–65; http://www.cs.umd.edu/hcil/pad++/papers/hypertext-98-padprints/hypertext-98-padprints.pdf

Landauer, T. K., Foltz, P. W., and Laham, D. (1998). Introduction to latent semantic analysis. *Discourse Processes*, 25, 259–284; http://lsa.colorado.edu/

Lynch, K. J. (1960). *The Image of the City*. Cambridge, MA: MIT Press.

Orendorf, J., and Kacmar, C. (1996). A spatial approach to organizing and locating digital libraries and their content. *Proceedings of 1st ACM International Conference on Digital Libraries*, ACM Press, pp. 83–89.

Petry, F., Buckles, B., Prabhu, D., and Kraft, D. (1993). Fuzzy information retrieval using genetic algorithms and relevance feedback. *Proceedings of ASIS Annual Meeting*, pp. 122–125, Knowledge Industry Publications.

Pirolli, P., and Card., S. K. (1995). Information foraging in information access environments. *Proceedings of CHI '95*, Denver, CO, ACM Press, pp. 51–58; http://www.acm.org/sigchi/chi95/proceedings/papers/ppp_bdy.htm

Raghavan, V. V., and Agarwal, B. (1987). Optimal determination of user-oriented clusters: An application for the reproductive plan. *Proceedings of 2nd International Conference on Genetic Algorithms and Their Applications*, Cambridge, MA, pp. 241–246, Lawrence Erlbaum Associates.

Robertson, G., Czerwinski, M., Larson, K., Robbins, D., Thiel, D., and van Dantzich, M. (1998). Data mountain: Using spatial memory for document management. *Proceedings of 11th Annual ACM Symposium on User Interface Software and Technology (UIST '98)*, pp. 153–162, ACM Press; http://www.research.microsoft.com/users/marycz/home.htm

Robertson, G., Dantzich, M. v., Robbins, D., Czerwinski, M., Hinckley, K., Risden, K., Thiel, D., and Gorokhovsky, V. (2000). The Task Gallery: A 3D windows manager. *Proceedings of Conference on Human Factors in Computing Systems CHI'2000*, The Hague, 1–6 April 2000, ACM Press, pp. 494–501.

Robertson, G. G., Mackinlay, J. D., and Card, S. K. (1991). Cone trees: Animated 3D visualizations of hierarchical information. *Proceedings of CHI '91*, New Orleans, LA, 28 April – 2 May 1991, pp. 189–194, ACM Press.

Russell, D. M., Stefik, M. J., Pirolli, P., and Card, S. K. (1993). The cost structure of sensemaking. *Proceedings of INTERCHI '93 Conference on Human Factors in Computing Systems*, Amsterdam, pp. 269–276, ACM Press.

Schatz, B. R. (1995). Building the Interspace: The Illinois Digital Library Project. *Communications of the ACM Computing Survey*, 38(4), 62–63.

Schatz, B. R., and Chen, H. (1996). Building large-scale digital libraries. *Computer theme issue on the US Digital Library Initiative* 29(5), (http://computer.org/computer/dli/).

Schvaneveldt, R. W. (1990). *Pathfinder Associative Networks: Studies in Knowledge Organization*. Norwood, NJ: Ablex.

Shneiderman, B. (1996). The eyes have it: A task by data type taxonomy for information visualizations. *Proceedings of Symposium on Visual Languages*, Boulder, CO, IEEE, pp. 336–343.

Shum, S. B., Motta, E., and Domingue, J. (2000). ScholOnto: An ontology-based digital library server for research documents and discourse. *International Journal on Digital Libraries*, 3(3), 237–248.

Tan, D. S., Stefanucci, J. K., Proffitt, D. R., and Pausch, R. (2001). The Infocockpit: Providing location and place to aid human memory. *Proceedings of Workshop on Perceptive User Interfaces*, Orlando, FL; http://www.cs.ucsb.edu/PUI/PUIWorkshop/PUI-2001/PUI2001Schedule.html

Thorndyke, P., and Hayes-Roth, B. (1982). Differences in spatial knowledge acquired from maps and navigation. *Cognitive Psychology*, 14, 560–589.

Vincow, M. A., and Wickens, C. D. (1998). Frame of reference and navigation through document visualizations: Flying through information space. *Proceedings of 42nd Annual Meeting of the Human Factors and Ergonomics Society*, Santa Monica, CA, Human Factors and Ergonomics Society, pp. 511–515.

Vinson, N. G. (1999). Design guidelines for landmarks to support navigation in virtual environments. *Proceedings of CHI 1999*, Pittsburg, PA, ACM Press.

Wickens, C. D., Liang, C.-C., Prevett, T. T., and Olmos, O. (1994). Egocentric and exocentric displays for terminal area navigation. *Proceedings of Human Factors and Ergonomics Society 38th Annual Meeting*, Santa Monica, CA, Human Factors and Ergonomics Society, pp. 16–20.

Chapter 8
Interactive Visualization of Paragraph-level Metadata to Support Corporate Document Use

Mischa Weiss-Lijn, Janet T. McDonnell and Leslie James

8.1 Introduction

Metadata is at the heart of the Semantic Web and it is important that effective applications of this resource are developed. The application described was created to look at whether the interactive visualization of paragraph-level semantic metadata can be used to facilitate the goal-directed search of corporate documents.

This research is motivated by the need of large corporations the world over to make better use of the knowledge they store in documents. There is much work currently looking at how to locate and automatically distribute relevant documents to employees. Our research, which was sponsored by Sainsbury's, a large UK retail organization, is therefore exploring a technology for improving the effectiveness of using documents once they have already been located.

We have focused on an important class of document use, where needs tend to be satisfied at the sub-document level: goal-directed reading. Adler et al. (1998) identify this as a prevalent class of reading in a study of work-related document use in a range of work settings. They describe it as "sampling information in the text which satisfies the goal of the search" (Adler et al., 1998). Van House (1995) concludes that "Workplace users [...] want to retrieve information rather than documents per se", hence information needs in digital library use are most commonly satisfied at the paragraph or section level. We have therefore developed a system to facilitate goal-directed search by helping the user to home in on paragraphs relevant to their goal.

To assess the merit of using metadata in supporting goal-directed search, paragraph-level metadata and accompanying taxonomies have been prepared for two sets of documents. An interactive system named GridVis has been built to give users access to the document using this metadata.

In this chapter the methods used to construct the metadata and taxonomies are laid out, then GridVis is described and various key design decisions are discussed using evidence from analyses, user trials, and experimental evaluation.

116

8.2 Creating Content-descriptive Paragraph-level Metadata for Business Documents

In order to properly create and evaluate a visualization of paragraph-level metadata, one needs to have high-quality metadata. Methods for the creation of metadata lie on a continuum; at one end of this low-quality metadata can be produced in a scalable manner with relatively little human involvement, at the other end high-quality metadata is painstakingly hand crafted. For the purposes of this research it is important to produce metadata of high quality. If the metadata is not of comparatively high quality then any negative evaluation of the visualization could be attributed to the shortcomings of the metadata. If the visualization is found to be valuable, then its efficacy with more scalable (and rapidly improving) methods of metadata production can be assessed. Here the methods used to produce the high-quality metadata needed for GridVis are described.

In the course of this research GridVis was trialled with two distinct types of documents internal to Sainsbury's. First analytical research reports were used, then later the system was trialled with weekly industry news digests.

8.2.1 Metadata Design and Production

The metadata was produced in what can broadly be broken down into two stages: an initial generation and a subsequent paring down or rationalization.

This was done on two separate occasions for the two different document types. For the first set of documents, both stages were executed using methods drawn from the ontology literature (i.e. Uschold and Gruninger, 1996; Jokela et al., 2000). For the second set of documents, these methods were enhanced in order to produce metadata more suited to supporting goal-directed search.

8.2.1.1 Tag Generation

The process for generating tags initially involved a number of stages and brought together a number of techniques from the literature. The first stage was to examine the documents' audience, as suggested in Jokela et al. (2000), and to gather information about requirements. The authors were interviewed to discover who the audience were, what their jobs entailed and how their interests differed. The next stage is akin to Uschold and Gruninger's (1996) brainstorming, where two of the documents were read and liberally tagged with the aim of generating a broad initial set of tags. This initial set was then complemented by reading domain-relevant documents such as business plans and systems documentation, and by attending key team and division meetings. The combined use of these methods led to a large and rich initial set of metadata tags. This tag set represented the important concepts and objects of the domain, but not necessarily those needed to discriminate topics of interest.

For the second set of documents, a number of methodological improvements were made to the tag-generation method described. As above, domain knowledge was required, but since the research continued in the same business environment, the tagging process could rely on the domain knowledge already gained from the investigations of the previous round of tagging. The improvements to the method were primarily derived from a set of eight interviews with a reasonably broad set of typical readers. They were asked what brought them to the documents and what they looked for when reading them. Each interviewee was also asked to go through one of the documents deciding what they would skip, which paragraphs they would read and what questions they would be trying to answer. This part of the interview provided a rich source of information about the document audience's needs, from audience members themselves instead of the documents authors used in the previous method.

These interviews were also used to generate tags tightly focused on supporting goal-directed search. Since goal-directed search involves finding text relevant to a goal, it should be possible to judge the relevance of a piece of text using tags alone. The interviews were used to tease out the kinds of information used in making relevance judgements when reading the types of document for which the tags were being developed. Interviewees were asked to articulate the rationales behind their choices of paragraph, i.e. what features of paragraphs (or sections) prompted them to read in depth or move on. These rationales revealed the minimal set of information, and hence metadata, needed to successfully discriminate material of interest. Moreover, the rationales, and hence the metadata they provide, were expressed in the everyday language of potential users. For example, one paragraph was rejected because "I already know about the picking centre in Manchester", so from this we see that the tags "picking centre" and "Manchester" could be fruitful, and more generally, that the location and business units need to be tagged. Once tags had been derived from these rationales, the insights gained were used to generate more tags through a liberal tagging of all the documents to be used with the tool. Hence data from interviews with document audience members allowed the generation of kinds of tags needed to make relevance judgements.

8.2.1.2 Tag Rationalization

The next stage in producing the tags was to refine and reduce the tag set to a functional minimum.

Following Uschold (1996), the tags were inspected for duplication and consistency, removing near synonyms and rewording analogues. The tags were also inspected and reworded for clarity by the researcher and company employees.

One other feature used to eliminate and improve the tags was to look at their "basicness". Uschold and Gruninger (1996) suggest that words that are "cognitively basic", in that they are couched at a common level of abstraction, are better candidates for use in taxonomies and as metadata. This is because it is at the basic level, "dog" instead of "mammal" for instance, where meaning is common to most people. The tags were rated for basicness by three potential users at Sainsbury's. This rating was used to locate tags that could be considered for elimination or rewording.

The tags were also screened for relevance. In the case of the first set of documents this was done by examining the tags while holding user needs (as expressed by a document author) in mind. For the second set of documents, information from the eight interviews described above was used. The interviews yielded a set of queries or questions that the tags needed to be able to express. They also produced a set of rationales behind relevance judgements. Again the tags could be tested to see whether they would provide the information required to form the rationales. This procedure allowed redundant tags, or types of tag, to be excluded, while also identifying what types of tag might be usefully added.

8.2.2 Metadata Taxonomy Design and Production

The structure, or taxonomy, that houses the metadata is crucial. If the tags were presented as a structureless mass they would be unwieldy, if not unusable, to the document reader and metadata author. The structure introduced by a taxonomy allows tags to be more rapidly located since it delimits a small subset of possibly germane tags. The taxonomy also allows the tags to be more easily and consistently authored, since parts of it (e.g. a class like "competitors") suggest appropriate tags (e.g. the instance "Tesco Supermarkets").

The taxonomies required share many features with several types of ontology. Consequently, the taxonomies were created using techniques developed for creating these ontologies. Although the taxonomies constructed in this research are not the fully fledged formal ontologies such as those produced by Uschold and Gruninger (1996), and Perez and Benjamins (1999) etc., they do correspond to the structured informal ontologies which serve as the basis for such formalization (Uschold, 1996). The taxonomies created here have more substantial similarities to the type of ontology defined by Jokela et al. (2000). This type of ontology is made up of a number of independent "dimensions" (e.g. Publication, Business Area) each containing an internal structure (e.g. for Publication, no structure, and for Business Area, a hierarchical one).

The following is a description of the methods used to construct the two taxonomies produced during the course of this research. First we examine the methods used to construct the taxonomy for the first set of documents, then we go on to describe how these were improved for the next set of documents.

The construction of the first ontology largely followed the methodology proposed by Uschold and Gruninger (1996). The first stage consisted of the tag generation described above. The taxonomy development was initiated by identifying natural semantic groupings of tags. To accomplish this, tags, each on a separate slip of paper, were moved around the surface of a large desk, grouped and regrouped, until a satisfying grouping had been found. By naming these groups the first version of the taxonomy was produced. These names were inspected for clarity and parsimony by both the researcher and Sainsbury's staff, and reworded if necessary. Many variations on the structure were considered in the search for something that was both parsimonious and concrete enough to be accessible to company employees. Once a structure had been settled upon, it was used in the tagging of some documents. These documents required some new tags, which themselves prompted some minor changes to the taxonomy. To summarize, the tags were first generated and semantically grouped, a taxonomy was created to describe these groupings, and it was then iteratively refined through inspection and use.

As with the methods initially used for tag generation, the methods described above do not focus on producing a taxonomy to support goal-directed search. They allow the construction of a reasonable taxonomy, but one that is organized solely around the structure of the domain. This structure is not tuned to the task of discriminating relevant content. The second taxonomy was developed with an improved method that used the audience interviews described above to produce a taxonomy organized around the structure of the domain and along the dimensions used to make relevance discriminations.

The improvements to the taxonomy construction method were derived from interviews of members of the documents' audience. A first draft of the taxonomy was generated by grouping rationales according to the types of information they used. For example, the decision to reject a paragraph on the basis "I already know about the picking centre in Manchester" uses information about a business unit, i.e. "picking centre" and a location, i.e. "Manchester". The grouping process allowed the common types of information used in decisions about relevance to be identified. A first draft of the taxonomy was constructed from these information types. Constructing the first draft in this way ensured that the taxonomy's main elements and structure supported the task of discriminating relevant paragraphs.

In order to ensure the taxonomy's completeness and parsimony, it was then tested and refined using Russell et al.'s (1993) learning loop process. This involved testing the taxonomy by applying it to the existing tag set. The tags that were not well housed, and the parts of the taxonomy that were not much used, motivated improvements. The improved taxonomy was then re-applied to the tag set, the taxonomy re-adjusted, the tag set re-applied and so on until a satisfactory fit was found. The learning loop process provided a much more methodical and principled approach then relying upon inspection as recommended by Uschold and Gruninger (1996). Once this had been done, the taxonomy's wording was inspected for clarity by potential users at Sainsbury's.

The second taxonomy was developed for a very different type of document to the first, but for the same community of users with the same "industry" concerns and concepts. It therefore should have been possible to use the previous ontology as a starting point, but interestingly, the two taxonomies ended up looking very different. This suggests that generic corporate taxonomies cannot be blindly applied to new document types; taxonomies of this kind need to be tightly coupled to the documents to which they must relate.

8.3 Visualization Design

Once high-quality paragraph-level document metadata is available, the next challenge is to provide a visualization that puts the metadata in the hands of the user. Here the GridVis visualization is described; first the design methods used are discussed, then a brief overview of the core features is given, followed by an illustrative scenario. Once the basics of the GridVis design have been made clear, we go on to look at the rationales behind the design and the more advanced functionality and enhancements that these have led to.

8.3.1 Design Methods

The design work was supported by a number of techniques: the close involvement of potential users, iterative prototyping, informal user testing and experimental evaluation. These techniques are only briefly described here. The results that impacted on the design of GridVis will be discussed in the next section.

The informal user testing and paper design work relied on potential users. These were the members of the team supporting this project. This team was not a software development team, but bona fide Sainsbury's head office workers. As such they provided an articulate and enthusiastic group of collaborators who were genuinely part of the target user group, conscious of its motivations, knowledge and limits. For the sake of conciseness this group will be referred to as the "frontier users".

Initial design ideas were refined and followed up by quickly assembled simple prototypes. The initial ideas were worked out on paper using general design and usability principles as guidelines (e.g. Schneiderman, 1993). These were then honed, in part through discussions with people at Sainsbury's, to make way for some simple implementations. The concretization of ideas and sketches in interactive mock-ups was itself helpful in spotting pitfalls and design trade-offs.

These prototypes were then used for informal user testing. The frontier users were asked to do various reading tasks using the prototypes. This allowed interaction problems to be uncovered and exposed limitations of the design. For the initial few iterations this provoked a radical change of design; later when the foundations of the GridVis design settled, user testing informed more localized changes and additions.

A quantitative empirical evaluation of an interactive implementation of GridVis was also carried out (see Weiss-Lijn et al., 2001a). Careful qualitative analysis of the data from this experiment enabled some fairly subtle interface design problems to be identified.

8.3.2 The Visualization Design

8.3.2.1 Overview

The GridVis client-side application contains a visualization of a document's metadata (see Figure 8.1). This visualization can be considered as three interlinked sections: the metadata tree on the left-hand side, the iconic document overview running along the top, and the grid sitting at the centre. The taxonomy is used to create a tree structure and the metadata tags are added to this as leaf nodes. Each tag has a corresponding row in the central grid. The iconic document overview is a miniature image of the document laid out horizontally along the top of the visualization. Each paragraph in this overview lines up with one of the columns in the grid below. The central grid shows which metadata tags apply to which paragraphs in the document: each column represents a paragraph and each row represents a tag. Hence, to show that a tag has been applied to a particular paragraph, the cell where the appropriate column and row meet is shaded. The colour of the cell is determined by the value of the applicability attribute given to the tag when it was applied to a paragraph: the higher the applicability the darker the colour (a legend for this scale is always visible in the top left-hand corner). The metadata tags and taxonomy, iconic document overview and grid, are thus brought together to produce a visual overview of the document.

The user can query the visualization with their mouse through a combination of dynamic querying and brushing (Card et al., 1999). When the mouse is placed

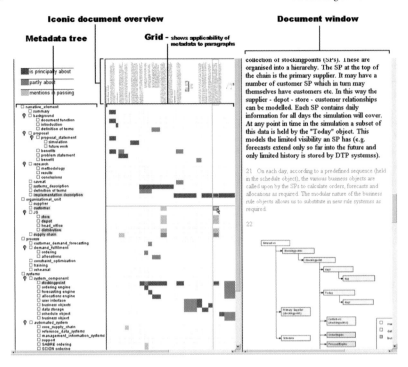

Figure 8.1   A screenshot of GridVis. By placing their mouse over a cell in the grid, the user has highlighted a paragraph in the iconic document overview and all the metadata terms in the metadata tree relevant to this paragraph.

over a cell in the grid, all the tags in the column are highlighted; hence the paragraph's content is described. By looking along the row of an interesting tag, the user can see where and to what extent that topic comes up in the document. So by moving the mouse in the central grid the user can explore what different parts of the document are about, and where in the document particular topics are covered.

The user can also query the document by clicking on any cell in the grid. Clicking on the grid will produce a query that is sent to the servlet formulated with the metadata and paragraph corresponding to the selected cell. The servlet will produce an HTML version of the document in which every paragraph tagged with the selected metadata is highlighted using a bold font. The document window will display the paragraph selected, thereby offering details on demand (Card et al., 1999).

8.3.2.2   An Illustrative Scenario

Scenarios (Carroll, 2000) have been found to be effective design and communication tools. Consequently the scenario below is included to give a better idea of how the functionality described above might be used in practice.

Clair, a Sainsbury's employee, sits down to look at this week's "industry update" newsletter, with a view to finding out whether the company plans to sell its US interests. She starts up GridVis and looks through the metadata to see if any of Sainsbury's US subsidiaries are mentioned. She scans down the top-level entries in the metadata taxonomy until she reaches "business unit". Then she scans the next level of entries under "business unit" until she reaches "Sainsbury's". Under Sainsbury's she sees an entry for "Shaws" which is a US subsidiary of Sainsbury's.

Having found a relevant tag, Clair proceeds to see if any of the paragraphs relevant to this tag will say anything about plans for a sell-off. She looks along the tag's row in the grid and sees that two cells have been coloured in. Passing her mouse over the first she sees coloured cell in the same column and its tag, become highlighted. The other cell's tag label reads "loyalty cards". Deciding that therefore the paragraph is not relevant she moves her mouse on to the next coloured-in cell. In this case the "acquisitions" and "USA" tags light up. This surprises Clair, since she expected Shaws to be on sale, not making acquisitions; she decides to look at the paragraph and clicks on the cell. The right-hand window is refreshed; the paragraph she wants now appears at the top of the screen with its text in bold.

8.3.2.3 Design Rational and Advanced Features

Descriptions of a design's end state misses out the many insights gained and put to work during its evolution. Since these insights are often portable to related applications we shall cover the more important ones here.

The core design decisions behind GridVis were initially developed alongside alternatives that were cast aside upon consideration of a task analysis. This task analysis made it possible to pick out key actions involved in using paragraph-level metadata. The different designs being considered at that stage were compared in their ability to support these key actions. Although each design provided some support for each action, it was clear that GridVis would support them best.

One insight gained from the early user testing was that subjects had trouble conceptualizing the visualization's horizontal representation of the document. This problem underlined the importance of the iconic document overview in providing a representation of the document's orientation. In later versions this function was bolstered by adding the ability to query the document directly from the iconic document overview; clicking on a paragraph in the overview would highlight the paragraph's column in the grid and bring this paragraph up in the document window.

The user testing and experimental evaluation showed that people would often revisit the same paragraphs. Some subjects commented on the value of this; being led to the same parts of the text from different tags, helped them see the text from different perspectives. Subjects also admitted that they had not expressly wanted to revisit paragraphs, but were simply going where the vis-ualization lead them. These problems lead to the design of history visualization features. These use colour markings on the grid to indicate which tags, cells and paragraphs have already been visited.

Similarly, it became clear that users would want to read the section title of any paragraph they selected in GridVis. In the user testing sessions and experimental evaluation, people tended to scroll upwards from a paragraph they had been offered by GridVis, in order to read the section title. The section titles perhaps offer a way to conceptualize paragraphs (e.g. "method" vs. "introduction"), thus making it easier to bring pre-existing knowledge to bear in the process of extracting relevant information.

The need to give paragraph context was resolved through several devices. Firstly, instead of displaying the selected paragraph at the top of the document window, the preceding paragraph was shown first, followed by the selected one. This proved very effective for documents with short sections such as news digest documents since it often brought the titles into view. A second device, which was brought in later, was to display the relevant section title above the "iconic document overview" as the mouse rolls over columns in the grid (see Figure 8.2).

Another important insight came from the task analysis based on data from the first round of user testing (Weiss-Lijn, 2001b). This showed that the act of tag selection was a pivotal part of using GridVis for goal-directed search (see Figure 8.3). Whereas the tags had been integrated into the grid in the mock-up interface, subsequently they were displayed in a separate and conventional vertical tree display. This change served to more clearly display the tags and hierarchical organization, using a sophisticated yet familiar interface.

Once a tag is chosen, a paragraph (i.e. cells) relating to it must be selected. This task has several components. First potentially relevant cells must be located, then these must be inspected in order to decide on the relevance of these paragraphs to the query. We shall start by looking at the design decisions that went into making the cells easy to locate, and then we shall look at what was done to make their relevance easier to assess.

Comments from user testing and the frontier user group suggested it was hard to locate the relevant cells. Also the task analysis (Weiss-Lijn, 2001b) showed that this was the second pivotal action in GridVis use (see Figure 8.3). The qualitative analysis of data from an empirical evaluation of GridVis allowed this task to be looked at in more detail (Weiss-Lijn, 2001a). It revealed that the task could be tackled using five different strategies (see Table 8.1 and Figure 8.3). The comments from frontier users and early user testing initially suggested that there were problems with the support for the first two strategies. Also, the fact that subjects did not seem to make much use of any co-occurrence strategies suggested that GridVis was not adequately supporting the use of co-occurrence information.

The problems with the support for the first two strategies in Table 8.1 came down to the difficulty of locating cells in the grid. Several features were added to make locating relevant cells easier. The essential problem here is that it is quite hard to look down a row or column in the grid to find coloured cells. This is because the eye can easily stray from the desired row or column. The first feature added, to deal with this problem, was a crosshair graphic. As the mouse was moved around in the grid, the borders of the column and row under the mouse would be drawn thicker and (in later versions) in a bright green colour. Although this helped, it forced users to bring their mouse into the correct row of the grid. This could be cumbersome, since the user's mouse movements over the grid would have to be coordinated with the highlighting of tags in the metadata tree.

A further set of features were implemented to avoid this problem and deliver better support. This required the user to simply select a tag of interest rather then the more complex positioning of the mouse in the correct row of the grid. Once the tag is selected the tag's row in the grid is highlighted with coloured borders

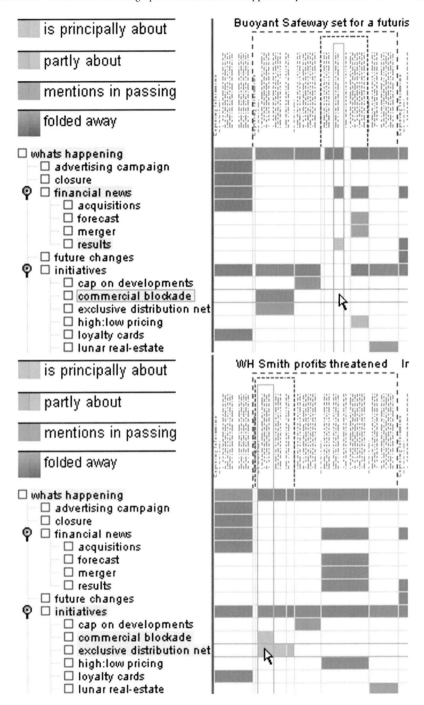

Figure 8.2 The two screenshots of GridVis illustrate the level of detail management feature. As the mouse is moved from one paragraph to another, only the paragraphs in the section the mouse is currently over are shown, the rest are shown at the section level. Also, the title of the section the mouse is currently over, is displayed above the iconic document overview.

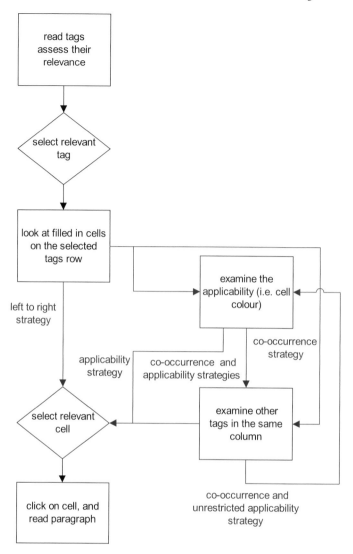

Figure 8.3 A schematic summary of the results of a task analysis based on an early round of user testing. The blue dotted arrows indicate the different possible cell-selection strategies uncovered in a qualitative analysis of results from an empirical evaluation of GridVis (Weiss-Lijn, 2001a).

and the columns of relevant paragraphs are given a different colour (see Figure 8.4). Giving the relevant cells a different colour is a particularly effective device. This is because it allows the cells to be located with an effortless pre-attentive visual search whose duration is independent of the number of cells in the display (Healey, 1996).

As mentioned above, users in the user trials and empirical evaluation made very little use of the potentially useful co-occurrence information when selecting cells. To gather co-occurrence information the users must look at the other tags

Table 8.1 The different possible strategies for cell selection.

Strategy	Information used
Left to right	None
Applicability	Applicability of cells on tag of interest
Co-occurrence only	Relevance of other tags in columns (paragraphs) of interest
Co-occurrence and restricted applicability	Applicability of cells on tag of interest
	Relevance of other tags in columns (paragraphs) of interest
Co-occurrence and applicability	Applicability of cells on tag of interest
	Relevance of other tags in columns (paragraphs) of interest
	Applicability of other tags in columns (paragraphs) of interest

on the paragraph of interest. Co-occurrence information is important because it gives the users a fuller understanding of a paragraph's content, thus allowing them to find the most apparently relevant cell and avoid reading irrelevant material. Users tendency to not use this information could be attributed to the fact that it is difficult to do so; upon locating a cell they would have to look up the column to find other cells that are filled in, then look along the rows of these cells to read their tag labels.

To tackle this problem, all the tags on a paragraph are highlighted when the mouse passes over its column. This relieves the user of the need to look up co-occurring tags on the grid before reading them; they need only pass the mouse over the appropriate column and read off the highlighted tags.

A qualitative analysis of the later experimental evaluation revealed that when selecting paragraphs relating to a tag of interest, users still seldom used co-occurrence information. A further analysis found that precision could be

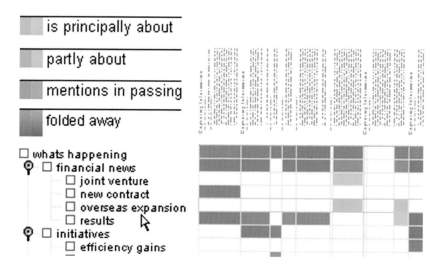

Figure 8.4 This shows how instance selection can be aided by selecting the tag of interest. The relevant row is highlighted to make tracing along it easier, and the cells of the relevant columns are made to "pop out" by giving them a different colour.

substantially increased by making full use of the co-occurrence information. Hence despite the possible rewards, the cost of using co-occurrence information was still too high.

New functionality has been added to GridVis, to further address this problem. The co-occurrence strategy was made easier through partial automation; if the user selects tags of interest, GridVis indicates which tags co-occur on each paragraph. This can be used in several ways. Most simply, it can be used to see which paragraphs relate to the largest number of interesting tags. Perhaps more *often* it can be used to find a paragraph that has *all* the tags of interest applied to it.

A related problem impeding the use of co-occurrence was revealed by a GOMS (Card et al., 1983) analysis of the cell selection. The GOMS analysis essentially decomposes the process of selecting a cell using the co-occurrence strategy into component actions for which standard time estimates can be made using results published in psychology literature. This analysis revealed that reading tag highlighting (for the column of interest) was *the* major contributor to task time. One way to reduce this contribution would be if the user only read the leaf tags. It is the leaf tags that are of major importance; the parent tags serve mainly to contextualize their leaf children. By only reading leaf tags, the GOMS model predicted that the task time for instance selection, using co-occurrence, would be reduced by between a third and half. To realize these gains a simple change was made to the interface which, it is hoped, will encourage the user to ignore parent tags. The highlight colour was made lighter for parent tags then for leaf ones, making them less obviously highlighted. Thus via a GOMS analysis a design problem was identified; this prompted a simple design change, which should substantially speed up the use of co-occurrence information in cell selection.

Another possible factor inhibiting the use of applicability and co-occurrence information is GridVis' voracious appetite for screen real estate. With longer documents, the users have to scroll horizontally to see the whole grid. This makes it impossible to see every paragraph relevant to a tag and therefore confounds attempts to select the most appropriate paragraph.

The screen real estate problem was addressed by an implementation that dynamically redraws the grid at varying levels of detail to only show in full the parts of the document relevant to the user's current activity (see Figure 8.2).

8.4 System Design

Since GridVis is designed for use on a corporate intranet in a corporation where software installation for low priority applications is problematic, it was given a client-server architecture; the visualization is generated by a client-side Java applet, the queries are answered by a Java servlet using XLS-T to produce customized HTML documents. The documents and taxonomy are encoded as XML. The document structure is described with a standard hierarchical XML structure; the metadata is embedded within this alongside the text it describes.

8.5 Related Work

In this section we briefly review other work on technologies which support the use of single digital documents and their relation to GridVis.

8.5.1 Visualization of Document Properties

Several systems have been developed to visualize aspects of individual document content. Eick et al. (1992) pioneered two important techniques in SeeSoft, a system for visualizing line-oriented software statistics (see Figure 8.5). In SeeSoft each file of code for a particular system was visualized as a single thin vertical rectangle whose length was proportional to the file size. Each line of code in the file was visualized as a one-pixel thick horizontal line in the rectangle. This allowed the whole file to be visualized on screen and since indentation and line length was depicted in the visualization, programmers found they could recognize files. GridVis has made use of this technique in its iconic document overview to enable the entire document to be recognizably, yet compactly, displayed.

SeeSoft allowed document metadata to be viewed by colouring the code lines. Once an attribute, e.g. "programmer name" or "time written", was chosen for visualization, its values were automatically mapped to particular colours that were in turn used to shade each line of code. The user could then inspect the colour distribution to look for interesting patterns. This technique is ideal when the data is continuous (e.g. time), or when it is categorical but there are relatively few values (e.g. programmer name). When the data is categorical but there are many values as (e.g. 70+ with GridVis), colours become impossible to clearly differentiate (Ware, 2000).

In TileBars, Hearst (1994) visualized the relevance of search terms to different parts of a document. Documents were divided up into topics and the relevance of a query to each was represented by a square: the darker the square the higher the

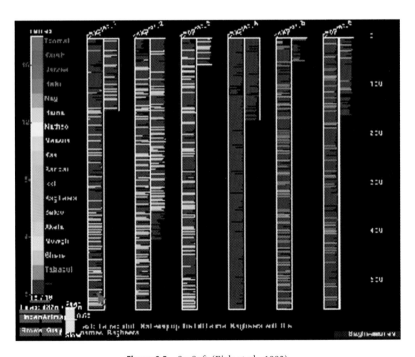

Figure 8.5   SeeSoft (Eick et al., 1992).

relevance of that topic. The squares were arranged in a row to represent the entire document. Several separate term sets can be incorporated at once by visualizing the relevance of each with a separate row of squares. In a sense, GridVis can be seen as an extension of the TileBars visualization. Each cell in GridVis corresponds to a tile, with shading brightness indicating relevance. The major advantages of the extensions made in GridVis are that the tags are applied at the paragraph level, the quantity of text is indicated by cell width, and many more terms are visualized. Visualizing every tag at once allows patterns to be spotted (e.g. "all the stuff about marketing Internet shopping is at the end of the document") and rapid visual inspection of tag co-occurrence.

8.5.2 Supporting Within-document Navigation

In the work done so far on supporting the use of single documents, no one has seriously looked at the potential of semantic metadata. Nevertheless, researchers in information visualization and hypertext have developed systems to support document use.

As with GridVis, in both SeeSoft and TileBars, the representation can also be used to navigate directly to the most relevant part of the documents. In TileBars (see Figure 8.6), clicking on a particular square will take the user to the start of that sub-topic. In SeeSoft, the user can display code in a reading window by placing a magnification rectangle over lines of interest. So, to a limited degree, both these systems support navigation within a single document.

A number of visualization systems from XEROX PARC have attempted to facilitate document navigation. The first of these is the Document Lens (Mackinlay and Robertson, 1993; see Figure 8.7), which allows the entire document to be viewed at once, fully displaying the page of interest while keeping the rest of the document viewable, if not readable. Keyword searches can be performed and the results are displayed by highlighting the word wherever it appears in the document. The mode of overview here is primarily visual as opposed to semantic, since text outside the focus region is very hard to read. It is unclear whether this kind of overview is very helpful and there has been no published evaluation to suggest that it is.

Another visualization from XEROX PARC is the 3D book (Card et al., 1996; Woodruff et al., 2000). Here an entire book or a collection of web pages is represented using a 3D book metaphor. The user is able to turn to specific pages, turn pages one at a time, or rifle through the pages seeing what is on each page as it turns. This visualization offers very intuitive navigation and a good metaphor for presenting collections of information. Nevertheless it does not directly attempt to support goal-directed search, and it is not clear that it would be able to do so.

Superbook (Egan et al., 1989) is a more clearly successful system for supporting goal-directed search. Using SuperBook, a large text can be searched using keywords. The number of query word occurrences in each section of the document is displayed beside their entries in a table of contents. The table of contents is displayed using a fisheye algorithm that automatically folds away irrelevant sections while keeping parent headings of relevant paragraphs visible for contextual orientation. The user can access any piece of text in the document by opening and selecting headings in the table of contents. Egan et al. (1989) performed three empirical evaluations of their tool, comparing its effectiveness for

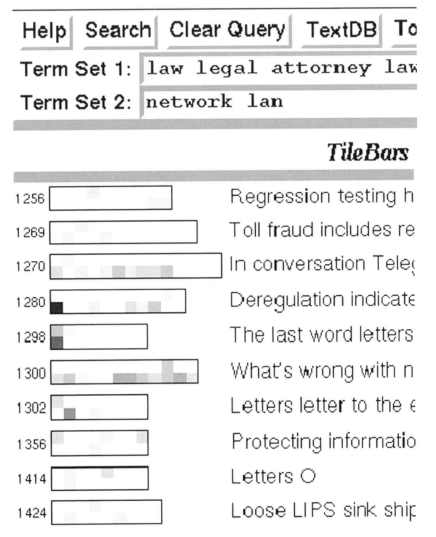

Figure 8.6 TileBars (Hearst, 1995).

simple goal-directed searches with that of printed journals. In the third evaluation, using an improved version of the software, they found that performance
with printed journals was approximately 25% slower and less accurate. A similar
study was carried out with a more conventional hypertext system (Mynatt et al.,
1992). Here subjects were asked to perform goal-directed searches of a non-
sequential text, either using a printed encyclopaedia or a hypertext tool incorporating a search tool, text links and a back button. The hypertext users did
slightly better overall, although they were not significantly faster. The modest
computational demands and reasonable empirical validation of these techniques
is perhaps what has led to many of their innovations being incorporated into

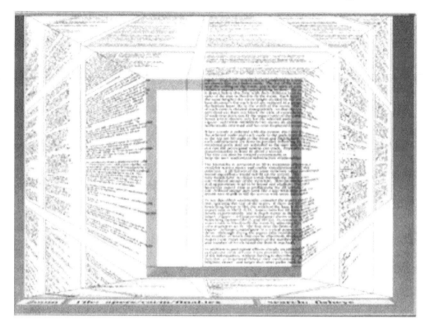

Figure 8.7   The Document Lens (Robertson and Mackinlay, 1993).

current commercial help systems which rely heavily on hypertext links, full text search, and expandable tables of contents.

8.5.3 Ontology Visualization

Finally we shall briefly turn to consider some of the work that has been done to make it easy to navigate through and understand taxonomies and ontologies. For the majority of work with ontologies there is little need to cater to needs of non-expert users. But in some cases systems have been built to make the ontologies accessible to a wider circle of users. Benjamins et al. (1999) use a hyperbolic tree visualization to allow the user to smoothly move through the hierarchy while maintaining an overview. Domingue (1998) use a simple force-directed graph layout to display the elements in their ontology and the relationships these have to each other. In GridVis we have used an explorer-style tree rather then a force-directed layout or hyperbolic visualization since this allows the metadata representation to be tightly coupled with the representation of a document.

8.6 Summary

This chapter has described the design and construction of an application for using semantic metadata to support the goal-directed search of corporate documents. This involved the careful production of high-quality metadata as well as the construction of taxonomies to house them. The metadata and taxonomies were constructed using methods from the formal ontology construction literature, as well as new methods based upon interviews with potential users, focusing on how they would distinguish the material they would read from that they wouldn't. The GridVis application was developed and refined through several rounds of evaluation and analysis. The rationales for design enhancements are discussed, drawing on evidence from user testing, empirical evaluation, and various analyses. Finally, previous work on digitally supporting single-document use is briefly discussed.

8.7 Acknowledgments

This research was sponsored by J Sainsbury plc and undertaken within the Postgraduate Training Partnership established between Sira Ltd and University College London. Postgraduate training partnerships are a joint initiative of the DTI and the EPSRC. The first author would also like to thank Dr John Gilby for his wise counsel and Anne Pomery for her spiritual support.

8.8 References

Adler A., Gujar A., Harrison B. L., O'Hara K., and Sellen A. (1998) A diary study of work-related reading: Design implications for digital reading devices. *Conference Proceedings on Human Factors in Computing Systems*, pp. 241–248, ACM Press.

Benjamins R. V., Fensel D., Decker S., and Perez A. G. (1999) (KA)2: Building ontologies for the internet: A mid-term report. *International Journal of Human–Computer Studies* 51, 687–712.

Card S. K., Moran T. P., and Newell A. (1983) *The psychology of human computer interaction.* Lawrence Erlbaum Associates.

Card S. K., Robertson G. G., and York W. (1996) The WebBook and the Web Forager: An information workspace for the World-Wide Web. *Proceedings of ACM CHI, '96 Conference on Human Factors in Computing Systems*, vol. 1, pp. 111–117, ACM Press.

Card S. K., Mackinlay J. D., and Shneiderman B. (Eds) (1999) *Information visualization: Using vision to think*, Morgan Kaufmann, p. 223.

Carroll J. M. (2000) Five reasons for scenario based design. *Interacting with Computers* 13, 43–60.

Domingue J. (1998) Tadzebao and WebOnto: Discussing, browsing and editing ontologies on the web. In B. Gaines and M. Musen (Eds), *Proceedings of the 11th Knowledge Acquisition for Knowledge-Based Systems Workshop*, 18–23 April, Banff, Canada, SRDG Publications.

Eick S. G., Steffen J. L., and Sumner E. E. (1992) SeeSoft – A tool for visualizing line oriented software statistics. *IEEE Transactions on Software Engineering* 18, 957–968.

Egan D. E., Remde J. R., Gomez L. M., Landauer T. K., Eberhardt J., and Lochbaum C. C. (1989) Formative design evaluation of SuperBook. *ACM Transactions on Information Systems* 7 (1), 30–57.

Healey C. G. (1996) Choosing effective colours for data visualization. *Proceedings of the Conference on Visualization '96*, p. 263, IEEE Computer Society Press.

Hearst M. (1994) Context and structure in automated full-text information access, PhD thesis, University of California, Computer Science Division.

Hearst, M. (1995) TileBars: Visualization of term distribution information in full text information access. *Proceedings of the ACM SIGCHI Conference on Human Factors in Computing Systems*, Denver, CO, May 1995, pp. 59–66, ACM Press.

Jokela S., Turpeinen M., and Sulonen R. (2000) Ontology development for flexible content. *Proceedings of the 33rd Hawaii International Conference on System Sciences*, IEEE Computer Society Press.

Mackinlay J. D. and Robertson G. G. (1993) The Document Lens. *Proceedings of the ACM User Interface and Software Technology Conference (UIST '93)*, pp. 101–108, ACM Press.

Mynatt B. T., Leventhal L. M., Instone K., Farhat J., and Rohlman D. S. (1992) Hypertext or book: Which is better for answering questions. *Proceedings of ACM CHI 1992*, ACM Press.

Russell D. M., Stefik M. J., Pirolli P., and Card S. K. (1993) The cost structure of sensemaking. *Conference Proceedings on Human Factors in Computing Systems*, pp. 269–276, ACM Press.

Shneiderman B. (1993) *Designing the user interface: Strategies for effective human–computer interaction.* Addison-Wesley.

Uschold M. (1996) Building ontologies: Towards a unified methodology. *Proceedings of Expert Systems '96, 16th Annual Conference of the British Computer Society Specialist Group on Expert Systems*, Cambridge, 16–18 December, Springer.

Uschold M. and Gruninger M. (1996) Ontologies: Principles, methods and applications. *Knowledge Engineering Review* 11 (2).

Van House N. A. (1995) User needs assessment and evaluation for the UC Berkeley electronic environmental library project. *Digital Libraries '95: The 2nd Conference on the Theory and Practice of Digital Libraries*, June, Austin, TX.

Ware C. (2000) *Information visualization: Perception for design.* Morgan Kaufman.

Weiss-Lijn M., McDonnell J. T., and James L. (2001a) Visualizing document content with metadata to facilitate goal-directed search. *International Symposium of Visualization of the Semantic Web, IV2001*, 25–27 July.

Weiss-Lijn M., McDonnell J. T., and James L. (2001b) A "best-case" evaluation of novel information retrieval applications. *8th European Conference on Information Technology Evaluation*, 17–18 September.

Woodruff A., Gossweiler R., Pitkow J., Chi E. H., and Card S. K. (2000) Enhancing a digital book with a reading recommender. *Proceedings of the CHI 2000*, The Hague, The Netherlands, April 2000, pp. 153–160, ACM Press.

Chapter 9
Web Services: Description, Interfaces and Ontology

Alexander Nakhimovsky and Tom Myers

9.1 Introduction

In this chapter, we compare the Semantic Web and Web Services, in the hope that such a comparison will shed light on each and help us understand the directions of their evolution. Both the Semantic Web and Web Services are young, rapidly changing technologies that overlap in significant ways. A better understanding of how they are similar and where they differ may add clarity to their development and mutual accommodation. If, as we believe is the case, they have complementary strengths and weaknesses, their mutual understanding can be of help to both.

We start with a high-level juxtaposition drawn in broad strokes, unavoidably inaccurate in small detail. Small detail will follow soon thereafter.

9.2 The Semantic Web and Web Services: A Comparison

The Semantic Web and Web Services share a vision. Both would like to see the web as one giant information store operated upon by loosely coupled co-operating applications. Both see XML as the main tool for making multiple pieces of the Web interoperable. A major difference between them is that the Semantic Web thinks of the Web as a repository of knowledge, while Web Services thinks of it as a marketplace. Hence there is more emphasis in the Semantic Web on knowledge representation and management, and more emphasis in Web Services on an actual action (frequently, but not necessarily a commercial transaction) that brings about a change in the world. While the Semantic Web's metaphor for the Web is an encyclopedia, the Web Services' metaphor is a telephone book where you or your agent can find a number to call to obtain a service.

A useful analogy from earlier programming languages and systems would be Prolog vs. C. The Semantic Web would like to see the Web as a Prolog-style database and an inference engine, while Web Services would like to see it as a more traditional information store and a distributed C/Java/C# application. The Semantic Web's roots are in AI: declarative knowledge representation and inference. Web Services' roots are in distributed programming; an introduction to Web Services frequently starts with a brief review of RPC, DCOM, CORBA and

RMI. Sociologically, too, the worlds of the Semantic Web and Web Services are quite different; people working on the Semantic Web frequently come from the "symbolic AI" tradition and bring to the Semantic Web the ideas of knowledge representation, planning and logic programming, while people working on Web Services are mostly professional programmers working for software companies. The Semantic Web worker tries to implement a vision. The Web Service worker has to deliver a product that fills a real or perceived need.

Any comparison between the Semantic Web and Web Services must recognize that Web Services are much closer to the "metal and wire" of the Web than the Semantic Web, with such items as ports, protocol bindings, and patterns of message exchange explicitly represented in software. This may point to a possible synergy; just as C is a level or two closer to the iron than Prolog, and Prolog interpreters can be and have been implemented in C, so it might be useful to think of the Semantic Web as being a level or two above Web Services, composed of meaning units that are built out of Web Services.

Another thing to recognize is that in practical terms, Web Services are way ahead of the Semantic Web and moving ahead faster. Web Services are backed up by huge investments and hundreds if not thousands of developers, while the Semantic Web is backed up by a grant from DARPA, a committee at W3C, and a relatively small group of mostly academic researchers. Web Services are designed so that, with relatively little additional training, currently existing and widespread programming skills can be re-deployed for Web Services programming. By contrast, to create a Semantic Web application, you need relatively exotic programming skills and a background in AI and logic. It does not help that the RDF/XML syntax of the initial RDF Model and Syntax Recommendation is arguably the worst formal notation ever invented.

As a result, Web Services are rapidly creating a set of conditions on the ground that the Semantic Web will have to contend with. It seems likely that the Semantic Web will come into existence within an infrastructure created by Web Services. The strength of the Semantic Web is in its foundations in logic and AI and a rigorous approach to software design. On the other hand, it should be remembered that Prolog never escaped a niche status, and the entire enterprise of symbolic AI has yielded relatively little in terms of working systems and market success.

9.3 Web Services Definition and Description Layers

A Web Service, most generally, is a distributed self-describing web application that uses an XML communication protocol and can be discovered and invoked on the basis of its self-description. More specifically, a Web Service uses

- Simple Object Access Protocol (SOAP) for communication and elements of self-description
- Web Services Description Language (WSDL) for a low-level description of SOAP connectivity and interfaces
- Universal Description, Discovery and Integration language (UDDI) for a higher-level description of functionality.

Although WSDL professes protocol-independence, and defines a SOAP binding as one of several possible bindings, in practice SOAP is firmly entrenched as the best-developed and most important layer. It is also closest to becoming a standard.

9.3.1 Standardization Efforts

In Web Services literature or presentations, one commonly encounters assertions to the effect that Web Services are "based on standards", meaning SOAP, WSDL and UDDI. This is misleading. Of the three specifications, only SOAP has been adopted by W3C as a recognized Activity, and its current status is a Working Draft (WD). (See SOAP, 2001b, 2001c.)

While a WD is by no means a standard, at least it has a very good chance of becoming a Recommendation. (W3C is not a standards body, so its Recommendations are not, strictly speaking, standards, but for all intents and purposes they are, or at least have been until now.) In addition, SOAP activity is wrapped into larger XML Protocol (XMLP) activity that is developing a context for, and extensions of SOAP, such as Security and Quality of Service. (See XMLP, 2001.)

By contrast, WSDL is just a W3C Note, with no commitment to ever making it into an area of activity and establishing a Working Group. (See WSDL, 2001.) The section entitled "Status" says:

> This draft represents the current thinking with regard to descriptions of services within Ariba, IBM and Microsoft... This document is a NOTE made available by the W3C for discussion only. Publication of this Note by W3C indicates no endorsement by W3C or the W3C Team, or any W3C Members. W3C has had no editorial control over the preparation of this Note.

Given these qualifications, it is misleading to call WSDL "a W3C specification". In fact, W3C is one of the movers behind Darpa Agent Modelling Language – Services (DAML-S), which is a possible competitor to WSDL. (See Ankolenkar et al., 2001.) On the other hand, WSDL is deeply embedded in all existing Web Services frameworks including Microsoft's .NET, IBM's Web Services ToolKit (WSTK), and Apache's Axis. (We will return to the frameworks shortly.)

As for UDDI, its only claim to standardhood is that it is supported by a very powerful industry consortium.

9.3.2 The Significance of SOAP

Technically, perhaps the strongest difference between the Semantic Web and Web Services is that Web Services are built on top of their own communications protocol. The significance of a separate, XML-based communications protocol is that it provides a platform-independent medium for describing APIs, specifying meta-level constraints (such as: this service must "understand" such and such a procedure call), and delivering level-specific error codes, as opposed to generic lower-level error codes. On the other hand, a separate protocol with its own rules of engagement between clients and servers creates a danger that Web Services will develop into an alternative Web, a web of SOAP servers and clients that has little or no connection to the HTML/HTTP Web; even the human front-end does not have to be a Web browser at all, and may, in fact, be platform-specific. We will return to this topic after we learn more about SOAP.

9.4 SOAP in Greater Detail

The current version of SOAP is WD 1.2. Compared with version 1.1, the specification is in two parts: the essential SOAP (Part 1; SOAP, 2001b) and SOAP Adjuncts (Part 2; SOAP, 2001c); there is also a Primer in Part 0 (SOAP, 2001a). We concentrate on Part 1, the Messaging Framework.

9.4.1 SOAP Message

Appropriately for a communication protocol, the main concept of SOAP is a *message*. A SOAP message is a one-way transmission from a SOAP sender to a SOAP receiver. However, SOAP messages can be combined to implement various Message Exchange Patterns (MEPs) such as request/response or multicast. SOAP messages can also travel from the message originator to its final destination via intermediaries that can simply pass the message on or process it and emit a modified message or a fault condition. *SOAP node* is a general name for the initial SOAP sender, the ultimate SOAP receiver, or a SOAP intermediary (which is both a SOAP sender and a SOAP receiver). Ultimately, a Web Service is a collection of SOAP nodes.

Within this picture, the main questions addressed by the specification are:

- What is the message structure as an XML document?
- How do the elements of the message correspond to programming objects that are manipulated by SOAP Nodes? (SOAP encoding)
- What is the underlying transport that actually delivers the message?
- What happens to the message along the way and at destination? (Message Exchange Model)
- How does SOAP report its own error conditions (called Faults)?

Our main interest is in message structure, but we briefly comment on the other parts of the specification here and in the context of SOAP examples.

As regards *encoding*, the biggest change between SOAP versions 1.1 and 1.2 is that SOAP encoding has been taken out of the main body of the specification and placed into Part 2, the Adjuncts. The intent is to indicate that it is ultimately up to individual applications and messages to decide on the details of XML encoding and data binding. The encoding used in our examples is the one specified in SOAP 1.1 and SOAP 1.2 Part 2.

As regards the *underlying transport*, all our examples will use HTTP. This means that the SOAP message will travel as the body of an HTTP message, using the HTTP POST method. In principle, SOAP can be used with a variety of protocols; in practice, HTTP is by far the most common, with SMTP a distant second.

The *Message Exchange Model* is mostly concerned with how individual elements of the message are processed at intermediary SOAP nodes along the path from origin to final destination. The processing is controlled by meta-information attached to such elements. The meta-information is expressed as the element's attributes, *actor* and *mustUnderstand*.

Fault elements are for specifying SOAP-level error or status conditions. A fault element must contain a fault code and a message string. Fault codes are qualified names as specified in XML Namespaces; they consist of a namespace URI and a local name. SOAP 1.2 defines a small set of SOAP fault codes covering basic SOAP faults. We will show examples of fault elements in our code.

9.4.2 The Structure of a SOAP Message

A SOAP message is an XML document and as such has an Infoset. (Infoset is a W3C specification that defines the object model of XML documents.) The SOAP specification defines the structure of SOAP messages in Infoset terms rather than in the more traditional way of defining the syntactic structure of the serialized XML document. Since Infoset is relatively recent and less well known that the syntactic notions, we will recast the definition in syntactic terms.

The root element of a SOAP message is *Envelope*, in the SOAP-Envelope namespace (http://www.w3.org/2001/12/soap-envelope). Three other elements are declared in that namespace: *Header*, *Body* and *Fault*. Several attributes are also defined in that namespace, including *encodingStyle* that specifies the SOAP encoding to be used in processing the message.

The Header and Body elements are children of the root, Header optional, Body required. Both Header and Body consist of *blocks*, i.e. children elements in their own namespace(s), with no constraints on their internal structure. The content of the Body, sometimes called the payload, is intended to be processed by the message's final destination. The content of the optional Header may be intended for intermediate nodes, with each Header block targeted individually, as specified in the Message Exchange Model. In general, Header blocks serve for application-specific extensions. We do not use headers in our examples.

9.4.3 Examples of SOAP Messages

Suppose we want to create a very simple Web Service that count the number of times a given pattern occurs within a given string. For instance, if the pattern is *an* and the string is *ananas*, the service will return the integer 2. The action of such a service can be expressed in Java as follows:

Listing 1. Java class for counting patterns in strings
```
public class CountPat{
  public int count(String string,String pat){
     int cnt = 0,pos = string.indexOf(pat);
     while(pos >= 0){
       cnt++;
       pos = string.indexOf(pat,pos+pat.length());
     }
     return cnt;
     }
  }
```

As defined in Listing 1, the service will count only non-overlapping occurrences of the pattern: if the pattern is *aa* and the string is *aaa*, the service will return 1, not 2. To count all occurrences, we would replace the line in boldface with the one below:

```
pos = string.indexOf(pat,pos+1);
```

This is not the most efficient way to search strings for patterns, but we are not
interested in algorithmic efficiency; we are interested in how and where the
difference in the semantics of the service can be expressed. We will return to this
question at the end of the chapter. In the meantime, we note that in either case
the service expects two inputs, both of them strings, and returns an integer.
A SOAP message addressed to such a service would look like this:

Listing 2. SOAP request

```
<?xml version = "1.0" encoding = "UTF-8"?>
<SOAP-ENV:Envelope
    SOAP-ENV:encodingStyle =
      "http://schemas.xmlsoap.org/soap/encoding/"
    xmlns:SOAP-ENV =
      "http://schemas.xmlsoap.org/soap/envelope/"
    xmlns:xsd = "http://www.w3.org/2001/XMLSchema"
    xmlns:xsi =
      "http://www.w3.org/2001/XMLSchema-instance"
  >
    <SOAP-ENV:Body>
      <count>
        <arg0 xsi:type = "xsd:string">
          alphabetaalphagammaalpha
        </arg0>
        <arg1 xsi:type = "xsd:string">
          alph
        </arg1>
      </count>
    </SOAP-ENV:Body>
</SOAP-ENV:Envelope>
```

The root element uses the global *encodingStyle* attribute to specify which
encoding to use. The value of the attribute is a URI that serves as an identifier of
the intended encoding. The encoding specified in our example is the encoding
that is defined in SOAP 1.1 and SOAP 1.2 Part 2. The *encodingStyle* attribute is in
the same namespace as the Envelope and Body elements. In addition to that
namespace (mapped to *SOAP-ENV*), two others are declared, mapped to *xsi* and
xsd. Both come from the XML Schema Recommendation and have to do with
assigning data types to element content of SOAP messages. Our message Body
consists of a single block whose name is the name of the remote procedure to
invoke. The block consists of two elements that are eventually converted to
arguments of the remote procedure call.

As we mentioned, this message will travel from origin to destination over
HTTP, as the body of an HTTP request. The header of the HTTP request looks
like this:

Listing 3. HTTP request whose body is SOAP request of Listing 2

```
POST /axis/CountPat.jws HTTP/1.0
Content-Length: 467
Host: localhost
Content-Type: text/xml; charset=utf-8
SOAPAction: "/count"
```

As you can see, this is standard HTTP, with one new header, SOAPAction, added for SOAP purposes. It specifies the programmatic action to be invoked on the SOAP server in response to the message. The generated HTTP response, containing the SOAP response in its body, is as follows (this time we show the entire HTTP message all together):

Listing 4. HTTP response containing SOAP response as its body

```
HTTP/1.1 200 OK
Content-Type: text/xml; charset=utf-8
Content-Length: 427
Date: Sun, 06 Jan 2002 16:52:50 GMT
Server: Apache Tomcat/4.0.1-b1 (HTTP/1.1 Connector)

<?xml version="1.0" encoding="UTF-8"?>
<SOAP-ENV:Envelope
    SOAP-ENV:encodingStyle=
      "http://schemas.xmlsoap.org/soap/encoding/"
    xmlns:SOAP-ENV=
      "http://schemas.xmlsoap.org/soap/envelope/"
    xmlns:xsd="http://www.w3.org/2001/XMLSchema"
    xmlns:xsi="http://www.w3.org/2001/XMLSchema-
    instance">
    <SOAP-ENV:Body>
      <countResponse>
        <countResult xsi:type="xsd:int">3</countResult>
      </countResponse>
    </SOAP-ENV:Body>
</SOAP-ENV:Envelope>
```

Now we need a SOAP client that is capable of sending out a message as in Listings 3 and 2 and interpreting the response as in Listing 4. Such a client can be constructed within the same framework that is used for deploying the SOAP server, or in a totally different one. In any case, there is a great deal of support for client construction built into the framework. (Just as there is a great deal of support for server construction.) The framework support can be framework-dependent, or it can be based on the framework-independent WSDL description of the service. It is time to look at how SOAP servers and clients are programmed.

9.5 What Is It Like for a Programmer?

It is essential to keep in mind the pragmatic or sociological aspect of Web Services; they are distributed applications consisting of modules that are familiar programming modules: Java/C++/C# classes, COM objects, and so on. All the major players in the "Web Services space" have invested a lot of thought and effort into making Web Services programming easy for a programmer. In particular, a lot of attention has been paid to the question of how familiar software modules within a client/server framework can become a SOAP server and how one generates a SOAP client for it. The goal is to automate as much of this process as possible. We present the tools of the open-source Apache Axis project (3d alpha release at the time of writing, see Axis, 2001). Comparable facilities are available within IBM's Web Services Development Toolkit (WSTK; see WSTK, 2000) and Microsoft's .NET framework (see MS .NET, 2001). Our first task is to describe the directory structure of an Axis installation.

9.5.1 Axis SOAP Server and Tomcat Servlet Engine

A SOAP server can be implemented as a J2EE Web Application. In other words, a Web Service can be implemented as a Java servlet or a JavaServer Page (JSP). To run servlets and JSPs, one needs a servlet/JSP engine attached to a Web server. If the incoming HTTP request is addressed to a servlet or JSP, the server will redirect it to the servlet/JSP engine that will generate a response to be sent to the client.

Apache Tomcat is a Web server and a servlet/JSP engine rolled into one piece of software. (It can also be attached as a servlet/JSP engine to a different server.) By default, the Tomcat server runs on port 8080. The directory in which Tomcat is installed (call it TOMCAT_HOME) has a subdirectory called webapps. This directory is the server root of the Tomcat web server. It is in this directory that we install Axis, in a directory called axis. Every Web Service (or SOAP server) run by Axis will be a subdirectory of **TOMCAT_HOME/webapps/axis**. If you look back in Listing 3, the first line specifies /axis/CountPat.jws as the destination of the SOAP message. The extension .jws stands for "Java Web Service". So how does the Java code of Listing 1, in file **CountPat.java** become a SOAP server in file **CountPat.jws**?

9.5.2 From Java Class to SOAP Server

There are three ways to convert a Java class into a SOAP server within the Axis framework. The simplest but least flexible one goes like this:

- Step 1. Make a copy of CountPat.java and rename it as CountPat.jws.
- Step 2. Place CountPat.jws into TOMCAT_HOME/webapps/axis/ directory.
- Step 3. There is no step 3, you are done.

A more flexible and powerful way of configuring a Web Service within Axis is by using an XML file in the Axis Web Services Deployment Descriptor (WSDD) format. The details of WSDD are outside the scope of this chapter but can be found in the Axis User Guide.

The third way of constructing a Web Service from a Java class is via the intermediate stage of a WSDL description of the service. We will discuss WSDL shortly.

9.5.3 Constructing a SOAP Client

To invoke the service deployed as described in the preceding section, we need to send an HTTP request whose header is Listing 3 and body is the SOAP message in Listing 2. Within Axis, we construct a client using classes within the org.apache.axis.client package. Here is a client for the CountPat service, implemented as a JSP. The punchline is the call of the invoke( ) method of the ServiceClient class that invokes the service. The method takes three arguments: the namespace of the method element (the empty string in our case), the local name of the method and its arguments as an array of Objects:

Listing 5. JSP SOAP Client for the CountPat Service

```
<%
String method = request.getParameter("method");
String arg1 = request.getParameter("arg1");
String arg2 = request.getParameter("arg2");
String endpoint =
"http://localhost:8080/axis/CountPat.jws";
org.apache.axis.client.ServiceClient client =
    new org.apache.axis.client.ServiceClient(endpoint);
  try {
      Object[] args = new Object [] { arg1, arg2 };
      Object obResult = client.invoke("",method,args);
  %>
  <html><body><h3></h3>
    The result is: <%= obResult.toString() %>
  </h3></body></html></h3>
  <%
    }catch(Exception ex){/* appropriate message */}
%>
```

The client is itself a Web application invoked from an HTML form with three input fields for the method name and its two parameters. The entire configuration of software is shown in Figure 9.1.

In the configuration of Figure 9.1, the GUI and the SOAP client do not have to be on separate machines. A SOAP client is a fairly lightweight piece of software that can easily be outfitted with a GUI of its own, such as a WindowsForm of the .NET framework. When this happens, the web of distributed SOAP applications may become rather tenuously connected to the HTTP/HTML Web of HTML documents.

While the code of our SOAP client is quite transparent and easy to compose, its creation, just as the creation of the SOAP server, can be further automated by first obtaining the WSDL description of the service. This is the subject of the next section.

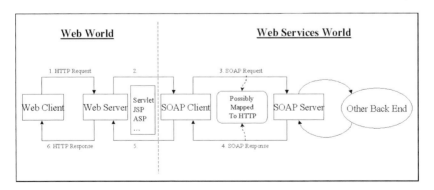

Figure 9.1   Software configuration for running a Web Service.

9.6 WSDL

WSDL is an XML language for describing Web Services. It is, in effect, an interface definition language for SOAP. Its design goals, from the beginning, included automation tasks, such as:

- Generate a WSDL description of a service from its implementation in a programming language.
- Generate a SOAP service from its WSDL description.
- In the case of request-response services, generate a client from the WSDL description of the server.

The Web Services toolkits and frameworks from Microsoft, IBM and Apache all implement these capabilities. We will continue using Axis for our examples. As we illustrate the structure of a WSDL document with samples of generated code, keep in mind that the URI of our CountPat service is **http://localhost:8080/axis/ CountPat.jws**, the name of the class is CountPat, and the name of the operation supported by the service is count. While the document structure is, of course, toolkit-independent, some of the naming conventions are those of Axis.

9.6.1 WSDL Document Structure and Examples

WSDL is primarily designed to describe exchange of typed messages between two endpoints: in effect, remote procedure calls. A partial list of elements defined in WSDL is shown below, in the order of appearance, with examples from generated code.

The root element is `definitions`. It declares several namespaces, including a generated namespace for service-specific elements, which is also the target namespace:

Listing 6. The root element and namespaces
```
<definitions
  targetNamespace = "http://localhost:8080/axis/
  CountPat.jws"
  xmlns = "http://schemas.xmlsoap.org/wsdl/"
  xmlns:serviceNS = "http://localhost:8080/axis/
  CountPat.jws"
  xmlns:soap = "http://schemas.xmlsoap.org/wsdl/
  soap/"
  xmlns:xsd = "http://www.w3.org/2001/XMLSchema">
```

Elements of type `message` describe requests and responses. In our example, we have:

Listing 7. Message elements
```
<message name = "countResponse">
    <part name = "countResult" type = "xsd:int"/>
  </message>
  <message name = "countRequest">
    <part name = "arg0" type = "xsd:string"/>
```

```
    <part name = "arg1" type = "xsd:string"/>
  </message>
```

As you can see, message elements have children parts that describe the data types of arguments and returned values. The data types are those of XML Schema. If application-specific data types are defined, a `types` element would precede message elements.

Elements of type `operation` describe operations supported by the message. They appear grouped within a port type element. Our example supports a single operation:

Listing 8. Port type and operations

```
    <portType name = "CountPatPortType">
      <operation name = "count">
        <input message = "serviceNS:countRequest"/>
        <output message = "serviceNS:countResponse"/>
      </operation>
    </portType>
```

Next, a `binding` element specifies the concrete protocol (SOAP) and provides protocol-specific details about the operation(s) supported by the service:

Listing 9. Binding to SOAP

```
    <binding
        name = "CountPatSoapBinding"
        type = "serviceNS:CountPatPortType">
      <soap:binding
          style = "rpc"
          transport = "http://schemas.xmlsoap.org/soap/
          http"/>
      <operation name = "count">
        <soap:operation soapAction = "" style = "rpc"/>
        <input>
          <soap:body
            encodingStyle =
              "http://schemas.xmlsoap.org/soap/encoding/"
            namespace = "" use = "encoded"/>
        </input>
        <output>
          <!-- identical to input -->
        </output>
      </operation>
    </binding>
```

Finally, `port` is a single endpoint defined as a combination of a binding and a network address, and `service` is a collection of related endpoints.

Listing 10. Service and port(s)

```
    <service name = "CountPat">
      <port
          binding = "serviceNS:CountPatSoapBinding"
          name = "CountPatPort">
        <soap:address
```

```
        location=
          "http://localhost:8080/axis/CountPat.jws"/>
    </port>
    </service>
  </definitions>
```

To obtain its automatically generated WSDL description we add the query string ?wsdl to the service URI: **http://localhost:8080/axis/CountPat.jws?wsdl**. The output, in outline and with references to Listings 6–10, is in Listing 11:

Listing 11. WSDL description of CountPat service

```
  <?xml version="1.0" encoding="UTF-8"?>
  <definitions
    namespace declarations see Listing 6
  >
    <message name="countResponse">...</message>
    <message name="countRequest">...</message>
    see Listing 7

    <portType name="CountPatPortType">...</portType>
    see Listing 8

    <binding name="..." type="...">
    see Listing 9

    </binding>
    <service name="CountPat">
    see Listing 10

    </service>
  </definitions>
```

9.6.2 Options and Alternatives

The generated WSDL of Listings 6–11 shows a WSDL description of a service that implements a remote procedure call using SOAP as the protocol and XML Schema data types for the call signature. These are not the only options, as the WSDL specification makes clear:

● WSDL can describe message exchange patterns other than remote procedure call.
● In addition to SOAP, two other protocols are provided for, plain HTTP and MIME.
● Data type libraries other than XML Schema Part 2 can be used.

However, the configuration of our example is by far the most common and fits the specification most naturally.

9.6.3 What Can One Do with WSDL?

Axis and other toolkits provide tools for automatic code generation from WSDL descriptions. In Axis, the tools are in the Wsdl2java class within the org.apache.axis.wsdl package. Here is a command line to build a stub for the service client:

```
java -cp wsdl4j.jar;axis.jar;clutil.jar;C:\cp\xerces.jar
    org.apache.axis.wsdl.Wsdl2java
     -verbose
    http://localhost:8080/axis/CountPat.jws?wsdl
```

This instructs the Java Virtual Machine to run Wsdl2java on our WSDL, in verbose mode, using several libraries including Xerces XML parser. The output (in verbose mode) is:

```
Parsing XML File:
http://localhost:8080/axis/CountPat.jws?wsdl
Generating portType interface: CountPatPortType.java
Generating client-side stub: CountPatSoapBindingStub.java
Generating service class: CountPat.java
```

The three Java files are indeed generated and the "client-side stub" contains a definition of the public count( ) method that takes two strings and returns an integer. The method, in turn, calls the invoke( ) method to invoke the service. Of course, the generated stub does not provide any mechanism for passing parameters and it has no idea what you would like to do with the returned result, but it can serve as a useful starting point. The WSDL description of a Web Service implemented in Java (and perhaps automatically generated from a Java class) can also be used to generate a SOAP client on a .NET platform. Finally, WSDL can be used to generate a starting point for SOAP servers, also in any framework, on either Java or .NET platform. In Axis, you would simply insert the – skeleton flag next to – verbose.

We can conclude that WSDL is a very useful XML language for describing SOAP-based Web Services and automating several aspects of Web Services programming. We can also conclude that it contains no facilities for describing the intended semantics of the service.

9.7 UDDI

UDDI, like WSDL, is a layer of description built on top of SOAP. While WSDL is an automation tool that provides a low-level XML description of SOAP-based services, UDDI is intended for more high-level tasks: service discovery and integration. At the centre of UDDI is the notion of a registry that would provide another XML description of a service, based on business semantics. The UDDI specification does not mention WSDL at all, but within the UDDI description of a service it provides an element, tModel, for a technical specification of the service interfaces and bindings. This is where WSDL fits into the UDDI view of the world; a "good practices" paper, Curbera et al. (2001), provides specific suggestions on how to use WSDL for tModel descriptions.

9.7.1 Components of a UDDI Entry

A UDDI entry describes a *business entity*, such as a firm or a non-profit organization. Each business entity can support a number of *business services*. Each service can be offered in a variety of binding templates that describe where to find a particular implementation of the service and how to connect to it. Each binding template contains a reference to a *tModel*, the technical description of the service's interface.

The XML Schema that defines UDDI entry (UDDI v2 Schema, 2001) specifies the following containments:

- A *businessEntity* element contains a *businessServices* element which in turn contains any number of *businessService* elements.
- A *businessService* element contains a *bindingTemplates* element that contains any number of *bindingTemplate* elements.
- Each *bindingTemplate* contains a *tModelInstanceDetails* that contains *tModel* elements each of which contains an *overviewDoc* element that contains an *overviewURL*. This is where a reference to a WSDL file would be inserted.

In addition to these other substantive elements, most UDDI elements have a key for easy retrieval and a name for easy reference.

9.7.2 UDDI and WSDL

The way WSDL descriptions find their way into UDDI entries can be summarized as follows (see Curbera et al., 2001 for more details):

- Industry groups define a set of service types, and describe them with one or more WSDL documents. The WSDL service interface definitions are then registered as UDDI tModels; the *overviewDoc* field in each new tModel points to the corresponding WSDL document.
- Programmers will build services that conform to the industry standard service definitions. In essence, they retrieve the WSDL definitions using the URL in the *overviewDoc* field and construct services on the basis of WSDL as described in the preceding section.
- The new service is entered into the UDDI registry as a *businessService* element within a *businessEntity*. Typically, some kind of a deployment descriptor can be generated at the same time. Much of this work can and will be automated by UDDI tools.

Our next question is: "Where in this process is the semantics of a Web Service defined?" As we have seen, WSDL has nothing to say about semantics. UDDI provides, on top of WSDL, three service taxonomies:

- services classified by industry, using the North American Industry Classification System (NAICS; see http://www.ntis.gov/product/naics.htm)
- services classified by product or service, using the Universal Standard Products and Services Classification (UNSPSC; see http://eccma.org/unspsc/)
- services classified by location, using ISO 3166 (see http://www.din.de/gremien/nas/nabd/iso3166ma/)

Additional taxonomies, such as those by Yahoo or Google, can be registered with UDDI and used to classify services. These taxonomic hierarchies constitute a simple semantic characterization of UDDI-registered services. However, as of UDDI 2.0, there are no inference rules associated with them, nor is there an agreed syntax for writing down such rules for use by automatic agents. This is

where Semantic Web initiatives, especially Darpa Agent Modelling Language –
Services (DAML-S), may (or may not) find an important role to play.

9.7.3 Semantic and Ontological Needs

Ankolenkar et al. (2001, p. 429) define DAML-S as follows:

> DAML-S is an attempt to provide an ontology, within the framework of the DARPA
> Agent Markup Language, for describing Web services. It will enable users and
> software agents to automatically discover, invoke, compose, and monitor Web
> resources offering services, under specified constraints. We have released an initial
> version of DAML-S. It can be found at the URL: http://www.daml.org/services/
> daml-s.

What does "to provide an ontology ... for describing Web services" mean? The
word "ontology" has been much used lately, with different intended meanings. In
this case, the authors mean providing a language such that we can logically prove
statements about its lexical items (which may include names of functions and
relations). Such languages usually can describe both individual facts and general
rules, and the language processor (also known as an *inference engine*) would
know how to combine facts and rules to infer new facts. For instance, consider
this formal notation:

Listing 12. A logical notation
```
father(abraham,isaac); // Abraham is the father of Isaac
father(isaac,esau); // Isaac is the father of Esau
father(X,Y),father(Y,Z):-grandfather(X,Z)
// X is the father of Y and Y is the father of Z
// implies X is grandfather of Z
```

On the basis of this information, an inference engine would be able to infer (and
add to the database of facts) the fact that Abraham is the grandfather of Esau. In
a similar fashion, if two web services, s1 and s2, offer the same widget w for
prices p1 and p2 respectively, and p1 < p2, an inference engine would infer
that, on some scale of preference, service s1 is preferable to s2.

This information can, of course, be expressed by a piece of code in a program
that, for instance, subtracts the price, multiplied by a weight factor, from the
preference metric so that lower price gets higher preference:

```
s1.preference - = s1.price(w)*PRICE_FACTOR;
```

Voluminous discussions of declarative vs. procedural semantics, both within AI
and within the theory of programming languages, have documented why it is in
many respects better to express a rule as a declarative statement in a specially
designed language than as a line of code in a program. (See, e.g., Date, 2000.)
Many years of practice have also demonstrated that it is very difficult to design
ontologies that are expressive enough to describe non-trivial programming tasks.
Even the simple distinction between counting overlapping vs. non-overlapping
patterns in our CountPat service would take a substantial amount of effort to
express in a rigorous way, using some algebraic notation. Note that CountPat is a
very simple example of a very simple type of Web Service that involves a single
request-response in which only integers and strings are exchanged.

Can DAML-S indeed deliver a language for describing Web services such that it will be possible for automatic agents to reason about them in reliably rigorous ways? The amount of work that would be required is staggering and the track record of similar endeavours is not very encouraging. However, as technical committees sit down to formulate industry-specific languages for describing UDDI web service entries, they must be aware of the semantic distinctions that those languages have to express. To the extent that those languages are capable of expressing those distinctions, the world of Web Services will move closer to the vision of the Semantic Web.

9.8 References

Ankolenkar, Anupriya, Mark Burstein, Jerry R. Hobbs, Ora Lassila, David L. Martin, Sheila A. McIlraith, Srini Narayanan, Massimo Paolucci, Terry Payne, Katia Sycara and Honglei Zeng (2001). "DAML-S: A semantic markup language for web services" In *Proceedings of SWWS' 01: The First Semantic Web Working Symposium*. Available: http://www.semanticweb.org/SWWS/program/full/SWWSProceedings.pdf
Axis (2001). *Axis User Guide*. Available: http://xml.apache.org/axis/index.html
Curbera, Francisco, David Ehnebuske and Dan Rogers (2001). *Using WSDL in a UDDI Registry 1.06*. Available: http://www.uddi.org/pubs/wsdlbestpractices-V1.06-Open-20011130.pdf
Date, C.J. (2000). *What Not How: The Business Rules Approach to Application Development*. Reading, MA: Addison-Wesley.
MS .NET (2001). *Microsoft .NET Development*. Available: http://msdn.microsoft.com/library/default.asp?url = /nhp/Default.asp?contentid = 28000519
SOAP (2001a). *SOAP Version 1.2 Part 0: Primer*. Available: http://www.w3.org/TR/soap12-part0/
SOAP (2001b). *SOAP Version 1.2 Part 1: Messaging Framework*. Available: http://www.w3.org/TR/soap12-part1/
SOAP (2001c). *SOAP Version 1.2 Part 2: Adjuncts*. Available: http://www.w3.org/TR/soap12-part2/
UDDI v2 Schema (2001). Available: http://www.uddi.org/schema/uddi_v2.xsd
WSTK (2000). *IBM Web Services Toolkit*. Available: http://www.alphaworks.ibm.com/tech/webservicestoolkit/
WSDL (2001). *Web Services Description Language (WSDL) 1.1*. Available: http://www.w3.org/TR/wsdl/
XMLP (2001). *XML Protocol Working Group*. Available: http://www.w3.org/TR/2001/WD-xmlp-reqs-20010319/

Chapter 10
Recommender Systems for the Web

Joseph A. Konstan and John T. Riedl

10.1 Introduction

As the web rapidly evolved into an immense repository of content, human users discovered that they could no longer effectively identify the content of most interest to them. Several approaches developed for improving our ability to find content. Syntactic search engines helped index and rapidly scan millions of pages for keywords, but we quickly learned that the amount of content with matching keywords was still too high. Semantic annotation helps assist automated (or computer-assisted) processing of content to better identify the real contents of pages. A Semantic web would help people differentiate between articles on "china" plates and articles about "China" the country. Recommender systems tried a different approach – relying on the collected efforts of a community of users to assess the quality and importance of contents. For example, a web page recommender may identify that a particular page is popular overall, or better yet, popular among people with tastes like yours.

Recommender systems are generally independent of syntactic and semantic approaches. Hence, recommenders are often combined with other technologies. For example, the search engine Google (www.google.com) combines syntactic indexing with a non-personalized recommender (the PageRank algorithm) that assigns higher value to pages that are linked to by high-value pages. Similarly, most recommender system interfaces allow users to first use search techniques to narrow down the set of candidates being evaluated.

The term "recommender systems" was first coined at a workshop in 1996, and has been used imprecisely and inconsistently in published work. For this chapter, we limit ourselves to discussing systems that have two key properties: (1) they incorporate the experiences or opinions of a community, and (2) they produce for the user a mapping of scores to items, a set of recommended items, a ranking of items, or a combination of these three. We further focus on personalized recommenders – those that produce different recommendations for different users – and automated recommenders – those that do not require explicit actions to send or receive recommendations. These are the recommender systems that have been most prominent and successful in industrial applications (Schafer et al., 2001).

This chapter provides a survey of research on recommender systems, focusing on recommenders that can be applied to the Web. While reflecting on research that was largely independent of the Semantic Web, it looks at how recommenders and the Semantic Web can be integrated to provide better information sources for users. Finally, it reviews a number of user interface issues related to recommenders on the Web.

10.2 The Beginning of Collaborative Filtering

As content bases grew from mostly "official" content, such as libraries and corporate document sets, to "informal" content such as discussion lists and e-mail archives, users began to experience a new type of overload. Pure content-based techniques such as information retrieval and information filtering were no longer adequate to help users find the documents they wanted. Keyword-based representations could do an adequate job of describing the topic of documents, but could do little to help users understand the nature or quality of those documents. Hence, a scholarly report on economic conditions in Singapore could be confused with a shallow message by a recent visitor who speculates that "the economy is strong – after all, I paid over $12 for a hotel breakfast!" In the early 1990s there seemed to be two possible solutions to this new challenge: (1) wait for improvements in artificial intelligence that would allow better automated classification of documents, or (2) bring human judgement into the loop. Sadly, the AI challenges involved are still formidable, but fortunately human judgement has proved valuable and relatively easy to incorporate into semi-automated systems.

The *Tapestry* system, developed at Xerox PARC, took the first step in this direction by incorporating user actions and opinions into a message database and search system (Goldberg et al., 1992). Tapestry stored the contents of messages, along with metadata about authors, readers, and responders. It also allowed any user to store annotations about messages, such as "useful survey" or "Phil should see this!" Tapestry users could form queries that combined basic textual information (e.g. contains the phrase "recommender systems") with semantic metadata queries (e.g. written by John OR replied to by Joe) and annotation queries (e.g. marked as "excellent" by Chris). This model has become known as *pull-active collaborative filtering*, because it is the responsibility of the user who desires recommendations to actively pull the recommendations out of the database.

Tapestry predates the Web, let alone the Semantic Web, but it carries several important lessons. First, there is a great deal of information to be gained from even simple semantic mark-up. Being able to select pages based on authors, modification dates, and other commonly available fields makes it easier for users to find the pages they want. Second, usage patterns from other users can be valuable, especially if those users are trusted. Pull-active collaborative filtering requires a community of people who know each other well enough to decide which opinions matter; I need to know that Chris's "excellent" means something, while Jean's may not. Finally, Tapestry reminds us that after a certain point, it becomes more effective to add deep (in this case human) semantic annotations, rather than wait for the technology to improve automated syntactic and surface semantic processing.

Soon after the emergence of Tapestry, other researchers began to recognize the potential for exploiting the human "information hubs" that seem to naturally occur within organizations. Maltz and Ehrlich (1995) developed a *push-active collaborative filtering* recommender system that made it easy for a person reading a document to push that document on to others in the organization who should see it. This type of push-recommender role has become popular, with many people today serving as "joke hubs" who receive jokes from all over and forward them to those they believe would appreciate them (though often with far less discriminating thought than was envisioned).

Tacit Corporation's KnowledgeMail (www.tacit.com) extends these ideas into a broader knowledge-management system. The system combines traditional information filtering with a push-distribution interface and query system to find experts. The system builds private profiles of each user's interests based on keyword analysis of their mail usage. Users can then choose which parts of their profile to make public (Figure 10.1). The push-distribution interface allows the sender of a message to ask the system to suggest recipients based on interest. In addition, users can seek expertise by asking the system to contact experts on the topic of a particular message. This hybrid of content and manual collaborative filtering can help an organization be more efficient in distributing information to those who need it without overwhelming everyone with everything.

So far, push-active recommenders lack the rich semantic annotation promised in the Semantic Web. There is great potential for improvement of these systems if

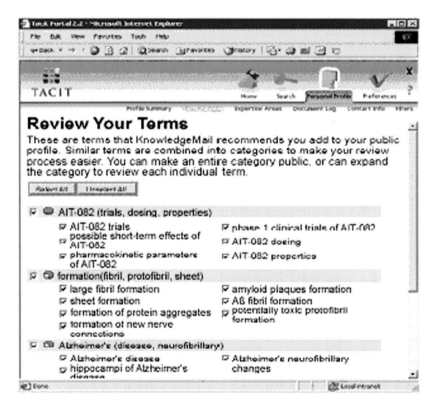

Figure 10.1 Tacit's KnowledgeMail provides an interface through which users make parts of their private profiles public. Other users can then push content to these users based on the profiles.

semantic tagging could be included – but only if it is automated. For example, if automated tagging could identify business-related semantic entities such as competitors, markets, products, etc., messages could almost certainly be routed more automatically, and profiles could be structured more sensibly and compactly.

10.3 Automated Collaborative Filtering

A limitation of active collaborative filtering systems is that they require a community of people who know each other. Pull-active systems require that the user know whose opinions to trust; push-active systems require that the user know to whom particular content may be interesting. Automated collaborative filtering (ACF) systems relieve users of this burden by using a database of historical user opinions to automatically match each individual to others with similar opinions. Another advantage of ACF systems is the ability for users to participate using a pseudonym, and therefore without revealing their true identity.

Intuitively, ACF systems follow a process of gathering ratings from users, computing the correlations between pairs of users to identify a user's "neighbours" in taste space, and combining the ratings of those neighbours to make recommendations. More formally, the early ACF systems – GroupLens (Resnick et al., 1994), Ringo (Shardanand and Maes, 1995), and Video Recommender (Hill et al., 1995) – all used variants of a weighted k-nearest neighbour prediction algorithm.

Later algorithm research has refined the basic algorithm (Herlocker et al., 1999), extended the algorithm to correlate items-to-items (which can be helpful when there are many more users than items; Sarwar et al., 2001), and incorporated a variety of different algorithmic approaches, including Bayesian networks (Breese et al., 1998), horting (Wolf et al., 1999), and dimensionality reduction through singular value decomposition (Sarwar et al., 2000). Algorithmic research continues, with an important focus being designing algorithms that support specific interfaces or unusual data sets.

Interfaces for recommender systems attempt to visually present recommendations in a manner useful to users.

The GroupLens recommender system (Resnick et al., 1994; Konstan et al., 1997) used a very explicit interface where ratings were entered manually by keystroke or button, and ratings were displayed numerically or graphically (Figure 10.2). Improvements to this type of interface have taken two forms: (1) less visible interfaces such as the implicit ratings discussed below and the use of subtle suggestions (e.g. product placement) in place of explicit predictions and identified recommendations, and (2) more information-intensive interfaces, which have generally been used to display additional data to help users make decisions, such as Ringo's community interaction interfaces and the explanations interfaces presented below.

Commercial users of recommender systems may classify interfaces according to the types of recommendations made. *Predictions* are forecasts of how much a user will like an item, and can be used in response to queries, as annotations to be used while browsing, or in combination with other techniques. *Suggestions* are lists of items, or individual items, presented to a user as recommended, often these are associated with the top levels of a site or a personalized "my site" page.

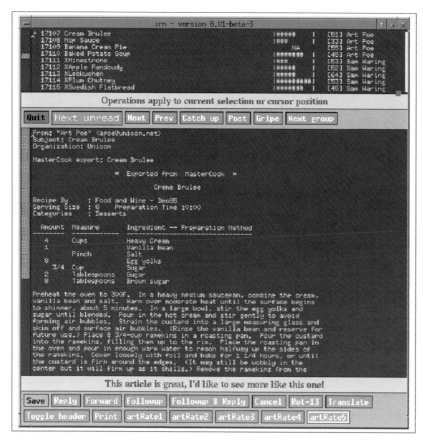

Figure 10.2   A modified Xrn news reader. The GroupLens project added article predictions (lines of ### on the top right) and article rating buttons (bottom).

Item-associated recommendations are displayed in conjunction with specific items, usually based on evidence that those who liked or purchased the item being viewed also liked the recommended ones. Finally, *organic* interfaces often remove the evidence of the recommendation, making the site simply appear natural, yet personalized. For example, a custom web-based newspaper may rearrange stories to place ones with high predicted interest at the front (Bharat et al., 1998).

The basic approach of automated collaborative filtering has been developed quite apart from the semantic tagging and analysis that is emerging in the Web. Indeed, one of the goals of early collaborative filtering was to be "content-neutral", and the early ACF software was completely ignorant of all content attributes. Later work has shown that this approach was too pure; humans care about content, and both their ratings and their usage of recommender systems can be content-specific. Accordingly, later systems, including commercial systems, support the definition of content attributes that can be used both to partition the space of items (to define subspaces with better correlations among users) and to support interfaces that allow users to overlay content and quality questions. A simple example of this approach is found in MovieLens, which allows users to receive recommendations for movies by genre and date.

Looking forward, however, there are areas of synergy between automated collaborative filtering and the Semantic Web. First, semantically tagged content can be better classified, and ratings of it can be better analysed to build models of user interest. Second, user opinions *are* semantic evaluations of content; they can be processed to supplement other techniques for semantic analysis. For example, if a semantic tagger cannot tell whether a particular web page refers to the old New York Giants baseball team, or the New York Giants football team, perhaps because the content is mostly in the overlap between the two, human ratings could well disambiguate the reference. Finally, automated collaborative filtering is still useful in a Semantic web, and may add more value to users when a topic is already well-established.

An interesting example of such overlap occurs in the Platform for Internet Content Selection (PICS) (Resnick and Miller, 1996). PICS was designed to provide a standard interface through which web browsers could access rating bureaus, and through which rating bureaus could provide page ratings for their subscribers. The idea was to unify the wide range of content rating and filtering services that were emerging with a standard interface, so that those who wanted to filter out pornography or immorality could do so, and so that others who might want to rate pages on other criteria (including automated collaborative filtering) could set up such rating bureaus. Though the rapid explosion and pace of the Web dissuaded many would-be ratings services, today we can think of PICS annotations as yet another source of semantic annotations for web pages and links. Indeed, a Semantic Web browser today may choose to consult the filtering services that identify content inappropriate for minors so that they can alter the display of a page (by omitting such links or obscuring inappropriate images, for example).

10.4 Enhancing Collaborative Filtering with Semantics

Content, and in particular semantic content, can be used to address two of the major problems facing collaborative filtering recommender systems: the start-up problem and the problem of changing moods. This section explores three different approaches to using content within ACF recommender systems.

10.4.1 New Users and New Items

One opportunity to improve collaborative filtering systems is during the start-up process for new users or new items. Collaborative filtering systems cannot recommend items that have never been rated by any user because they have no data on which to base a recommendation. Similarly, collaborative filtering systems offer little value to new users who have not yet rated items. The Semantic Web can help these users find items of interest immediately, according to their past interest profile. For instance, a user navigating to a new site might be recommended items that are labelled the same as items she has liked on other sites she has visited. Over time, the recommendations could be tuned based on the user's specific interactions with the new site in addition to the Semantic Web data. Incorporating both types of recommendations in the same interface would enable users to smoothly switch from startup situations to long-term personalization relationships with Web sites.

Semantic web information can be used in other ways to improve the performance of collaborative filtering on Web sites. One idea is to use the Semantic Web categories to provide a partitioning of the information on a Web site into categories that should be separately recommended. Experience with collaborative filtering has shown that recommendations made based on data from closely related items are more accurate than recommendations made across broad categories. For instance, if a Web site has medical data on both strength training and cardiovascular fitness, recommendations of content may be more valuable if they are within those categories rather than across categories.

Alternately, collaborative filtering can be used to identify potential areas for improvement within the Semantic Web labelling for a Web site. For instance, the collaborative filtering engine might point out areas of the site that are rated very similarly though they are far apart in the Semantic Web hierarchy. These differences may point out areas in which the Semantic Web labelling differs from the way users look at data on the site – and may provide an opportunity to improve the usability of the site.

Another possible type of convergence between collaborative filtering and the Semantic Web is the use of collaborative filtering to choose among several possible labellings for a Web site. As the Semantic Web spreads, there are likely to be competing alternatives for labelling popular sites. A new visitor to one of those sites may use collaborative filtering to choose the most useful of the labellings for her.

10.4.2 Integrated Content/Collaborative Filtering Solutions

Combining the Semantic Web and collaborative filtering to solve the startup problem is related to a general approach to collaborative filtering problems in which classical content filtering is combined with collaborative filtering to produce better recommendations. Pure collaborative filtering is impractical in many domains because of the rate of new items (that arrive unrated) and because of the high sparsity (and high desired sparsity) of the domain. Domains where items are created frequently but have a short useful lifespan are particularly problematic, limiting the effectiveness of recommender systems for news, live discussions, and live or scheduled entertainment. Several researchers are examining approaches to better integrate content filtering with collaborative filtering to take better advantage of the strengths of each.

Filterbots are one such example. The GroupLens Research group completed two different studies of automated filtering agents. Sarwar et al. (1998) found that simple ratings agents for Usenet news articles correlated with some users, increasing the quality and coverage of their predicted ratings. These agents used very basic text-analysis techniques, looking at the length of the articles, the percentage of new content, and the quality of spelling within the new content. Results showed that different newsgroups and users benefited from different agents, but that overall the agents could be used to improve the recommender system.

Good et al. (1999) extended this work by testing a variety of personally trained movie-rating agents (as well as non-personalized ones). The agents were trained using rule-induction systems, TFIDF information filtering systems, and basic linear regression; they used a variety of data including genre information, cast lists, and descriptive keywords. In experiments using data from a small user community (50 users), the best agents outperformed collaborative filtering using users, but the combination of users and agents in a collaborative filtering system outperformed all other combinations. Later results suggest that as communities get larger, they reach a cut-off point at which agents stop adding much value.

Other examples include P-Tango, Claypool et al.'s (1999) online newspaper project and Baudisch's (1998) TV-Scout system. P-Tango creates a personalized newspaper for each user by combining collaborative filtering with user-selected categories and keywords. P-Tango is able to provide better recommendations for users by combining the two techniques than with either technique separately. Figure 10.3 shows the P-Tango front page for an established user.

Fab takes a very different approach to the same goal of combining content and collaborative filtering (Balabonovic and Shoham, 1997). In Fab, user profiles are created using classical content filtering techniques. Distances between neighbours are computed directly on the content-based profiles, rather than on user ratings vectors. These distances are then used by a collaborative filtering algorithm to select neighbours and make predictions in more or less the usual way.

Linton et al.'s (2000) Organization-Wide Learning (OWL) system uses semantic information in a different way. The system observes usage of word-processing software and delivers personalized advice about commands that the user might benefit from learning. Since word processing commands have heavy overlap, the system includes a semantic model of the commands. Hence, when making recommendations, the system consults both normal use of that command and the user's use of alternatives.

Figure 10.3 The Tango personalized newspaper combines collaborative and content-based filtering. It provides an appealing rating scale on the right.

All of these techniques can also be applied to the Semantic Web. Filterbots have been proposed as automatic semantic labelling agents for Web sites. The information in the Semantic Web on a site can be used to provide content hierarchies that can be used by systems like P-Tango that combine collaborative and content filtering. The Fab approach suggests that neighbourhoods can be selected based on other types of data than ratings, such as Semantic Web labels a user tends to prefer. The OWL approach can be used to incorporate semantic understanding of the structure of a Web site, such as by recognizing tags that identify alternative presentations of similar content. The Semantic Web may prove a platform for bringing together content and collaborative techniques, improving value to users.

10.4.3 Situational Recommenders

Collaborative filtering recommenders usually work to find the best recommendations according to a user's complete history of interactions with a Web site. This is, after all, one of their benefits; they learn what you want based on what you've done in the past. In many cases, though, a recommendation that is based on a less complete history, but that is more appropriate to a particular task, is preferred. For instance, a visitor to a medical Web site might be a long-standing visitor to the site who usually reads expert information about a chronic disease her daughter has been suffering from for years. However, on this particular visit she might be looking for information about a disease her mother has just been diagnosed with. In this case, she does not want the site to steer her towards the chronic disease she usually reads about, and she also does not want to see the expert information she usually reads. Instead, she wants to focus on a new disease, and wants to be treated as a novice. A situational recommender might give her the tools she needs to specify her short-term interest in contrast to her long-term profile.

MetaLens is an example of one approach to a situational recommender (Schafer, 2001). MetaLens is an extension of our MovieLens framework in which users can specify attributes of the show they want to go to, including its cost, distance to the theatre, show times, appropriateness for children, and many other attributes. Figure 10.4 shows a sample MetaLens screen shot of an experiment we did in which users were given specific instructions about a particular situation in which they might need recommendations. The users could use MetaLens controls to select the movies that were recommended to them.

Another situational recommender we have studied in the context of MovieLens enables users to create a set of profiles based on groups of movies (Herlocker and Konstan, 2001). Each profile is a group of movies that have something in common to the user. For instance, one such profile might be "Intelligent Spy Flicks". When the user asks for recommendations, the situational recommender looks for movies that are closely related to those in the group, and that are appropriate according to his long-term interest profile.

Situational recommenders like these would benefit from the Semantic Web. The semantic hierarchy on a Web site could serve as information that would be used by a situational recommender to create recommendations appropriate to a particular user at a particular time. For instance, the labels on content at the medical Web site might be used to select content appropriate to the user's newly

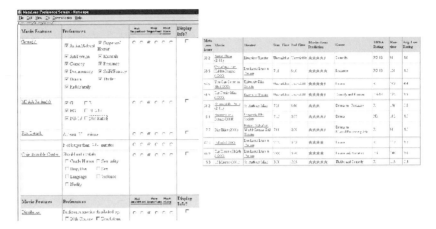

Figure 10.4 Query formation and combined recommendation screens from MetaLens. Users form query profiles by specifying preferences, their strengths, and which features to display. The recommendation list is sorted by a single, composite score.

discovered interest. Collaborative filtering could select the novice information on the new disease that the user would be most likely to find interesting.

10.5 Explanation and Inference

Recommender systems have two principal interfaces – the recommendation interface and the rating interface. This section discusses one of the more important examples of research to improve each interface by better matching it to user tasks and needs.

10.5.1 Explaining Recommendations

Recommender systems do not exist for their own sake, rather they exist to help users engaged in a task which would otherwise have too many alternatives to adequately consider. In some low-risk domains, users may simply be grateful for the suggestion, and may follow it; in other domains, however, they need to be convinced. In particular, they need to understand enough about a recommendation to decide whether and when to trust it.

Explanations can provide more general information to a user to aid in her decision-making process. Four common models of explaining collaborative filtering recommendations are process, recommendation data, track-record, and external data. Process explanations address the manner in which recommendations were produced, helping users determine whether that manner is appropriate for the decision being considered. Recommendation data can be explained generally, through summarization, or it can be presented or visualized in greater detail. The recommender system's track record for the user or in similar cases may help users gauge how well the system is likely to perform for them. Finally, external data, while not used in the recommendation process, can provide additional input to help users determine whether to follow a particular recommendation. These explanation models can be combined to create more elaborate recommendations. Additional explanation models can be used to address social navigation systems with data other than ratings.

Herlocker et al. (2000) studied 21 different explanations for movie recommendations. Six of these explanations had a statistically significant positive effect on decision-making: three simple displays of neighbour ratings, one measure of historical correctness, and two directly content-focused explanations – the similarity of the recommended movie to other movies rated and the assertion that one of the user's favourite actors is in the cast. It should not be surprising that explanations that tie to content and semantics would be appealing to users – these explanations speak directly to user interests. A key conclusion is that web recommender system effectiveness, overall, can be enhanced by providing explanations that exploit any available semantic data. Similarly, automated markup systems may help users better cope with mistakes by offering users explanations for the markups made.

10.5.2 Focusing Implicit Ratings

Recommender system researchers have been studying ways in which ratings can be collected from users with the least effort and the most value. One promising approach is *implicit ratings*. Implicit ratings are measures of interest that are derived from observing the user's interaction with a site without asking the user to modify his behaviour in any way. For instance, Tapestry stored annotations with documents identifying whether a user had printed or replied to a message (Goldberg et al., 1992). Other users could base their decisions on these annotations if they chose. The GroupLens project experimented with time-spent-reading as an implicit rating for Usenet news articles (Miller et al., 1997). Building on the work by Morita and Shinoda (1994) that showed that users spent more time reading articles they preferred, the GroupLens project was able to show that collaborative filtering was able to predict ratings for substantially more articles by using time-spent-reading and that the ratings predicted were of similar quality to explicit rating-based predictions.

Another implicit rating is available in the link structure of the Web. Web links, in addition to providing direct access from one web page to another, represent the web page author's endorsement of the target page as useful and relevant, at least in context. Terveen and Hill (1998) found this data to be useful in classifying sites – specifically for identifying authoritative sites and information hubs. The Google search engine employs a similar technique to rank results returned from a search in an attempt to present the most important sites first; sites that are linked to from many other authoritative sites are considered more important than sites that are sparsely linked to. Hill and Terveen (1996) even found that cross-medium recommendations were effective, mining endorsements of web pages from Usenet news articles in the PHOAKS system shown in Figure 10.5 (Terveen et al., 1997). Both Terveen and Hill's systems and Google use only information already created by authors for another purpose, benefiting from both the availability and the relative objectivity of implicit ratings.

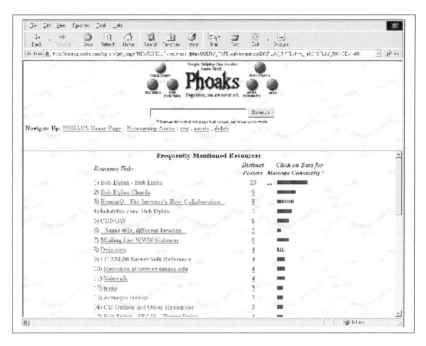

Figure 10.5 A set of recommendations from PHOAKS. Each recommendation shows the number of distinct posters who mentioned the page, and provides links to their messages, a form of explanation (Terveen et al., 1997).

These implicit ratings could be improved if the meaning of the pages or links was understood better. Did the author link to the page because it was an example of a bad page on a given topic? The Semantic Web might be able to record this information so it could be used by recommenders. Further, if a user frequently visits Web pages on many sites that have particular Semantic Web tags, that user may like Web pages on other sites that have those same tags. Typical implicit ratings systems would not detect the similarity between these pages, since the URLs are different. Combining the technology for extracting implicit ratings with the Semantic Web's rich data about each page, might make possible richer implicit ratings systems that would be even more effective at extracting meaning for users.

10.6 Socially Aware Recommenders

Recommender systems started as systems that used group information to help each individual, but too often these systems ignore the importance of the groups themselves. This section discusses social navigation systems, which make community behaviour visible in aggregate, and recommenders for smaller subgroups of a larger community.

10.6.1 Social Navigation

Social navigation systems have emerged as a broad array of techniques that enable people to work together to help each other find their way through crowded spaces. In a social navigation system, each user who visits a Web site does a small amount of work to untangle which of the paths from that Web site are most valuable. Early users leave information signposts that help later users make sense of the wealth of alternatives available to them. Later users benefit from the signposts, because they are able to direct their attention to the parts of the site that are most valuable to them. Some forms of social navigation are very closely related to collaborative filtering. For instance, Munro et al. (1999) discuss ways in which the passage of users through an information space can leave footprints that help other users find their way more readily through that same space (see Figure 10.6). As information spaces become more crowded with users, we may find it important to have automated systems that show us only those footprints that are most useful to us.

Social navigation may fit into the Semantic Web in many different ways. Most directly, social navigation may extend to systems in which visitors to Web pages explicitly label those pages according to their semantic content. After all, labelling only by the authors of the pages is limiting because the authors are generally at a very different level in their understanding of the content than most visitors. As different visitors label pages, collaborative filtering can be used to select the view of the Semantic Web that is most valuable for each visitor, according to his viewing history and relationships with the previous visitors.

Social navigation can also fit into the Semantic Web by making visible which of the labels on a page seem most appropriate with respect to what visitors to that

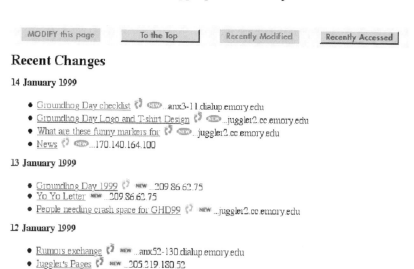

Figure 10.6 Footprints show web visitors which links the community has followed.

page actually do. For instance, one page might be labelled as having information on both sailing and windsurfing; however, if all visitors to that page end up following links to windsurfing information, social navigation could adjust the relative strengths of the labels to indicate that windsurfing is a more important label for that page.

Social navigation and the Semantic Web have similar goals. Both provide facilities that make navigating the Web more efficient and successful for users. The two techniques are complementary, and over time we anticipate that they will be used synergistically.

10.6.2 Recommending for Groups

Most automated collaborative filtering systems have focused exclusively on recommending items to individuals. In some domains, such as Usenet News (Resnick et al., 1994; Konstan et al., 1997; Miller et al., 1997), this limitation is understandable. Few users read articles collectively. In other domains such as books or music (Shardanand and Maes, 1995), it is common both to enjoy the media alone and in groups. Moreover certain items, among them board games and movies (Hill et al., 1995), are more commonly enjoyed in groups. Recommender systems that identify items such as movies for individuals do not address the user's key question, which is not "what movie should I see?" but rather "what movie should we see?" Recommendations can be provided to a group either by extending the automatic recommender to automatically recommend for the group, or by creating a new interface that displays individual recommendations for each member of the group, so the users can form their own group recommendation. In either case, the problem requires extending existing recommendation algorithms.

We built such a group recommendation interface for our MovieLens research Web site. We call the group interface PolyLens. PolyLens encourages users to form groups of other MovieLens users, using either the email address or MovieLens pseudonym of the other users. Once a group is formed, each user in the group can get lists of recommended movies with the PolyLens prediction of how much that user will like the movie, and a separate prediction of how much the whole group will like the movie (see Figure 10.7). Overall, our experience has been that users are enthusiastic about group recommenders, and that group recommenders would help users make choices (O'Connor et al., 2001).

MusicFX is another system that supports group formation, though without using collaborative filtering (McCarthy and Anagnost, 1998). MusicFX was

Group: Dantost		Back To Individual Recommendations				
TITLE	GENRE	REVIEWS	GROUP	YOUR	cosley@cs.umn.edu	cosley@quasar
Pixute (198')	Drama		★★★★	★★★★★	★★★★	★★★★
Wmng 'm sers, The (1993)	Animation, Comedy		★★★★★	★★★★★	★★★★★	★★★★★
After Life (1998)	Drama		★★★★✦	★★★★✦	★★★★✦	★★★★★
King of Masks, The (Biao Lian) (1996)	Drama		★★★★✦	★★★★★	★★★★✦	★★★★★

Figure 10.7 PolyLens group recommendation display. Iterative user testing showed that users preferred a single list with separate recommendations for the group and for each individual group member.

designed to address the challenge of selecting music for the often large groups of people using a corporate gym. Each person filled out a taste profile describing their music preferences. The computer that tracked who was in the gym also kept track of what type of music would be most appropriate for the current group of people who were working out. Over time, some people changed their work habits to arrange to be at the gym when other people, often strangers, with similar musical taste were there. Figure 10.8 shows the system's view of five workout participants and their taste in music.

Currently most Web navigation is solo. Group navigation is likely to become increasingly important over time, much as multi-player games are becoming prevalent, and multi-user support is now expected in document authoring systems. For instance, MultECommerce supports a group of shoppers visiting a virtual store together (Puglia et al., 2000). A recommender system in such a store should be integrated into the group experience, perhaps providing recommendations of items for individuals in the group, but basing the recommendations in part on the taste of the entire group. For instance, the recommendations of clothing shown to a group of teenage girls shopping alone might be very different from the clothing recommendations shown to one of the girls shopping with her mother.

Similar to the changes in recommender interfaces that have been necessary to support groups, the interface to the Semantic Web will have to change to support groups. One such interface might be a recommender supporting a group of

j	Genre	Person	A	B	C	D	E	GP,	Pr,
1	Alternative Rock		2	2	0	2	2	68	0.48
2	Hottest Hits		1	1	2	0	-2	38	0.27
3	New Music		1	1	1	0	0	35	0.25
4	Hot Country		2	0	0	0	-2	28	0.00
5	Dance		2	-1	1	-1	-1	28	0.00
6	World Beat		0	1	-1	1	-2	23	0.00
7	Traditional Country		1	0	0	-2	-2	17	0.00
8	50's Oldies		0	0	0	-1	-1	14	0.00
9	Heavy Metal		-1	-1	-1	-1	-2	4	0.00
10	Polka		-1	-1	-2	-2	-2	2	0.00

Figure 10.8 Example preferences from the MusicFX system. Users A–E are the five users currently in the gym. Each of the users A–E has specified her preference for each radio station that could be chosen to be played in the gym. MusicFX has computed an aggregate preference score for each of the radio stations for the five users. The stations are sorted by aggregate preferences. In this case, the top three stations dominate for these five users, so those stations will be played most of the time. Note that MusicFX is not a winner-takes-all system: stations with lower aggregate preference will still be played, though less frequently. From McCarthy and Anagnost (1998).

people navigating together, and using both collaborative filtering and Semantic Web information to make its recommendations. Such an interface might provide a view of the Semantic Web that would be appropriate to the group of individuals navigating together. Each member of the group might see some pages that are selected to be appropriate for just him, a group view that is appropriate for the group together, and see or hear comments made by group members about the pages. So little work has been done in this area that it is hard to know which interface will be most successful, but experience suggests that making navigating the Web a social experience will be important over the long term.

10.7 Conclusion

Recommender systems already provide substantial user value by personalizing a number of sites on the Web. The Semantic Web brings forward rich opportunities for improving these interfaces, and for striking a better balance between content and collaborative personalization methods.

10.8 Acknowledgements

We gratefully acknowledge the contributions of the students who are current and alumni members of the GroupLens Research Group at the University of Minnesota, without whom this work could not have been done. This work was supported by the National Science Foundation under grants IIS 9613960, IIS 9734442, IIS 9978717, and DGE 9554517. Support was also provided by Net Perceptions Inc., a company that we co-founded that sells an automatic collaborative filtering system.

10.9 References

Balabanovic, M. and Shoham, Y. 1997. Fab: Content-based, collaborative recommendation. *Communications of the ACM*, 40(3).
Baudisch, P. 1998. Recommending TV programs on the Web: How far can we get at zero user effort? *Recommender Systems: Papers from the 1998 Workshop*. AAAI Press, Technical Report WS-98-08, pp. 16–18.
Bharat, K., Kamba, T., and Albers, M. 1998. Personalized, interactive news on the web. *Multimedia Systems*, 6(5), pp. 349–358.
Breese, J., Heckerman, D., and Kadie, C. 1998. Empirical analysis of predictive algorithms for collaborative filtering. In *Proceedings of the 14th Conference on Uncertainty in Artificial Intelligence (UAI-98)*, Morgan Kaufmann, pp. 43–52.
Claypool, M., Gokhale, A., Miranda, T., Murnikov, P., Netes, D., and Sartin, M. 1999. Combining content-based and collaborative filters in an online newspaper. *Proceedings of the SIGIR 1999 Workshop on Recommender Systems: Algorithms and Evaluation*. Available: http://www.cs.umbc.edu/~ian/sigir99-rec/
Goldberg, D., Nichols, D., Oki, B. M., and Terry, D. 1992. Using collaborative filtering to weave an information tapestry. *Communications of the ACM*, 35(12), pp. 61–70.
Good, N., Schafer, J. B., Konstan, J. A., Borchers, A., Sarwar, B., Herlocker, J., and Riedl, J. 1999. Combining collaborative filtering with personal agents for better recommendations. *Proceedings of AAAI-99*, AAAI Press, pp. 439–446.

Herlocker, J. and Konstan, J. A. 2001. Content-independent task-focused recommendation. *IEEE Internet Computing*, 5(6).

Herlocker, J., Konstan, J. A., Borchers, A., and Riedl, J. 1999. An algorithmic framework for performing collaborative filtering. *Proceedings of SIGIR'99*, ACM, pp. 230–237.

Herlocker, J., Konstan, J. A., and Riedl, J. 2000. Explaining collaborative filtering recommendations. *Proceedings of the ACM 2000 Conference on Computer-Supported Cooperative Work*, ACM, pp. 241–250.

Hill, W. and Terveen, L. 1996. Using frequency-of-mention in public conversations for social filtering. *Proceedings of the ACM 1996 Conference on Computer-Supported Cooperative Work*, ACM, pp. 106–112.

Hill, W., Stead, L., Rosenstein, M., and Furnas G. 1995. Recommending and evaluating choices in a virtual community of use. In *Proceedings of ACM CHI'95 Conference on Human Factors in Computing Systems*, ACM, pp. 194–201.

Konstan, J. A., Miller, B., Maltz, D., Herlocker, J., Gordon, L., and Riedl J. 1997. GroupLens: Applying collaborative filtering to Usenet news. *Communications of the ACM*, 40(3), pp. 77–87.

Linton, F., Joy, D., Schaefer, H.-P., and Charron, A. 2000. OWL: A recommender system for organization-wide learning. *Educational Technology and Society*, 3(1), pp. 62–76.

Maltz, D. and Ehrlich, E. 1995. Pointing the way: Active collaborative filtering. In *Proceedings of ACM CHI'95 Conference on Human Factors in Computing Systems*, ACM, pp. 202–209.

McCarthy, J. and Anagnost, T. 1998. MusicFX: an arbiter of group preferences for computer supported collaborative workouts. *Proceedings of the ACM 1998 Conference on Computer Supported Cooperative Work*, ACM, pp. 363–372.

Miller, B., Riedl, J., and Konstan, J. A. 1997. Experiences with GroupLens: Making Usenet useful again. *Proceedings of the 1997 Usenix Winter Technical Conference*, USENIX, January 1997.

Morita, M. and Shinoda, Y. 1994. Information filtering based on user behavior analysis and best match text retrieval. *Proceedings of the 17th Annual International SIGIR Conference on Research and Development*, ACM, pp. 272–281.

Munro, A., Hook, K., and Benyon, D. 1999. Footprints in the snow. In *Social Navigation of Information Space*, eds Munro, Hook and Benyon. Springer-Verlag, London.

O'Connor, M., Cosley, D., Konstan, J. A., and Riedl, J. (2001). PolyLens: A recommender system for groups of users. *Proceedings of ECSCW 2001*, Kluwer Academic, Bonn, Germany.

Puglia, S., Carter, R., and Jain, R. 2000. MultECommerce: A distributed architecture for collaborative shopping on the WWW. In *Proceedings of the 2nd ACM Conference on Electronic Commerce*, ACM, Minneapolis, MN, pp. 215–224.

Resnick, P. and Miller, J. 1996. PICS: Internet access controls without censorship. *Communications of the ACM*, 39(10), 87–93.

Resnick, P., Iacovou, N., Suchak, M., Bergstrom, P., and Riedl, J. 1994. Grouplens: An open architecture for collaborative filtering of netnews. In *Proceedings of ACM CSCW'94 Conference on Computer-Supported Cooperative Work*, ACM, pp. 175–186.

Sarwar, B., Konstan, J. A., Borchers, A., Herlocker, J., Miller, B., and Riedl, J. 1998. Using filtering agents to improve prediction quality in the grouplens research collaborative filtering system. In *Proceedings of 1998 Conference on Computer-Supported Collaborative Work*, ACM.

Sarwar, B. M., Karypis, G., Konstan, J. A., and Riedl, J. 2000. Analysis of recommender algorithms for e-commerce. *Proceedings of the ACM E-Commerce 2000 Conference*, ACM.

Sarwar. B. M., Karypis, G., Konstan, J. A., and Riedl, J. 2001. Item-based collaborative filtering recommendation algorithms. *Proceedings of WWW 2001*, WWW10 Ltd.

Schafer, J. B. 2001. MetaLens: A framework for multi-source recommendations. PhD thesis, Department of Computer Science and Engineering, University of Minnesota, 2001.

Schafer, J. B., Konstan, J., and Riedl, J. 2001. Electronic commerce recommender applications. *Journal of Data Mining and Knowledge Discovery*, January.

Shardanand, U. and Maes, P. 1995. Social information filtering: Algorithms for automating "word of mouth". In *Proceedings of ACM CHI'95 Conference on Human Factors in Computing Systems*, ACM, pp. 210–217.

Terveen, L. and Hill, W. 1998. Finding and visualizing inter-site clan graphs. *Proceedings of ACM CHI 98 Conference on Human Factors in Computing Systems*, ACM, pp. 448–455.

Terveen, L., Hill, W., Amento, B., McDonald, D., and Creter, J. 1997. PHOAKS: A system for sharing recommendations. *Communications of the ACM*, 40(3), pp. 59–62.

Wolf, J., Aggarwal, C., Wu, K.-L., and Yu, P. 1999. Horting hatches an egg: A new graph-theoretic approach to collaborative filtering. In *Proceedings of ACM SIGKDD International Conference on Knowledge Discovery and Data Mining*, ACM, San Diego, CA.

Chapter 11
Interactive Interfaces for Mapping E-commerce Ontologies

Vladimir Geroimenko and Larissa Geroimenko

11.1 XML-Based Communication Between Companies: Visualizing a Mutual Understanding

XML is a metalanguage that allows a company of any size to create its own markup languages that describe its business domain in a way that is most suitable and convenient for the company. This is one of the main advantages of using XML – it can provide a company with its own domain-specific language, a highly specialized set of tags (metadata labels) also called a vocabulary. The problem arises when two companies start to communicate with each other using their own XML-based languages. Because the languages use vocabularies that are partly or even completely different, it is impossible for computers to translate automatically from one language into another. One of the aims of the Semantic Web is to enable such translation requiring no human intervention. But before the new generation of the Web reaches that stage of maturity, there is a need for some simple but effective techniques to establish XML-based communication between companies.

To solve the problem, the co-operation of at least two people is required. One should be an expert in the business domain, able to say for sure that, for example, `<sale_price>` for Company 1 means the same as `<our_price>` for Company 2. The other has to be a programmer who can create appropriate XSLT (Extensible Stylesheet Language Transformations) stylesheets that will translate XML documents of Company 1 into those of Company 2 (and back if needed). This job can be partly automated. Generally speaking, a domain expert does not really need to involve a programmer if they are able to manipulate XML metadata labels directly in order the show what pieces of metadata have the same meaning. On this basis, a specialist program can write an appropriate stylesheet automatically. It is not even particularly difficult, because an XSLT stylesheet is nothing other than a specialist XML document.

A domain expert cannot (and does not need to) work with the complex codes of the XSLT language. All that they need is clear and comprehensive visualizations of two different vocabularies in order to match them. Usually, a list of words used as metadata labels (i.e. a vocabulary) is not enough to model a business domain. A more advanced conceptual model has to include explicitly all relationships between the entries of a vocabulary. Such a model is called an ontology. In other words, an ontology is an explicit specification of a conceptualization (Gruber, 1993). Ontologies are a fundamental technology for implementing the Semantic Web. They are important because they make it possible to establish a common conceptual description and a joint terminology between members of communities of interest (human or autonomous software agents).

This chapter explores the possibility of developing interactive visually rich interfaces to enable Web users (especially domain experts) to access and manipulate XML metadata and underlying ontologies. Native visualizations, i.e. those that are integral parts of the process of creating and displaying XML documents, are analysed in order to utilize their potential in our interface design. By adapting and merging various native visualizations, a novel and efficient representation of the XML document ontology has been developed: the Generalized Document Object Model Tree (G-DOM-Tree) Interface. This interface represents XML metadata and their structure in a comprehensive, intelligible and compact way that is suitable for the Web-based manipulation of its elements. After reviewing the main existing technologies for implementing the G-DOM-Tree Interface, a working prototype of an XML Ontology Translator is presented. This application dynamically generates ontological models of two XML documents in the G-DOM-Tree form, and then allows Web users to map them in order to establish XSLT-based communications between XML dialects that are syntactically dissimilar but describe the same domain. This demonstrates that visual interaction with XML ontologies can provide a simple but effective way of dealing with the problem of semantic interoperability of XML documents within real-life Web-based applications.

Due to the novelty of the field, significant results to date are restricted those described in a few recent publications (Berder et al., 2000; Bonfire, Casadei and Salomoni, 2000). At the same time, there is an enormous arsenal of previously developed techniques and metaphors for information visualization (Card, MacKinlay and Shneiderman, 1999; Chen, 1999; Ware, 2000). Many of them may be adopted creatively for an effective use on the XML-based Web.

11.2 The Process of Creating and Reading XML Documents and Its Native Visualizations

The process of designing and parsing (reading) an XML document necessarily includes several visual representations of the document content and structure. We will call them the native visualizations of XML documents. Although they are currently being used exclusively for design and programming purposes, our hypothesis is that they might also be helpful within visual interfaces for XML documents. Of course, they will probably need to be transformed and adapted in order to do their new job efficiently.

To analyse and compare the main native visualizations, we will take the process of creating a simple Product Catalogue as an example. This process starts with choosing words and phrases that are able to describe all the required aspects of the Product Catalogue content, and which can therefore be used as tag names (i.e. a vocabulary). The next step is to show relationships between vocabulary entries, or in other words, to create an ontology of the Product Catalogue

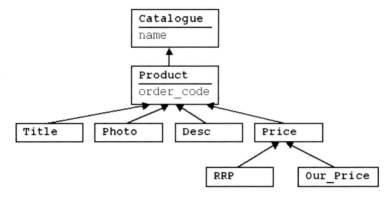

Figure 11.1   The UML-based visualization of the Product Catalogue ontology.

domain. A common way of doing this is by using UML (Unified Markup Language), its diagrams and notations.

The UML-based ontology shown in Figure 11.1 is the initial native visualization of the content of the XML documents to be created. Such diagrams are much more human-oriented than any other native visualization. They are thorough conceptual models that capture a human view of the domain, its objects (elements), their properties (attributes) and relationships. Therefore, they have a very high heuristic potential for user interfaces that enable visual interaction with XML ontologies.

Figure 11.2 shows the XML schema of the Product Catalogue, presented in a visual, diagrammatic form. It looks very similar to the UML ontological model. In principle, a UML model can be converted into an XML schema automatically, although in the case of complex XML documents it may be difficult to achieve without human intellectual help. In comparison with a UML ontology, an XML schema contains some additional technical components that are necessary for computers but are not so important for human understanding of the domain structure.

Once an XML schema is constructed, it can be used as a template for creating an unlimited number of XML documents. The design process is finished, and the next stage of reading and displaying the created documents lies ahead. The first step in this stage is parsing (reading) an XML file using a special program called

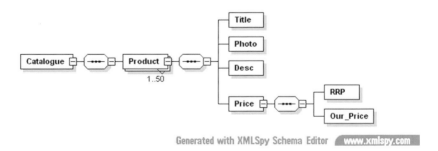

Generated with XMLSpy Schema Editor   www.xmlspy.com

Figure 11.2   The XML Schema visualization of the Product Catalogue ontology.

the XML parser. It can be a standalone parser or an integral part of a Web browser. A parser reads an XML file and constructs a hierarchical tree of nodes in the computer memory (called the XML Document Object Model or the XML DOM). The DOM of our Product Catalogue created by a Java-based parser is shown in Figure 11.3. Every structural component of an XML document (elements, data, etc.) is represented within its DOM as a node. Basically, a proper XML DOM contains nothing else but nodes. The DOM visualization looks quite technical from the user's point of view. Since it contains the maximal number of structural components (nodes) that may be extracted from an XML document, it is very difficult for the user to traverse the node tree of a complex XML document. Nevertheless, as it will be shown later, it is possible to use a DOM tree as a navigational aid within a graphical user interface.

Thus, the process of designing and parsing XML documents involves at least three native visualizations. They have more similarities than differences. These visualizations may be of use for creating visual interfaces that facilitate user interaction with XML metadata.

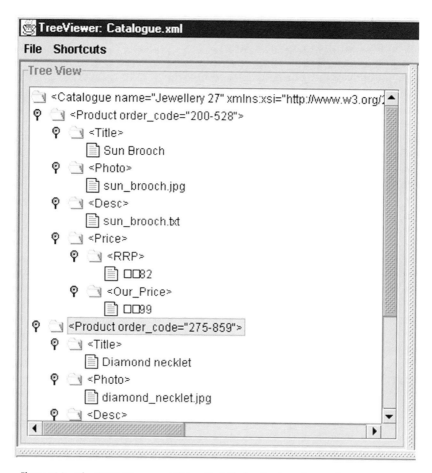

Figure 11.3   The DOM (Document Object Model) visualization of a Catalogue document.

11.3 Technologies for Visualizing XML Documents

If the visualizations that are native to the XML development process can be useful in designing interfaces for XML applications, what about technologies and languages available for the implementation of visually rich interfaces? First at all, it should be noted that an XML document as such has no specific visual form other than the plain text view. Indeed, an XML file (unlike an HTML file) does not contain any formatting tags and therefore requires specialist external files, or even applications, for its visual rendering.

Figure 11.4 shows how the "Catalogue.xml" file appears in Microsoft Internet Explorer 5. The main difference between this view and a plain text view (for example, in Notepad) is that Internet Explorer allows collapsing and expansion of XML elements that have child nodes.

It is possible to format an XML document in order to display it in a browser as a normal HTML page that includes links, tables, a variety of fonts, colours, etc. Cascading Style Sheets (CSS) are suitable for simple formatting, whereas the Extensible Stylesheet Language (XSL) allows more complex formatting and also transformation of XML documents. Although displaying XML as HTML or XHTML documents seems to be the main technique of their presentation on the Web (at least, in the foreseeable future), it does not provide the level of inter-activity required for creating effective visual interfaces. It lacks direct manipulation features, which are hard to implement even using Dynamic HTML (DHTML).

If the HTML/XHTML rendering has a distinctly limited potential for contributing to visually rich interactive interfaces, what languages and techniques are more suitable? In principle, any programming language may be equally

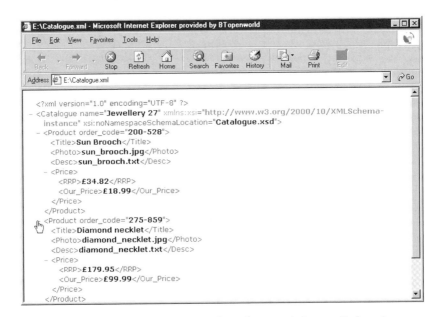

Figure 11.4   The Rendering of a Catalogue document in Internet Explorer 5.

relevant, as XML is language independent. Although this is true in theory, the real-world situation is much more complicated. For various reasons, only a few languages will be of wide use on the XML-based Internet. An analysis of today's situation and trends reveals the two major players – Java and ActionScript.

It is no surprise that Java is the closest companion to XML. Like XML itself, Java is platform independent. This means that a combination of XML documents and Java applications or applets provides e-commerce developers with a universal and portable solution. Combining XML with any other programming languages (such as C or C++) may result in losing its cross-platform features. Another reason for using Java for developing XML applications is that Java has become the *de facto* number one programming language, and so it is a natural choice for most programmers.

Sun Microsystems Inc. (http://java.sun.com) provides developers with the following core Java technologies for XML: the Java API for XML Parsing (JAXP), the Java API for XML Messaging (JAXM) and the Java API for XML Data Binding (JAXB). These key APIs will be included in the next releases of the Java 2 Platform (both Standard and Enterprise Editions). Together, these three Java technologies provide developers with a powerful and easy-to-use tool set. JAXP allows them to integrate any XML parser with a Java application in order to read, manipulate and generate XML documents. JAXM enables B2B messaging through support of a variety of XML messaging methods, including the ebXML standard. JAXB offers two-way mapping between Java objects and XML documents, including the automatic generation of Java classes from XML schemas. With the delivery of JAXP, JAXM and JAXB, Java increases its potential as the main programming language for XML development by offering even more simplified and integrated solutions.

Whilst Java is the obvious choice for XML developers, the ActionScript programming language is hardly known to most of them at this moment. What is ActionScript and why can it be cited, along with Java, as one of the most important tools for the future of XML development?

ActionScript is a complete JavaScript-like language that allows Macromedia Flash 5 developers to read, transform and generate XML documents. The methods of the ActionScript XML object can be used for downloading XML data from a server, accessing and manipulating XML nodes, sending XML documents to a server and displaying them within a Flash interface. Additionally, ActionScript provides a predefined XMLSocket object for establishing a continuous connection with a server.

Generally speaking, ActionScript offers the same opportunities for XML development as any other programming language. What makes it unique is that it is based on the Flash paradigm. Macromedia Flash is one of the most popular Web technologies. It allows designers to create reliable, dynamic and graphically rich Web sites for entertainment and e-commerce. According to Macromedia, seven of the top ten visited sites on the Internet deploy Macromedia Flash authored content, and 92% of current online users are able to experience this engaging content immediately using a pre-installed Macromedia Flash Player (www.macromedia.com/flash). Although Flash began its life as a simple vector-graphics and animation tool, it has evolved into a new platform for developing entire Web sites that is presently used by over half a million Web authors world-wide.

Thus, the Java and ActionScript languages seem to be the two main contenders for XML development. They complement each other very well; Java is a good

Figure 11.5   The Rendering of a Catalogue document using Flash 5.

choice for complex and serious B2B applications, Flash ActionScript is good for graphically rich interactive Web pages, portals and standalone e-commerce applications. Although Java applets and Flash movies have the same mission as interfaces for XML-based applications, Flash technology offers a simpler and more engaging solution. The history of the Internet (e.g. Java applets versus GIF animations) shows that such solutions have a good chance of survival.

Thus, Macromedia Flash technology is at present the best choice for creating visually rich and highly interactive interfaces because multimedia, animation and interaction is the true nature of this Web leading technology. By adding an embedded XML parser and the ActionScript language with its specialist XML objects, version 5 of Flash has become the most powerful tool for developing real-life Web-based applications. For example, Figure 11.5 shows an application we created using Flash 5 and its ActionScript. This application can read a Product Catalogue XML file and display it in an attractive and interactive visual form that enables the user to browse the Catalogue.

11.4 A Generalized Interface for Visualizing XML Metadata and Their Structural Relationships

There are several possibilities for designing graphical user interfaces to XML documents based on existing or novel visualization techniques. We have tried to develop a new interface that enables effective visual interaction with XML metadata. Our research was based on the above analysis of the native XML visualizations as well as some further logical and experimental exploration of the possibilities of their mutual use and integration. The result of the investigation was embodied in a novel interface that we call the Generalized Document Object Model Tree Interface (or, for short, the G-DOM-Tree Interface).

This Interface is based on the XML DOM visualization, generalized and enhanced to make it more suitable for effective visual interaction with metadata. Basically, it is a part of a DOM tree where all logical and structural components of an XML document are represented as nodes. The main difference from a DOM tree is that our model borrows from a standard DOM only its recurring metadata structure. By implementing this, it becomes very similar to an XML schema or a UML model. But, at the same time, the G-DOM-Tree model inherits the structural organization of a DOM rather than of a schema or a UML diagram.

Figure 11.6 shows the G-DOM-Tree representation of the Product Catalogue. Both types of metadata (elements and attributes) are represented as nodes that show element/attribute names and their places within the XML document structure. Each attribute has the status of a special child element of its parent element. The letter and colon "a:" in front of a node name is the only difference

Figure 11.6 The generalised DOM tree model of the Product Catalogue.

between an attribute and an element. To make the organization of the node tree more apparent, each structural level is indented and also marked with a different colour.

The features of the G-DOM-Tree view that make it an efficient and promising visualization of XML metadata include:

- The ontology of an XML document is represented in a comprehensive form, which, at the same time, is much more compact than a UML model or an XML schema.
- It is easy to read and understand because of its indentation-based form that matches the recurring structural pattern of an XML document and also because of the use of document tag names.
- All attributes are displayed as specialist children elements marked with the "a:" prefix, making it easy to transform an element into an attribute and back simply by adding or deleting the attribute prefix "a:".
- From a technological point of view, this visualization can be easily implemented as a Flash movie or Java applet, essentially by exploiting their techniques for generating dynamic menus.

Thus, the Generalized DOM Tree is a novel technique for visualizing ontologies of XML documents, on the fly, within Web-based user interfaces. Its practical use in a variety of XML applications may therefore be expected.

11.5 A Web-based Ontology Translator for E-commerce Documents

To implement the concept of the G-DOM-Tree-based visualization, a working prototype of a simple Ontology Translator has been developed using Flash technology. This application can read XML files and generate dynamically their Generalized DOM Trees. Any interface object can be manipulated directly. By dragging and dropping an object (i.e. a framed element or attribute name) on a specific target (another interface object), the user triggers the underlying ActionScript that can rename, add and delete appropriate nodes in the XML documents directly or write an XSLT stylesheet for all documents of this type.

The following example, shown in Figure 11.7, illustrates and explains the use of the Ontology Translator.

Suppose there are two collections of XML documents on the Web that describe the same domain using different XML dialects. In other words, they are employing two dissimilar sets of tags, most or all of them synonymous to human domain experts, but not to computers.

Comparison of the ontologies of the two Product Catalogues reveals the following main differences and similarities:

- The root element names ("Catalogue" – "Catalog") are written in British English and American English respectively.
- The metadata tag "Product" has the same meaning in the first catalogue as the "Item" in the second one.
- The same synonymy exists between the following pairs of tags: "Our_Price" – "Price", "Desc" – "Info", "Photo" – "Image".

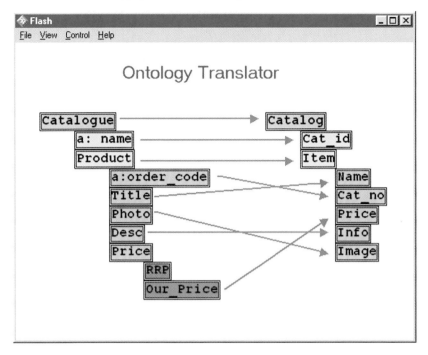

Figure 11.7 Matching ontologies using direct manipulation within an interactive Flash interface.

● The nodes "a: name" – "Cat_id" and "a: order_code" – "Cat_no" are synonyms, but they have different status (an attribute versus an element in each
  pair respectively).

Now imagine that you need to establish Web-based real-time communication
between the two XML-based languages, for example, in order to merge the
"British" and "American" catalogues. It is quite obvious that as of today there
is no software like "intelligent agents" that could accomplish this task for you.
A straightforward way is to develop an XSLT stylesheet for these documents but
it requires time and technical knowledge.

   The Ontology Translator allows any person, expert in the domain, but without
XML or XSLT knowledge, to map the two ontologies easily and efficiently. For
example, dragging the "Catalogue" element and dropping it onto the "Catalog"
can rewrite the name of the root tag in the "American" Product Catalogue or,
more generally, establish an XSLT rule for translating one element into another.
Deleting or adding the "a:" changes the node status in terms of "element –
attribute" not only on the interface but also in the XML document itself. Figure
11.8 shows the mechanism of establishing a mutual understanding by mapping
the two ontologies using direct manipulation of their metadata elements. As a
result, an XSLT stylesheet is generated that enables an automated translation
from "British" Product Catalogues into "American" ones.

   Thus, the Ontology Translator is a prototype application that enables visual
interaction with ontologies of two XML-based domain-specific languages in
order to establish communication between them. This Web application

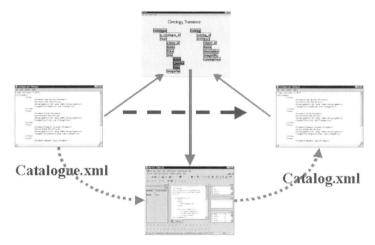

XSLT Style Sheet (XSLT Processor)

Figure 11.8   The mechanism of communication between the two types of catalogues that based on an XSLT stylesheet generated as a result of visual interaction with the ontologies.

implements both the G-DOM-Tree Interface and the Flash XML technology. It allows domain experts to work effectively in order to solve real-life problems of interoperability of Web-based XML documents.

11.6 Future Work

Our research to date has focused on the possibility of developing interactive visually rich interfaces that enable Web users to access and manipulate XML document ontologies. Native XML visualizations were analysed and, on the basis of their integration, a novel and efficient interface for displaying XML document ontology (the Generalized DOM Tree) has been developed. It has been implemented in an Ontology Translator working prototype using Macromedia Flash XML technology. Our research and prototype implementation has shown that visual interaction with XML ontologies provides a comprehensible but efficient way of dealing with the problem of semantic interoperability of XML documents within Web-based applications. The next logical step in the development of G-DOM-Tree-based interfaces is to use them within some real-life e-commerce applications to reveal aspects that need to be enhanced or rethought. A Java version of the interface may be required for its integration with Java-based B2B applications.

11.7 References

Berder M, Klein R, Disch A and Ebert A (2000) A functional framework for web-based information visualization systems. *IEEE Transactions on Visualization and Computer Graphics* 6(1): 8–23.

Bonfire ME, Casadei G and Salomoni P (2000) Adaptive intelligent hypermedia using XML. *Proceedings of the 2000 ACM Symposium on Applied Computing 2000* Vol. 2, ACM Press, New York, pp. 922–926.

Card S, MacKinlay J and Shneiderman B (Eds) (1999) *Readings in Information Visualization: Using Vision to Think*. Morgan Kaufmann.

Chen C (1999) *Information Visualization and Virtual Environments*. Springer-Verlag.

Gruber TR (1993) A translation approach to portable ontologies. *Knowledge Acquisition* 5(2):199–200.

Ware C (2000) *Information Visualization: Perception for Design*. Morgan Kaufmann.

Chapter 12
Using Scalable Vector Graphics and Geographical Information Systems in a Back Pain Study

Gheorghita Ghinea and David Gill

12.1 Introduction

According to a Department of Health survey, in Britain back pain affects 40% of the adult population, 5% of which have to take time off to recover (Boucher, 1999). This causes a large strain on the health system, with some 40% of back pain sufferers consulting a GP for help and 10% seeking alternative medicine therapy (Boucher, 1999). Due to the large number of people affected, back pain alone cost industry £9090 million in 1997/8 (Frank and De Sousa, 2000), with between 90 and 100 million days of sickness and invalidity benefit paid out per year for back pain complaints (Frank and De Sousa, 2000; Main, 1983; Papageorgiou et al., 1995). Back pain is not confined to the UK alone, but is a worldwide problem; in the USA, for instance, 19% of all workers' compensation claims are made with regard to back pain. Although this is a lot less than the percentage of people affected by back pain in the UK, it should be noted that in the USA not all workers are covered by insurance and not all workers will make a claim for back pain (Jefferson and McGrath, 1996). Any improvement in the way that patients with back pain can be analysed should therefore be viewed as one potentially capable of significantly saving both benefit expenditure and lost man-hours.

The problem with back pain is that "there exist no standardized clinical tests or investigations by which all people with low back pain can be evaluated" (Papageorgiou et al., 1995). Nor will there ever be, as different people have different pain thresholds and will be affected differently. It is also difficult for medical personnel to know what has caused the back pain, as there are potentially many different causes (Frank and De Sousa, 2000; Matsen, 2001).

Not only is evaluation difficult, but unfortunately, like most types of pain, back pain is difficult to analyse, as the only information that can be used is suggestive descriptions from the patient. Usually, the back pain that a patient is suffering from can be categorized in one of three groups: chronic, sub-acute and acute. Chronic back pain is described as pain that lasts for longer than three months and affects between 10% and 15% of the population (Matsen, 2001). The majority of people affected by this type of back pain fall into the over-65 age group, where 28% of its members suffer from this type of pain (Boucher, 1999). Sub-acute pain lasts between seven days and seven weeks and is normally mild. Acute back pain, however, lasts a short time, is usually characterized by severe pain and affects some 80% of back pain sufferers (Matsen, 2001).

Due to the debilitating effect that back pain has on society, our research aimed to find a method which would allow correlations and patterns to be found between patients' data, and therefore allow the medical world to draw conclusions as to the cause and effect of back pain. We devised and implemented three methods for visualization of back pain datasets, which would enable the user to carry out deeper analysis on a dataset than is usually possible using standard database queries. This is so because a human is able to compare and contrast diagrammatic information far faster and to a higher degree than statistical or numerical values.

12.1.1 Back Pain Questionnaires

The main medical work done to resolve back pain tends to be with patients who have chronic back pain. However, these patients may have developed psychological and emotional problems, due to having to deal with the pain. Because of these problems, patients can have difficulty describing their pain, which can lead to problems during the treatment. In some patients, the psychological problems may have aided the cause of the back pain, by adding stress to the body, or the stress of the back pain may itself have caused psychological problems (Ginzburg et al., 1988; Hildebrandt et al., 1988; Main, 1983; Mann et al., 1992; Parker et al., 1995; Ransford et al., 1976; Uden et al., 1988; Von Baeyer et al., 1983). Because of this, patients suffering from back pain are usually asked to fill out questionnaires in order to help the medical staff, not only to know where the pain is located, but also to identify the patient's mental state before treatment begins.

The main questionnaires used for this purpose are:

- the Modified Somatic Perception Questionnaire (MSPQ), which assesses somatic anxiety (Main, 1983);
- the Roland and Morris (1983) questionnaire, which is used to measure the patient's back pain-caused disability; and
- the Zung (1965) questionnaire, which assesses depression via the respondent giving answers to 20 questions using a self-rating scale.

In addition, the patient is usually required to mark on a diagram of a human body, where the pain is located, and the type of pain. This type of diagram is known as a "pain drawing" and forms the primary focus of our chapter. Accordingly, the structure of the chapter is as follows. The next section looks at pain drawings in more detail, examining the different types used in practice and their scoring methods, and finishes by highlighting limitations of current approaches. The subsequent section examines the feasibility of various technological solutions to overcome these limitations, and is followed by a description of the implementation of these solutions in practice. Finally, the developed solutions are compared with respect to one another and the set of requirements they set out to fulfil, and conclusions are subsequently drawn.

12.2 The Pain Drawing

Pain drawings, an example of which is shown in Figure 12.1, have been successfully used in pain centres for over 45 years (Palmer, 1949) and act as a simple

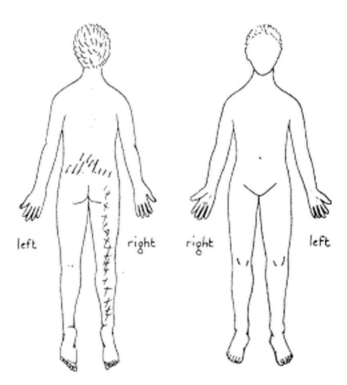

Figure 12.1   Pain drawing from NHS Northwick Park Hospital.

self-assessment technique, originally designed to enable the recording of the spatial location and type of pain that a patient is suffering from (Ohlund et al., 1996; Parker et al., 1995; Rankine et al., 1998). They have a number of advantages, including being economic and simple to complete, and can also be used to monitor the change in a patient's pain situation (Ohnmeiss et al., 1995). Over the years, different ways of evaluating and using pain drawings have been suggested.

Ransford et al. (1976) concluded that pain drawings could be used not only as a location and pain recorder, but also as an economical psychological screening instrument to see if a patient would react well to back pain treatment. As previously mentioned, back pain can be caused by psychological and emotional problems, as well as occupational factors, and hence medical treatment alone may not remove the cause of the pain, making the patient no better (Chan et al., 1993; Hildebrandt et al., 1988; Uden et al., 1988).

In order to evaluate the patient's psychological state the Minnesota Multiphasic Personality Inventory (MMPI), a standard American psychological questionnaire, can be used (Waddell et al., 1980). This has been proved in a double-blind study to indicate hypochondriasis (Hs) and hysteria (Hy) scores for patients, factors which have both been linked to treatment outcomes (Wiltse and Racchio, 1975). However, the MMPI is expensive and takes on average around one and half hours to complete, also requiring the respondent to understand English to high school level in order to be able to complete the questionnaire (Von Baeyer et al., 1983). Therefore, research was done by Ransford et al. (1976) to link the pain drawing with the MMPI, and see if it would be capable of acting as a simple screening device, filtering those in need of further psychological evaluation. This worked by using a scoring system for the pain drawing, which gave points for abnormalities in the pain drawings (drawings that did not match accepted patterns of pain). If this score was greater than three, the patient could be psychologically distressed. Ransford et al. (1976) found that they could predict 93% of the patients that needed further psychological evaluation just by looking at the patient's pain drawing, a conclusion later corroborated by Chan et al. (1993), and to a lesser extent by Von Baeyer et al. (1983). The latter concluded that while a relationship between the pain drawing score and the Hs and Hy scores in the MMPI was present, the magnitude of this relationship was much smaller than that published by Ransford et al. (1976).

Uden et al. (1988) assessed pain drawings using different categories of pain, ranging from nonorganic to organic: *nonorganic, possibly nonorganic, possibly organic* and *organic*. They conclude that cases that fall into the nonorganic category should undergo further psychological evaluation. This is because pain that is not of organic nature tends to mean that there are psychological or emotional problems. Using the same approach, Chan et al. (1993) found that there was a relationship between the pain drawing and the physical signs of nonorganic pain described by Waddell et al. (1980).

Mann et al. (1992) tried to link the pain drawing to causes of pain. In their paper, five lumbar spine disorder categories were used, and analysis was made of the number of patients that were correctly identified. The identification was done using a number of systems, including statistics, expert and computer evaluations. It was found that physicians averaged 51% accuracy, while the computer systems achieved 48% accuracy. They conclude that computer systems could be used to help with the diagnosis of back pain patients and could be used to bring down the costs of this type of evaluation.

12.2.1 Scoring Methods

In order to try and link the pain drawing to either psychological, emotional or causes of pain, several scoring systems have been developed. With the *grid method*, a grid overlay is placed over the pain drawing (Gatchel et al., 1986). The grid is designed so that each cell is approximately the same size. By using the grid, unskilled testers could calculate the amount of surface area that was in pain. *Sensation scoring*, on the other hand, allows not only the placement of pain to be noted but also the type of pain (e.g. numbness, stabbing, pins and needles) in the respective area. This type of scoring is done using a key, therefore allowing more information to be collected, and could act as an indicator as to what the cause of the pain is.

In the *simple body region* approach, the body is broken down into very simple regions, in order to indicate large areas that are in pain (Ohnmeiss et al., 1999), whereas in the *body region* method the pain drawing is broken down into regions using anatomical landmarks, such as joints (Margolis et al., 1986). In contrast, *visual inspection* uses trained evaluators, who look at the pain drawings and from their experience are able to say what they believe to be wrong with the patient, or if psychological testing is needed (Chan et al., 1993). Lastly, *penalty point methods* work by awarding points for every un-natural placement of pain on a pain drawing. Different areas and rules are made so that there is a weighting depending on the irregularities in the drawing. If more points than normal are scored, then the person in question may have a psychological problem that needs addressing (Ransford et al., 1976).

Many investigations have been carried out to assess the various processes involved with data collection and dissemination using pain drawings. These include the patient's ability to redraw the pain drawing after a time delay (Ohnmeiss, 2000), as well as the drawing evaluator's ability to interpret the information the same way each time (Hildebrandt et al., 1988; Margolis et al., 1988; Von Baeyer et al., 1983). Further investigations have been carried out into the ability of two different evaluators to agree on their interpretation of pain drawings (Chan et al., 1993; Uden et al., 1988). The findings showed that patients remain constant in the way that they fill in pain drawings, even if the time between filling them in is quite lengthy. It has been found that this was correct across all scoring systems used in pain drawings, except sensation scoring (Ohnmeiss, 2000). As to the ability of evaluators to agree on their interpretation of the pain drawing, Chan et al. (1993) report agreement between evaluators 78% of the time, and between evaluators and a registered nurse 74%. This, they claim, proves that the pain drawing is as reliable as any other commonly used process.

12.2.2 Pain Drawings – Conclusions

The overall consensus of the literature seems to be that, while the pain drawing is a powerful tool in the role for which it was originally designed, namely to record the spatial location and pain type, it is not as useful when it comes to acting as a psychometric test (Von Baeyer et al., 1983). This is because there are a number of problems with the way that patients behave towards the tests when filling them out, especially regarding the way that they like to present themselves to medical staff (Hildebrandt et al., 1988).

The literature regarding the pain drawing and the way that it can be analysed seems to have caused some confusion about what the pain drawing is actually to be used for, with little research into what it actually measures. It has been used by different organizations and at different times to measure a wide spectrum of factors, ranging from psychological distress, type of pain, to disability (Ohlund et al., 1996; Parker et al., 1995). Most of the methods investigated cannot be used on their own (Ohlund et al., 1996; Parker et al., 1995) or need further evaluation (Ginzburg et al., 1988; Hildebrandt et al., 1988; Margolis et al., 1986).

Although there are several methods of analysing the current datasets, none of the methods seem to be robust enough to be able to work on their own, or with complete certainty. Moreover, pain drawings are usually stored in a paper format, which allows no further evaluation of the data that is stored in them and makes searching through the data a somewhat arduous task. To compound the issue, if information regarding the pain drawing is stored, usually it is simply just a numerical result of statistical analysis that has been carried out on it, inevitably resulting in a loss of information. This is due to the fact that current systems used for analysis of the pain drawings and the associated questionnaires revolve around statistical packages, such as Excel and SPSS, which are incapable of handling diagrammatic data. Thus, although diagrammatic data is collected, it is not used as a key component of the data analysis. This is a problem, as people find it easier to show how they feel through a diagram, instead of answering closed questions in questionnaires. Such data cannot therefore be used to its full potential and, in particular, cannot be used in helping with queries within the dataset.

We have sought to alleviate this problem and have investigated various visual technological solutions that use the pain drawing as an actual aid to analysing the dataset. Furthermore, we have enhanced data management by digitally storing the data in ways that allow it to be analysed more easily, and have employed user-friendly visual techniques for data querying. Lastly, recognizing the importance in healthcare of distributed systems such as the World Wide Web providing ubiquitous information, all our approaches use Web-based technologies or technologies that could be implemented in this manner if required.

12.3 Back Pain Data – Technological Solutions

The back pain drawing that a patient completes can be stored in one of two ways: either the image can be scanned, or the image can be subjected to *regionalization*. In the latter case, the image is first broken down into regions, and only information relating to those regions of the human body affected by pain is recorded. The drawback of this approach is that pain location is *generalized*; for instance numbness in the hand might be generalized to numbness in the whole arm, if that is the smallest region encompassing the hand. However, regionalization leads to simple *image maps*: digitized drawings, broken down into regions, each region being hyperlinked using HTML (HyperText Markup Language, used for writing Web pages) to a specific document, such as a patient's medical records. Therefore each region becomes an image map hotspot linking to records that relate to that region. Use of image maps allows for easy data cross-examination, a feature absent if the image is simply scanned. However, scanning an image does allow for the drawing to remain intact, with precise indications of the location and types of pain. If it is scanned to appropriate storage formats such as GIF or JPEG, it can be hyperlinked to the rest of the dataset.

In our approach, web-based image maps were constructed either by using a GIF image (broken down into regions using Macromedia's Fireworks package) in conjunction with HTML, or by using Scaleable Vector Graphics (SVG), a new technology which allows zoomable and panable image maps to be designed. Both types of image maps can be used together with Active Server Pages (ASP) to dynamically update and present data. In our work we have also used Geographical Information Systems (GIS) a specialist analyst tool, which inherently works on image maps. These technologies are now presented in more detail.

12.3.1 SVG

SVG is a new markup-based vector graphics format, which the World Wide Web consortium (W3C) has made into an open Web standard. SVG is an XML styled tag language, which allows a text file to store the way that a vector graphic should be displayed. This has advantages over raster-based formats such as GIF and JPEG, which store data about each of the pixels in the image, resulting in large files. Another problem associated with raster images is that zooming tends to turn the image blocky. Vector graphics on the other hand, just store the end coordinate points that define lines, thus allowing the creation of polygons which not only can be colour filled, but which *may have their own attributes*. Because only data about the end points of a line are stored zooming and panning of the image are possible at any size. Moreover, this type of image requires less storage than a raster image (Boye, 1999). Lastly, the fact that SVG is XML-based, and is therefore a text-based graphics language with semantic markup, enhances the ability of search engines to hunt through the format and extract meaningful information for the end-user.

12.3.2 ASP

ASP allows for dynamic content to be used on the Web. The text document that is used to build the Web page contains either Visual Basic or Javascripting and requests the server to carry out some functions, such as database data retrieval or updates, before the HTML page is built dynamically, at run-time. Once the server has carried out its operation, the instructions for laying out the Web page are sent to the client. One of the main uses of this technology is to allow Web pages to interface with, and get results from, a database (VB123, 1999). In order to make use of this technology, the ASP queries and the database have to be stored on either an IIS (Microsoft Information Interchange Server) or a PWS (Personal Web Server), thereby allowing the server to carry out the queries on the database and return the information requested.

12.3.3 GIS

With the advent of computing and information systems, the analysis of complex geographical datasets and their related databases and flat files has been greatly enhanced by GIS technology (Bernhardsen, 1992). GIS tools such as ArcView allow the user to visualize data that may have gone unseen in spreadsheets, charts and other types of reports (ESRI, 1999b). However, GIS does not need to be a single system, as it can be made up of a number of different hardware and software components, each performing a role in the storing and integration of digital images and related geographical data, thereby allowing for fast information retrieval (Bretas, 1996).

Using GIS, several methods of analysis can be carried out on the data, such as selection by geographic criteria for the spatial dataset, or using standard database functions such as sum, maximum, minimum, average, frequency distribution, and standard deviation on the nonspatial data held in the database. As most GISs are built using relational databases, SQL (Standard Query Language) statements can also be used in such systems (Bretas, 1996). As the system is visual, it removes the complexity of paper files or large spreadsheets and allows users to point and click in logical ways through the datasets (Theodore, 1998). For instance, if an area of the visual image is selected, the selected area will be highlighted and all corresponding data in the related tables will also be highlighted and vice versa.

In order to build a GIS, a base map is used, where every point, line and area are given a unique identification code. These codes can then be linked to the database by inserting a new linking attribute into the database. The GIS software then automatically builds all the links that are needed for the system to work.

12.3.4 Medical GIS

Over recent years, the medical community, particularly in the USA, has realized how much geographical-related information it stores and the advantage of being able to visualize it. The medical community have therefore been developing ways to harness the data integration and spatial visualization abilities of GIS (ESRI, 1999a). Below is a list of functions that GISs have been used for (ESRI, 1999b):

- Track infectious diseases and identify gaps in child immunizations.
- Conduct market studies and document health care needs of a community.
- Manage materials, supplies, human resources, and logistics.
- Maintain location inventories of health care facilities, providers and vendors.
- Route health care workers, equipment and supplies to service locations.
- Publish health care information using maps on the Internet.
- Manage patient care environments and clinical resources.
- Distribute clinical data in a visual and geographic form.
- Locate the nearest health care facility or health care provider on the Web.

As an example, Loma Linda University Medical Centre has developed a GIS system, based on the Environmental Systems Research Institute's ArcView, which has a base map of the bed locations in the centre. This is linked to patients' clinical information, thus allowing doctors and other medical personnel to find the position of a patient in the centre in a visual manner (ESRI, 1999a).

It must be understood that GIS is not restricted to maps of the "real" world, for if something can be broken down into regions and areas, then GIS could be used to store the relating information. Thus ESRI and GeoHealth Inc. have devised a new software package that allows the human body to be visualized, namely

Bodyviewer. It uses the International Classification of Diseases (ICD-9) codes to link the human base image to databases containing information about patients and other relational clinical database management systems (ESRI, 1999a; Theodore, 1998).

12.3.5 Web-based GIS

The Web has opened up a number of new possibilities for GIS. These include the distributed sharing of data, the capture and analysis of new datasets, as well as the possibility of GIS data being accessed by a large number of users using simple, visual across multi-platform environments (Peng and Nebert, 1997; Plewe, 1996, 1997; Strand, 1998). The use of HTML in conjunction with GIS also allows the linking of documents, a feature unavailable in older systems. The main advantage of Web GIS is that the user does not need to be able to understand the complexities of specialist software, as all the information and technical ability that they need is to be able to work an Internet browser. This allows people who understand the data to analyse its geographical trends without needing to understand how the two are tied together within the GIS software (Plewe, 1997). However, for the purposes of our research, only local GIS was used.

12.4 System Requirements and Development

In our research, we have worked with back pain data provided by NHS Northwick Park Hospital. Here, medical staff currently collect data relating to patients with back pain by the use of a number of questionnaires including the three questionnaires described earlier in the chapter, as well as pain drawings, where the pain drawing is stored on paper and the questionnaire results are stored in a spreadsheet. The latter allows for a small degree of analysis, however any complex queries are out of the question. Moreover, as the diagrammatic data is stored in paper format, it only allows for simple one-to-one comparisons and makes cross-examination and data recovery between patients difficult.

After consultations with medical staff at NHS Northwick Park Hospital, it became clear that they needed a system which would allow back pain data to be analysed fully. In order to achieve this goal, both the questionnaire data and the diagrammatic data would have to be converted into more analysable methods of digital data storage using technologies such as HTML, SVG, ASP and GIS, which would allow for easy cross-examination and recovery of the data. The developed solution should allow medical personnel to enter new data and images, as well as to examine the information stored in the system, using a user-friendly visual-based interface. Moreover, the medical staff stressed that it would be an advantage if the system could not only allow the use of the back pain diagram to select the appropriate records, but conversely could enable the highlighting on the diagram of the region(s) corresponding to the selected records. Lastly, it would also be of use if the system could be run over an Intranet or the Internet.

Based on these requirements, a total of eight different design solutions were initially suggested. These were then assessed as to their practicality and three solutions were selected for development, in order to allow Northwick Park the flexibility of choosing between the competing designs. Thus, the following systems were implemented:

- ASP related database accessed by a GIF image map
- ASP related database accessed by an SVG image map
- GIS-based solution.

All of the developed systems interact with a database of back-pain data. Whilst the design of the database itself is beyond the scope of this book, it was modelled and normalized using the methods given in Connolly et al. (1999).

As the issue of relating the digitized pain drawings to the corresponding datasets was primordial in our work, we shall now describe our approach in achieving this goal, followed by a more detailed examination of each developed system.

12.4.1 Regional Diagram for Visual Interaction

In order to allow the digitized diagrams to be interactive with the dataset, thereby allowing the display of information relating to patients that had a particular type of pain in a specific region, the pain drawing itself had to be broken down into regions. It was decided that the best way to split the human body into regions was to use the dermatome map. This map was chosen because most medical staff understand what dermatomes represent and their mapping on the human body, so this is a simple system of body regionalization that everyone either would already understand or would understand after simple training. In order to allow for a better resolution of pain regions, the body was split into quarters, thus giving a rear left and right, and a front left and right for each dermatome. These regions had to be made into hotspots for SVG and GIF systems as well as GIS, with all regions following a standard code, as described in Table 12.1 and graphically depicted in Figure 12.2.

12.4.2 ASP with GIF Image Map

With this design, the GIF image map contains links which open other options, displayed in frames on the Web page. These allow a selection of the type of pain and data required, relating to the selected dermatome. When one of these is selected, ASP queries stored on a Web server would then operate on the resident back pain database using SQL, before returning the result in an HTML Web page, as shown in Figure 12.3. As the original scanned images are also stored on the Web server, this approach also allows any generalization errors to be checked for.

Table 12.1 Dermatome regions and their abbreviations

RRT1	Rear right dermatome T1
RLC2	Rear left dermatome C2
FRL1	Front right dermatome L1
FLS2	Front left dermatome S2

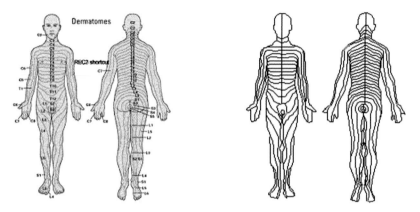

Figure 12.2   The original dermatomes used in our work, and the corresponding regions used in the research.

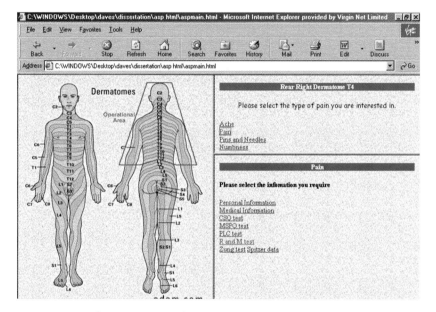

Figure 12.3   ASP with GIF image map – system snapshot.

12.4.3 ASP with SVG Image Map

This implementation works the same way as the previous one, however instead of having a GIF image map for use as the shortcut to the ASP queries, it uses an SVG image map, comprising four dermatome drawings, one for each different type of pain. Because the system uses four different SVG images of the dermatomes, it allows users to select the pain type that they wish to review from a visual representation instead of a hyperlink (as is the case with the preceding solution).

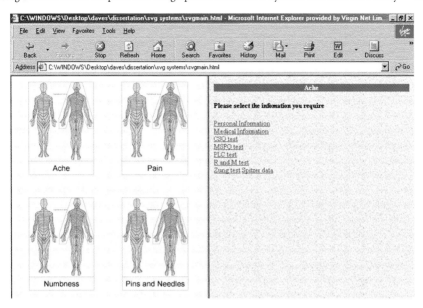

Figure 12.4 ASP with SVG image map – here the user selects region and type of pain from the graphic, which in turn gives the user the option of choosing the type of data needed.

SVG aids this, in that although the diagrams are relatively small, they can be zoomed and panned to allow the user to click directly on the region needed. All possible queries, relating to a specific area and pain type, were stored on the PWS on the machine, in ASP format. XLink functions were then used so that if a region was selected, a Web page would be loaded with hyperlinks to all the different tables that may contain information relating to patients that had pain of the specified type and in the specified region. Once one of these hyperlinks was selected, the ASP would run and load a new page, which would show the resulting data, as depicted in Figure 12.4.

Study_numb	Area	Pain	Ache	Numbness	Pandn
20003				RLL5	
20003				RLS1	
20003		RLS1			
20003		RLS2			
20003					RLL5
20003		RRS1			
20003		RRS2			
20003		RRL5			
20003		FRC4			
20003		FRC5			
20003		FRC6			
20003		FLC1			

Figure 12.5 Linking table in the GIS solution.

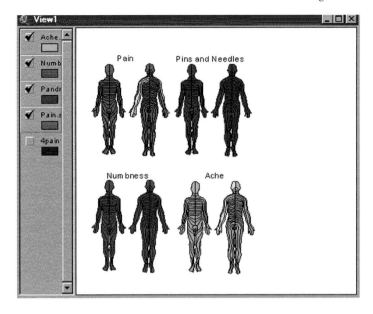

Figure 12.6 Simultaneous selection of dermatomes and types of pain in the GIS solution.

12.4.4 GIS

The GIS solution was created by digitizing the outline of each dermatome, stored as spatial co-ordinated polygons. This was then copied four times, one for each type of pain. Each polygon created in this manner was then given a unique

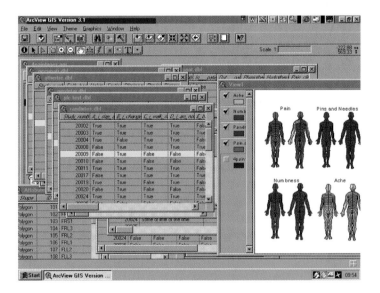

Figure 12.7 GIS solution – snapshot showing the pain areas and details of patient 20009.

identification number and therefore could be easily linked to the database via its keys. Each polygon was also given a dermatome code name (e.g. "RRT1"), which related to the corresponding region. A new flat file table was created, containing the four types of pain across the top, and the study number and the area of pain in each row; an example is shown in Figure 12.5.

This table stored under different attributes the areas of pain that each patient suffered from (Figure 12.6). Each of the different attributes was then linked to the corresponding dermatome image, as well as the rest of the database, as shown in Figure 12.7.

12.5 Review and Comparison of Solutions

We now review how the developed systems satisfied the original requirements set by Northwick Park Hospital, followed by a detailed comparison of the solutions. All of the implemented solutions stored patient questionnaire data, and the ASP systems also stored the scanned pain drawings, linking the database relations with the corresponding pain drawings. All the systems, with the possible exception of the GIS solution, where supplementary training is required to be able to take advantage of its full functionality, use standard, familiar, Web interfaces and point and click functionality to remove the complexity of the database from the user. Adding new patient records is straightforward in all the solutions. Moreover, all the information relating to a patient can be edited or deleted, including the pain drawing, though with the ASP-based systems this has to be done by someone with access to the Web server. However, all other solutions work under a client/server framework and place their data on a Web server.

All the systems allow linking between the dermatome image and the information in the database, enabling the largest part of the query to be done graphically, as region selection is done by point and click instead of a complex query written by the user. However, the only solution that highlights the regions on the dermatome image when corresponding data have been highlighted in tables is the GIS. This is part and parcel of the GIS functionality, as not only does a GIS show highlighted regions on the diagram, it also highlights all corresponding data on all the tables related to it.

Lastly, because of the distributed nature of the ASP systems, removing users' ability to carry out analysis that has not already been predetermined by the system, i.e. an ASP query is not constructed, the GIS-based solution provides the highest functionality. For instance, the user can, in the same query, select multiple regions (e.g. "back of the head") and different pain types (e.g. "numbness and pins and needles"), and then look for correlations in the dataset.

12.5.1 Comparisons

All these solutions use a dermatome image in order to allow the user to select an area of interest. This is where the similarity between the systems ends, however. The GIF-based solution uses an image map in order to allow the user to select the region of interest; the rest of the selection is done via hyperlinks which allow the pain type and type of information to be selected. The main advantages of this system are that users do not need to understand the underlying technologies employed; they just have to be able to use a Web browser. The database also does not need to be stored locally. The user can only update the database if they have administrator privileges. However, this solution is useful because it allows comparisons across the dataset to be made without understanding of the complexity of the database.

The SVG-based solution works the same way as the GIF-based system, but allows a more detailed zoomable and panable graphic system to be used, which contains an image for each of the different types of pain that the patient has described. It therefore replaces the hyperlink pain-selection process with the corresponding choice being made via dermatome-image selection. After consultations with specialists from Northwick Park Hospital it was decided that, due to the enhanced functionality of its interface, the SVG solution is the more adequate of the two.

Whilst the other methods only allow the selection of one area of interest on the dermatome map at a time, the GIS allows users to select as many as they want at the same time. This means that, when using this solution, patients that had pain in the left leg and left arm could be selected concurrently. If the user made this selection by pointing and clicking, all the results would be returned, i.e. pain in leg only, pain in arm only, and pain in both. Using the GIS query builder, the user can select that the pain has to be in the leg and the arm of the same patient.

Moreover, whilst the GIF and SVG-based solutions only allow users to request certain datasets, i.e. personal datasets, medical etc., with the GIS users can also query the database, using the query builder. This allows users to construct queries such as "show me the position of pain for everyone that answers question 6 of the MSPQ in a particular manner".

Thirdly, whilst the other solutions only allow users to look at each dataset as a separate entity, as normally users would look at one table at a time, GIS highlights on each table the information regarding the currently selected record(s). This allows users to carry out a much more in-depth type of analysis than can be done with the other methods, making this solution the most suited for finding patterns. GIS needs a high level of training compared with the other systems, but the rewards are a lot higher. The main drawbacks of this system are its complexity and set-up costs.

Our findings, therefore, are that the most appropriate solutions are the SVG and GIS systems. The SVG system is the best when it comes to allowing a lot of people to access the data in an inexpensive manner and with minimal training. The problem is that this removes the amount of control that the users have over the system. The GIS solution, on the other hand is best suited for analysis of the actual data, though it adds complexity and cost, and at the moment needs specialist technologies in order to allow it to be distributed. These results are summarized in Table 12.2.

12.6 Conclusions

Back pain is one of the most prolific health problems within the population and costs industry lost revenue due to the amount of days people have to take off in

Table 12.2 SVG vs. GIS solutions

	SVG	GIS
Separate diagram for each pain type	Yes	Yes
Panning and zooming	Yes	Yes
Multiple selections of regions	No	Yes
Distributed	Yes	Yes
Update of database	No	Yes
SQL	No	Yes
Highlight linked records	No	Yes
Training needed	No	Yes
Data analysis	No	Yes
Cost of system	Economical (SVG freeware plug-in + Web browser)	Can be expensive

order to recover. For several decades now hospitals have been collecting data in order to help analyse back pain patients. These have included several different psychometric and after-treatment questionnaires, as well as pain drawings recording position and type of pain. However, little or no work has been done in which pain drawings and questionnaires are used to check for data patterns between patients. Even positional data existed, no one seemed to have devised a system that made use of it to link pain areas to the corresponding datasets.

We proposed a number of solutions to this problem, three of which have been presented in this chapter. The most appropriate solutions were found to be an SVG-enabled system, which used ASP for remote data access, and one based on GIS technology. The former allowed users to use Web technology and pan around the drawings, before clicking on the data that they wished to view. The GIS made full use of the Geo Spatial analysis tool in order to view and analyse the data. Furthermore:

- GIS technologies can be used in non-geographical fields, as long as the dataset contains or can contain, spatial data. In this case the GIS was used to map the body. This allows the whole spatial analysis toolset to be used on non-geographical data, and helps the user to find correlations or patterns which may have taken a lot longer using standard glance methods. Queries such as: "Does a patient with pain in both limbs feel worse than a patient with pain in only one, and are they more likely to take time off work?" can easily be undertaken using the GIS solution. SVG makes for better image maps than the standard GIF images. This is due to the scale and pan features of this new technology, which allow the user to zoom in and get a better idea of the region areas, as well as the image taking up less space on the screen, as the whole image need not be shown at a large scale.

Moreover, our work has raised some interesting future research questions. Chief among these is the issue of body regionalization. Although we have split the body region into dermatomes, is this the best grid possible for back pain analysis, especially bearing in mind generalization effects? Would a finer resolution grid, albeit resulting in a more complex and resource-hungry solution, be more beneficial? Finally, work can also be done to explore how SVG can be combined with other XML-based medical markup languages in order to harness SVG's powerful graphic capabilities with XML's enhanced search and analysis potential.

12.7 References

Bernhardsen, T. (1992) *Geographical Information Systems,* Viak IT, Norway.

Boucher, A. (1999) *The Prevalence of Back Pain in Great Britain in 1998.* Department of Health. Available: http://www.doh.gov.uk/public/backpain.htm

Boye, J. (1999) *SVG Brings Faster Vector Graphics to Web.* Available: http://www.tech.irt.org/articles/js176/.

Bretas, G. (1996) *Geographic Information Systems for the Study and Control of Malaria.* GIS for Health and the Environment. Available: http://www.idrc.ca/books/focus/766/bretas.html

Chan, C. W., Goldman, S., Ilstrup, D. M., Kunselman, A. R. and O'Neill, P. I. (1993) The pain drawing and Waddell's nonorganic physical signs in chronic low-back pain. *Spine* 18, 1717–1722.

Connolly, T. C., Begg, D. and Strachan, A. (1999) *Database Systems: A Practical Approach to Design, Implementation, and Management.* Addison Wesley, Harlow.

ESRI (1999a) *GIS for Health Care Today and Tomorrow.* Environmental Systems Research Institute. Available: http://www.esri.com/news/arcuser/0499/umbrella.html

ESRI (1999b) *Health: GIS Solutions for Health Sciences and the Business of Health Care.* Environmental Systems Research Institute. Available: http://www.esri.com/library/brochures/pdfs/heathbro.pdf.

Frank, A. and De Sousa, L. H. (2000) Conservative management of low back pain. *International Journal of Clinical Practice* 55, 21–31.

Gatchel, R. J., Mayer, T. G., Capra, P., Diamod, P. and Barnett, J. (1986) Qualifications of lumbar function, Part 6: The use of psychological measures in guiding physical function restoration. *Spine* 11, 36–42.

Ginzburg, B. M., Merskey, H. and Lau, C. L. (1988) The relationship between pain drawings and the psychological state. *Pain* 35, 141–145.

Hildebrandt, J., Franz, C. E., Choroba-Mehnen, B. and Temme, M. (1988) The use of pain drawings in screening for psychological involvement in complaints of low-back pain. *Spine* 13, 681–685.

Jefferson, J. R. and McGrath, P. J. (1996) Back pain and peripheral joint pain in an industrial setting. *Archive Physical Medicine & Rehabilitation* 77, 385–390.

Main, C. J. (1983) The modified somatic perception questionnaire. *Journal of Psychosomatic Research* 27, 503–514.

Mann III, N. H., Brown, M. D., Hertz, D. B., Enger, I. and Tompkins, J. (1992) Initial-impression diagnosis using low-back pain patient pain drawings. *Spine* 18, 41–53.

Margolis, R. B., Tait, R. C. and Krause, S. J. (1986) A rating system for use with patients pain drawings. *Pain* 24, 57–65.

Margolis, R. B., Chibnall, J. T. and Tait, R. C. (1988) Test-retest reliability of the pain drawing instrument. *Pain* 33, 49–51.

Matsen, F. (2001) *Back Pain.* University of Washington. Available: http://www.orthop.washington.edu/arthritis/types/backpain/01.

Ohlund, C., Eek, C., Palmblad, S., Areskoug, B. and Nachemson, A. (1996) Quantified pain drawing in subacute low back pain. *Spine* 21, 1021–1031.

Ohnmeiss, D. D. (2000) Repeatability of Pain Drawings in a Low Back Pain Population. *Spine* 25, 980–988.

Ohnmeiss, D. D., Vanharanta, H. and Guyer, R. D. (1995) The association between pain drawings and computed tomographic/discographic pain responses. *Spine* 20, 729–733.

Ohnmeiss, D. D., Vanharanta, H. and Ekholm, J. (1999) The relationship between pain location and disc pathology: A study of pain drawings and CT/discography. *Clinical Journal of Pain* 15, 210–217.

Palmer, H. (1949) Pain charts: A description of a technique whereby functional pain may be diagnosed from organic pain. *New Zealand Medical Journal* 48, 187–213.

Papageorgiou, A. C., Croft, P. R., Ferry, S., Jayson, M. I. V. and Silman, A. J. (1995) Estimating the prevalence of low back pain in the general population: Evidence from the South Manchester Back Pain Survey. *Spine* 20, 1889–1894.

Parker, H., Wood, P. L. R. and Main, C. J. (1995) The use of the pain drawing as a screening measure to predict psychological distress in chronic low back pain. *Spine* 20, 236–243.

Peng, Z. R. and Nebert, D. D. (1997) An internet-based GIS data access system. *Urban and Regional Information Association Journal* 9, 20–30.

Plewe, B. (1996) A primer on creating geographic services: Mapping on the Web. *GIS World* 9, 56–58.

Plewe, B. (1997) So you want to build an online GIS. *GIS World* 10, 58–60.

Rankine, J. J., Fortune, D. G., Hutchinson, C. E., Hughes, D. G. and Main, C. J. (1998) Pain drawings in the assessment of nerve root compression: A comparative study with lumbar spine magnetic resonance imaging. *Spine* 23, 1668–1676.

Ransford, A. O., Cairns, D. and Mooney, V. (1976) The pain drawing as an aid to psychologic evaluation of patients with low-back pain. *Spine* 1, 127–134.

Roland, M. and Morris, R. (1983) A Study of the Natural History of Low Back Pain Parts 1 and 2. *Spine* 8, 141–150.

Strand, E. J. (1998) XML provides web-based GIS a path to scalable vector graphics. *GIS World* August, 28–30.

Theodore, J. (1998) ESRI Announces BodyViewer Extension for ArcView GIS.

Uden, A., Astrom, M. and Bergenudd, H. (1988) Pain drawings in chronic back pain. *Spine* 13, 389–392.

VB123 (1999) Understanding how ASP can interrogate your database. VB123.com. Available: http://www.VB123.com/toolshed/99_dbWeb/05ASPintro.htm

Von Baeyer, C. L., Bergstrom, K. J., Brodwin, M. G. and Brodwin, S. K. (1983) Invalid use of pain drawings in psychological screening of back pain patients. *Pain* 16, 103–107.

Waddell, G., McCulloch, J. A., Krummel, E. D. and Venner, R. M. (1980) Nonorganic physical signs in low-back pain. *Spine* 5, 117–125.

Wiltse, L. L. and Racchio, P. D. (1975) Preoperative psychological tests as predictors of success of chemonucleyolsis in treatment of the low back pain syndrome. *Journal of Bone and Joint Surgery (am)* 57, 478–483.

Zung, W. W. K. (1965) A self-rating depression scale. *Archives of General Psychiatry* 32, 63–70.

Concluding Remarks: Today's Vision of Envisioning the Semantic Future

Vladimir Geroimenko and Chaomei Chen

In this book, we have explored some significant topics in the emerging research area of visualizations for the Semantic Web. A new version of the Web is a vision that is incredibly quickly becoming a reality. Visual techniques and metaphors that the Second-Generation Web is bringing to life depend very much on its future implementations and building blocks. No one can predict how the real-life development of the Semantic Web will turn out, and what novel visualization techniques will be needed. Because of this, drawing a more or less detailed picture of the new research area will be possible only as a result of several years of thorough exploration, and we hope that with our pioneering book we help to make it happen sooner. As with any other novel area, we were trying our best to investigate the topics that seem to be of primary importance at this moment in time. We think that in general we have achieved our goal and that the reader will not judge us too severely for not presenting those aspects that could not be covered today because they require research that can be done only after the main structure of the Semantic Web has been implemented.

The next generation Web will be rich both semantically and visually. Since XML and related technologies separate content from presentation rules, any form of presentation has "equal opportunities" and therefore visually rich ones have a better chance of being implemented in semantic human–computer interfaces. The intensive use of semantics will change the nature of the visual aspect of the Web. In addition to today's images, pictures and animations, the future Web will enable the user to visualize much more conceptual things such as the meaning and structure of Web data. The next generation will be not only the Web of formalized meanings, understandable by machines, but also the Web of visualized meanings that increase human understanding of Web data. In other words, computers will be able to comprehend the future Web because it includes machine-processable semantics; humans can better comprehend this Web because of the use of visualized semantics.

Visually rich 2D and 3D worlds of meanings, common to the Semantic Web, will comprise a variety of different levels and forms of metadata – from simple XML DOM trees to RDF Schemas, Topic Maps and very complex ontologies. They will allow the user to interact with data and metadata in an efficient and desirable way (for example, navigate, manipulate, transform, zoom, filter, etc.). If a picture is worth a thousand words, a semantic visualization is worth a thousand metadata tags. Visual interaction with Web data, metadata, schemas and ontologies will be effectively used for a wide variety of purposes such as searching the

Web using semantically enhanced search engines, customizing Web pages and sites on the fly, instructing autonomous software agents, navigating through huge sets of data and metadata, accessing any part of any Web document, etc.

The Semantic Web will also change the nature of images that we are used to seeing on the current Web. Since they will be presented in an SVG, X3D or other XML-based format, it will be possible to put them to an active use, similar to any other XML documents. This means that computers will be able to understand the meaning of not only Web data but also Web images. Both computers and humans can access any parts of such images, "recognize" them by their tags, find them on the entire Web, compose new images on the fly using XSL, etc. For example, a software agent will be able to find an appropriate map of a city you plan to visit, and then put on it all images of your places of interest, link them to available Web resources, etc. Moreover, it can refine an existing X3D virtual model of the city in question by leaving only the streets you have to use, and by putting more visual signs and aural clues.

As of today, the future of the Semantic Web looks extremely bright. It will be a Web of meanings. These meanings will be formalized in a smart way to make them automatically processable by machines. The same meanings will be very often visualized in an effective way to help humans to comprehend them. Such a Web will make sense.

Index